UDDH

The Last Message of Sri Krishna

Text with English Translation and notes

SWAMI MADHAVANANDA

(Publication Department)
5 Dehi Entally Road
Kolkata 700 014

Published by
Swami Mumukshananda
President, Advaita Ashrama
Mayavati, Champawat, Himalayas
from its Publication Department, Kolkata
Email: mail@advaitaonline.com
Website: www.advaitaonline.com

© *All Rights Reserved*
Nineth Impression, January 2003
2M2C

ISBN 81-7505-115-9

Printed in India at
Trio Process
Kolkata 700 014

UDDHAVA GITA

OR

THE LAST MESSAGE OF SHRI KRISHNA

FOREWORD

Shrimad-Bhāgavatam is one of the most authoritative of Hindu scriptures. Tradition ascribes its authorship to the great Vyāsa, by whom it was taught to his illustrious son, Bhagavān Shuka. The Bhāgavata is a high authority on Bhakti or devotion. But devotion, as depicted here, is not divorced from Jnâna, as it is popularly understood, but rather Jnana is exceedingly helpful to its perfect attainment. Bhagavan Shri Krishna is the central figure of this wonderful work, and in the Eleventh Book, the Lord on the eve of His exit from the arena of the world gives His parting instructions to His beloved devotee and follower, Uddhava. The lessons comprise a variety of subjects, but in and through all, the necessity of seeing the Lord in everything and living a life of perfect self-surrender and non-attachment is passionately inculcated. The Bhāgavata amply fulfils the chief task of the Purânas, viz popularising the Vedic truths by means of narratives and such other aids. "It is", as Shri Ramakrishna aptly expressed it, "fried in the butter of Jnana and soaked in the syrup of Bhakti." The study of such a book cannot but be of the greatest help to a seeker after Truth.

The present edition comprises the two volumes which were first published with the title *Shri Krishna and Uddhava* and corresponds to chapters six to twenty-nine of the Eleventh Skandha of the Bhāgavata. The difficulty of the original will, it is hoped, be greatly overcome by the translation and notes here given. Of the many commentaries extant, Shridhara Swami's is the most famous, and it is this which we have mainly followed. We have every reason to hope that the present work will form a fitting sequel to the celebrated Shrimad-Bhagavad-Gitā.

MADHAVANANDA

CONTENTS

CHAPTER		PAGE
	FOREWORD	iii
I.	INTRODUCTION : THE GODS PRAY FOR THE LORD'S RETURN	1
II.	THE AVADHUTA AND HIS EIGHT TEACHERS	20
III.	NINE OTHER TEACHERS OF THE AVADHUTA	45
IV.	SEVEN MORE TEACHERS OF THE AVADHUTA	59
V.	THE REAL NATURE OF THE WORLD	71
VI.	SOULS BOUND AND FREE; CHARACTERISTICS OF A SAINT AND A DEVOTEE	83
VII.	THE EFFECT OF HOLY ASSOCIATIONS; THE TREE OF SAMSARA	99
VIII.	KNOWLEDGE THROUGH THE DESTRUCTION OF GUNAS, THE LORD TEACHES AS A SWAN	110
IX.	THE GLORY OF DEVOTION; DIRECTIONS ON MEDITATION	126
X.	POWERS RESULTING FROM YOGA	141
XI.	DIVINE MANIFESTATIONS	153
XII.	CASTES AND ORDERS OF LIFE	167
XIII.	FOREST LIFE AND MONASTICISM	185
XIV.	PRACTICE OF DEVOTION	201

VI

CHAPTER		PAGE
XV.	JNANA-YOGA, KARMA-YOGA, AND BHAKTI-YOGA	216
XVI.	MERITS AND DEFECTS WITH REGARD TO PLACE, TIME, ETC.	230
XVII.	CATEGORIES : THEIR NUMBER, DISTINCTION BETWEEN PURUSHA AND PRAKRITI; LIFE AFTER DEATH	246
XVIII.	HOW TO BE ABOVE INSULT, ILLUSTRATED BY THE STORY OF A MENDICANT	268
XIX.	THE SANKHYA SYSTEM	290
XX.	THREE GUNAS : THEIR EFFECTS	300
XXI.	RESULTS OF EVIL ASSOCIATION; THE STORY OF EMPEROR PURURAVAS	311
XXII.	METHODS OF WORSHIP	322
XXIII.	THE CAUSE OF DELUSION	339
XXIV.	AN EASY WAY TO SELF-REALISATION	356
	INDEX	373

CHAPTER I

श्रीशुक उवाच ।

अथ ब्रह्मात्मजैर्देवैः प्रजेशैरावृतोऽभ्यगात् ।
भवश्च भूतभव्येशो ययौ भूतगणैर्वृतः ॥१॥

Shuka said:

1. One day came Brahmâ surrounded by His sons,[1] the Devas and the Prajâpatis;[2] and Shiva, the Lord of things created and yet to be created, came surrounded by His Demons.

[1] *Sons*—Sanaka, Sanandana, and others.
[2] *Prajâpatis*—the ten lords of created beings.

इन्द्रो मरुद्भिर्भगवानादित्या वसवोऽश्विनौ ।
ऋभवोऽङ्गिरसो रुद्रा विश्वे साध्याश्च देवताः ॥२॥

2. Bhagavân Indra with the Maruts,[1] the Âdityas, the Vasus, the Ashvins, the Ribhus, the offspring of Angiras, the Rudras, the Vishvadevas, the Sâdhyas—

[1] *The Maruts etc.*—Different classes of superhuman beings are mentioned here.

गन्धर्वाप्सरसो नागाः सिद्धचारणगुह्यकाः ।
ऋषयः पितरश्चैव सविद्याधरकिन्नराः ॥३॥

UDDHAVA GITA

3. The Gandharvas, the Apsarâs, the Nâgas, the Siddhas, the Châranas, the Guhyakas, the Rishis, the Pitris, together with the Vidyâdharas and the Kinnaras—

द्वारकामुपसंजग्मुः सर्वे कृष्णदिदृक्षवः ।
वपुषा येन भगवान्नरलोकमनोरमः ।
यशो वितेने लोकेषु सर्वलोकमलापहम् ॥४॥

4. All came to Dvârakâ with a view to seeing Krishna—in which body the Lord, being the delight of human beings, spread his glory throughout the universe—the glory that takes away the impurities of all beings.

तस्यां विभ्राजमानायां समृद्धायां महर्द्धिभिः ।
व्यचक्षतावितृप्ताक्षाः कृष्णमद्भुतदर्शनम् ॥५॥

5. In that brilliant city enriched with great splendours they beheld Krishna, of wonderful form, with unsatiated gaze.

स्वर्गोद्यानोपगैर्माल्यैश्छादयन्तो यदूत्तमम् ।
गीर्भिश्चित्रपदार्थाभिस्तुष्टुवुर्जगदीश्वरम् ॥६॥

6. Covering the best[1] of the Yadus with garlands of flowers growing in the gardens of heaven, they began to praise the Lord of the Universe with sentences full of beautiful words and sentiments.

[1] *The best etc.*—i.e. Shri Krishna.

THE LAST MESSAGE OF SHRI KRISHNA 3

देवा ऊचुः ।

नताः स्म ते नाथ पदारविन्दं
बुद्धीन्द्रियप्राणमनोवचोभिः ।
यच्चिन्त्यतेऽन्तर्हृदि भावयुक्तै-
र्मुमुक्षुभिः कर्ममयोरुपाशात् ॥७॥

The gods said:

7. Lord, to Thy lotus-feet which those seeking liberation from the strong meshes of work[1] fervently meditate upon within the heart, we bow[2] with our Buddhi,[3] organs, vital powers, Manas,[4] and speech.

[1] *Work*—done for the satisfaction of desires.
[2] *Bow etc.*—i.e. surrendering ourselves completely.
[3] *Buddhi*—the determinative faculty.
[4] *Manas*—which raises doubts.

त्वं मायया त्रिगुणयाऽऽत्मनि दुर्विभाव्यं
व्यक्तं सृजस्यवसि लुम्पसि तद्गुणस्थः ।
नैतैर्भवानजित कर्मभिरज्यते वै
यत्स्वे सुखेऽव्यवहितेऽभिरतोऽनवद्यः ॥८॥

8. O Thou Invincible One, through Thy Mâyâ[1] consisting of the three Gunas, and resting[2] in them Thou dost create, maintain, and destroy in Thyself[3] this unthinkable universe, but these activities do not touch Thee, for Thou art unimpeachable, being immersed in the unobstructed bliss of the Self.[4]

UDDHAVA GITA

4

[1] *Mâyâ*—is the indescribable power of the Lord, being the equilibrium of Sattva or balance, Rajas or activity and Tamas or dullness.

[2] *Resting etc.*—i.e. seeming to identify Himself with the Gunas.

[3] *In Thyself*—The universe in all its stages is not apart from Brahman.

[4] *Self*—which is His Essence.

शुद्धिर्नृणां न तु तथेड्य दुराशयानां
विद्याश्रुताध्ययनदानतपःक्रियाभिः ।
सत्त्वात्मनामृषभ ते यशसि प्रवृद्ध-
सच्छृद्धया श्रवणसंभृतया यथा स्यात् ॥६॥

9. O Adorable One! O Supreme! Mental worship, scriptural study, charity, austerities, and work do not confer such purity on men of unsatisfied desires as the men of balanced minds obtain through a heightened true regard for Thy glories developed by means of hearing (of them).

स्यान्नस्तवाङ्घ्रिरशुभाशयधूमकेतुः
क्षेमाय यो मुनिभिरार्द्रहृदोह्यमानः ।
यः सात्वतैः समविभूतय आत्मवद्भि-
र्व्यूहेऽर्चितः सवनशः स्वरतिक्रमाय ॥१०॥

10. May Thy feet[1] be the fire to consume our evil desires, the feet which sages, for their welfare, carry[2] with tender hearts, which are worshipped by

THE LAST MESSAGE OF SHRI KRISHNA

devotees in diverse forms for attaining equal glories[3] with Thee, and by the spiritually-minded thrice a day with a view to transcending heaven!

[1] *Feet etc.*—i.e. being meditated upon.

[2] *Carry*—think of.

[3] *Equal glories etc.*—One of the five kinds of liberation known among the dualists. This is a lower Bhakti than the next kind described.

यश्चिन्त्यते प्रयतपाणिभिरध्वराग्नौ
त्रय्या निरुक्तविधिनेश हविर्गृहीत्वा ।
अध्यात्मयोग उत योगिभिरात्ममायां
जिज्ञासुभिः परमभागवतैः परीष्टः ॥११॥

11. Thy feet, O Lord, which are meditated upon in the prescribed manner in the sacrificial fire[1] by priests taking oblations with folded palms, and by Yogis desirous of knowing Thy Mâyâ—through spiritual union; and which are worshipped all around by the highest devotees![2]

[1] *Sacrificial fire etc.*—The god of whom they think while offering the oblation is not distinct from Brahman.

[2] *Highest devotees*—who look upon the whole universe as Brahman.

पर्युष्ट्रया तव विभो वनमाल्ययेयं
संस्पर्धिनी भगवती प्रतिपत्निवच्छ्रीः ।
यः सुप्रणीतममुयार्हणमाददन्नो
भूयात्सदाङ्घ्रिरशुभाशयधूमकेतुः ॥१२॥

UDDHAVA GITA

12. O Omnipresent Lord, the Goddess Lakshmi is jealous[1]—as from a co-wife—of Thy garland of wild flowers, even though withered; Thou dost accept the worship done with this (garland) as duly offered.[2] Oh, may Thy feet ever be the fire to consume our evil desires!

[1] *Jealous etc.*—The garland also hangs on the Lord's breast, a place reserved for His Divine Spouse, Lakshmi.

[2] *Duly offered*—The Lord makes much of even the humblest offerings of His devotees—this is the idea.

केतुस्त्रिविक्रमयुतस्त्रिपतत्पताको

यस्ते भयाभयकरोऽसुरदेवचम्वोः ।

स्वर्गाय साधुषु खलेष्वितराय भूमन्

पादः पुनातु भगवन्भजतामघं नः ॥१३॥

13. O Infinite, O Lord, may Thy foot rectify the sins of us, Thy devotees—the foot which with its three steps[1] became Thy banner,[2] as it were, with the Gangâ[3] flowing in three regions as its pennon; which caused fear and fearlessness to the armies of the Asuras and the Devas respectively; which conduce to heaven in the case of the good, and to hell[4] in that of the wicked!

[1] *Three steps etc.*—The reference is to the Vâmana or "Dwarf" Incarnation of the Lord, in which He for the sake of Indra begged of Bali, the Asura usurper of heaven, as much space as would be covered by His three steps. The king consenting, the Lord assumed a mighty form, one step of His covering the earth and the second the heaven, while there was no space for the third, whereupon Bali—whose name is a household word in India for generosity—

THE LAST MESSAGE OF SHRI KRISHNA

offered his head for this purpose and was asked by the Lord to go and live in the nether regions.

[2] *Banner*—because they proclaim His glory.

[3] *Gangâ etc.*—The Gangâ is believed to have sprung from Shri Vishnu's feet, and to flow through heaven, earth, and the nether regions under the names of Mandâkini, Bhâgirathi, and Bhogavati.

[4] *Hell etc.*—because they commit outrages in defiance of the eternal moral principles and are degraded thereby.

नस्योतगाव इव यस्य वशे भवन्ति

ब्रह्मादयस्तनुभृतो मिथुरर्द्य मानाः ।

कालस्य ते प्रकृतिपूरुषयोः परस्य

शं नस्तनोतु चरणः पुरुषोत्तमस्य ॥१४॥

14. May Thy feet contribute to our welfare! Thou art the Supreme Being, Thou art Time, beyond Prakriti and Purusha,[1] under whose sway[2] are Brahmâ and all other embodied beings—who fight mutually—like unto bullocks with strings passing through their noses!

[1] *Prakriti and Purusha*—Sânkhyan phraseology. The Prakriti corresponds with certain vital differences to the Avyakta of Vedanta, and the Purusha to the Jiva or individual aspect of the Soul; and Brahman is of course beyond all relative aspects.

[2] *Sway etc.*—because Brahman is disembodied Existence-Knowledge-Bliss Absolute.

अस्यासि हेतुरुदयस्थितिसंयमाना-

मव्यक्तजीवमहतामपि कालमाहुः ।

सोऽयं त्रिणाभिरखिलापचये प्रवृत्तः

कालो गभीररय उत्तमपूरुषस्त्वम् ॥१५॥

UDDHAVA GITA

15. Thou art the cause of the origin, continuity, and dissolution of this universe, (the Vedas) call Thee the Ruler of the Undifferentiated,[1] the Jiva, and the Mahat[2] also. Thou also art Time with its three naves,[3] which we know to be of immense power— which destroys everything. Ah, Thou art the Supreme Being.

[1] Undifferentiated—same as Mâyâ.

[2] Mahat—the first modification of Prakriti. This is designated as Brahmâ in the Purânas.

[3] Three naves—The year is divided into three groups of four months each.

For the ideas of these two verses compare Katha Upanishad, III. 11 and Gitâ, XV. 16-18.

त्वत्तः पुमान्समधिगम्य ययास्य वीर्यं
धत्ते महान्तमिव गर्भममोघवीर्यः ।
सोऽयं तयानुगत आत्मन आण्डकोशं
हैमं ससर्ज बहिरावरणैरुपेतम् ॥१६॥

16. Receiving energy from Thee, the Purusha,[1] of infallible power, along with Mâyâ, holds within Himself the Mahat, like the embryonic state of this universe. This mahat, backed by the same Mâyâ, projected from within itself the golden sphere[2] of the universe, provided with outer coverings.[3]

[1] The Purusha etc.—In this verse Shri Krishna is addressed as Brahman, next to which comes the Ishvara aspect, then Mâyâ, then Mahat or Cosmic Intelligence, and lastly, the manifested universe—this seems to be the order.

[2] Sphere—lit. egg.

[3] Outer coverings—layers of varying density.

THE LAST MESSAGE OF SHRI KRISHNA

तत्तस्थुषश्च जगतश्च भवानधीशो
यन्माययोत्थगुणविक्रिययोपनीतान् ।
अर्थान्जुषन्नपि हृषीकपते न लिप्तो
येऽन्ये स्वतः परिहृतादपि बिभ्यति स्म ॥१७॥

17. Therefore, art Thou the Lord of the movable and immovable, for Thou, O Ruler of the organs, art untouched by the sense-objects—even though enjoying them—which are presented by the activity of the organs created by Mâyâ, and of which others[1] are afraid, even when[2] these are themselves absent.

[1]*Others*—including even saints.

[2]*Even when etc.*—because nobody is too sure that he has no attachment at heart for them.

स्मायाऽवलोकलवदर्शितभावहारि-
भ्रूमण्डलप्रहितसौरतमन्त्रशौण्डैः ।
पत्न्यस्तु षोडशसहस्रमनङ्गबाणै-
र्यस्येन्द्रियं विमथितुं करणैर्न विभ्व्यः ॥१८॥

18. Thou whose mind sixteen thousand wives failed to unbalance with their love-shafts and allurements: their smiling glances expressing their ardour which rendered beautiful their eyebrows from which love-messages were sent forth to strengthen those love-shafts.

विभ्व्यस्त्वामृतकथोदवहास्त्रिलोक्याः
पादावनेजसरितः शमलानि हन्तुम् ।

UDDHAVA GITA

आनुश्रवं श्रुतिभिरङ्घ्रिजमङ्गसङ्गै-
स्तीर्थद्वयं शुचिषदस्त उपस्पृशन्ति ॥१९॥

19. The streams carrying the waters of Thy glory[1] that confer immortality, as well as those[2] which have sprung from the washing of Thy feet, are potent enough to destroy the sins of the three worlds. Those who abide[3] by their (respective) duties touch both these streams, the former—set forth in the Vedas[4]—through their ears, and the latter—issuing from Thy feet—by physical contact.

[1] *Streams . . . glory*—i.e. the rivers of Thy glory sung in the sacred books.

[2] *Those etc.*—as, for instance, the Gangâ which is believed to have thus sprung.

[3] *Who abide etc.*—i.e. virtuous people.

[4] *The Vedas*—are called *anushrava* because they are heard from the lips of the Guru.

बादरायणिरुवाच ।

इत्यभिष्टूय विबुधैः सेशः शतधृतिर्हरिम् ।
अभ्यभाषत गोविन्दं प्रणम्याम्बरमाश्रितः ॥२०॥

Shuka said:

20. Thus praising the Lord, Brahmâ with the gods and Shiva saluted Him and ascending the sky said:

ब्रह्मोवाच ।

भूमेर्भारावताराय पुरा विज्ञापितः प्रभो ।
त्वमस्माभिरशेषात्मंस्तत्तथैवोपपादितम् ॥२१॥

THE LAST MESSAGE OF SHRI KRISHNA

11

Brahmâ said:

21. O Lord, we formerly besought Thee to reduce the burden of the earth. O Thou Self of all, Thou hast done it exactly as we wished.

धर्मश्च स्थापितः सत्सु सत्यसन्धेषु वै त्वया ।
कीर्तिश्च दिक्षु विक्षिप्ता सर्वलोकमलापहा ॥२२॥

22. Thou hast placed religion in the hands of the virtuous who are devoted to Truth, and hast spread in all directions Thy fame that takes away the impurities of all.

अवतीर्य यदोवंशे बिभ्रद्रूपमनुत्तमम् ।
कर्माण्युद्दामवृत्तानि हिताय जगतोऽकृथाः ॥२३॥

23. Having incarnated in Yadu's line and assuming a matchless form Thou hast done deeds of surpassing valour for the good of the world.

यानि ते चरितानीश मनुष्याः साधवः कलौ ।
श्रृण्वन्तः कीर्तयन्तश्च तरिष्यन्त्यञ्जसा तमः ॥२४॥

24. Hearing and reciting which deeds of Thine, O Lord, good people will easily get beyond ignorance in this iron age.

यदुवंशोऽवतीर्णस्य भवतः पुरुषोत्तम ।
शरच्छतं व्यतीयाय पञ्चविंशाधिकं प्रभो ॥२५॥

25. O Lord, O Thou Supreme Being, a hundred and twenty-five years have passed since Thou didst incarnate in Yadu's line.

UDDHAVA GITA

नाधुना तेऽखिलाधार देवकार्यविशेषितम् ।
कुलं च विप्रशापेन नष्टप्रायमभूदिदम् ॥२६॥

26. O Thou Support of the universe, Thou hast now no more work to do for the gods, and this line[1] also is almost at the point of destruction owing to the Brâhmanas' curse.[2]

[1] *This line*—i.e. the Yâdava line.

[2] Curse—This alludes to the curse which some Rishis coming to Dvâraka gave the Yâdava boys, who played a trick on them.

ततः स्वधाम परमं विशस्व यदि मन्यसे ।
सलोकाँल्लोकपालान्नः पाहि वैकुण्ठकिंकरान् ॥२७॥

27. Therefore, if Thou thinkest fit, deign to go back to Thy own supreme abode,[1] and protect us, the lords of beings, together with our people—for we are but servants of Vaikuntha.

[1] *Own...abode*—i.e. Vaikuntha mentioned in the last line.

श्रीभगवानुवाच ।
अवधारितमेतन्मे यदात्थ विबुधेश्वर ।
कृतं वः कार्यमखिलं भूमेर्भारोऽवतारितः ॥२८॥

The Lord said:

28 I have already decided what Thou art saying, O Lord of the god; I have finished Your entire work and taken off the burden of the earth.

तदिदं यादवकुलं वीर्यशौर्यश्रियोद्धतम् ।
लोकं जिघृक्षद्रुद्धं मे वेलयेव महार्णवः ॥२९॥

THE LAST MESSAGE OF SHRI KRISHNA

29. This famous line of Yadu, haughty with the splendour brought on by strength and prowess, is bidding fair to overrun the world, and is only stopped from doing so by Me, like the ocean by its coast.

यदसंहत्य दृप्तानां यदूनां विपुलं कुलम् ।
गन्तास्यनेन लोकोऽयमुद्धतेन विनङ्क्ष्यति ॥३०॥

30. If I leave without destroying this extensive line of the proud Yadus, they will overstep all bounds and put an end to this world.

इदानीं नाश आरब्धः कुलस्य द्विजशापतः ।
यास्यामि भवनं ब्रह्मन्नेतदन्ते तवानघ ॥३१॥

31. O Brahman, now has the destruction of this line set in, consequent on the Brâhmanas' curse, and I shall visit[1] Thy abode, O pure One, at the end of this.

[1] *Visit etc.*—on His way to Vaikuntha.

श्रीशुक उवाच ।
इत्युक्तो लोकनाथेन स्वयंभूः प्रणिपत्य तम् ।
सह देवगणैर्देवः स्वधाम समपद्यत ॥३२॥

Shuka said:

32. Being thus accosted by the Lord of the Universe, the Lord Brahmâ saluted Him and went back to His abode, along with the gods.

UDDHAVA GITA

अथ तस्यां महोत्पातान्द्वारवत्यां समुत्थितान् ।
विलोक्य भगवानाह यदुवृद्धान्समागतान् ॥३३॥

33. Then beholding dire calamities overtaking the city of Dvâraka, the Lord addressed the assembled elders of the Yadus:

श्रीभगवानुवाच ।
एते वै सुमहोत्पाता व्युत्तिष्ठन्तीह सर्वतः ।
शापश्च नः कुलस्यासीद्ब्राह्मणेभ्यो दुरत्ययः ॥३४॥

The Lord said:

34. See how the direst calamities are visiting this city everywhere, and there has been an irremediable curse upon our line from the Brâhmanas.

न वस्तव्यमिहास्माभिर्जिजीविषुभिरार्यकाः ।
प्रभासं सुमहत्पुण्यं यास्यामोऽद्यैव मा चिरम् ॥३५॥

35. O revered ones, we must not dwell here (any more) if we wish to live. We shall repair to the exceedingly holy Prabhâsa even today; there should be no delay.

यत्र स्नात्वा दक्षशापाद्गृहीतो यक्ष्मणोडुराट् ।
विमुक्तः किल्बिषात्सद्यो भेजे भूयः कलोदयम् ॥३६॥

36. Bathing in which place Chandra (the moon), who was afflicted with consumption by Daksha's curse,[1] was instantaneously cured of his evil and again had his digits restored.

THE LAST MESSAGE OF SHRI KRISHNA

[1] *Curse*—According to Hindu mythology Chandra married twenty-seven daughters of the Prajâpati Daksha (27 constellations). Daksha cursed his son-in-law for his undue partiality for his favourite wife, Rohini, to the exclusion of some of his other wives.

वयं च तस्मिन्नाप्लुत्य तर्पयित्वा पितॄन्सुरान् ।
भोजयित्वोशिजो विप्रान्स्नानागुणवताऽन्धसा ॥३७॥
तेषु दानानि पात्रेषु श्रद्धयोप्त्वा महान्ति वै ।
वृजिनानि तरिष्यामो दानैर्नौभिरिवार्णवम् ॥३८॥

37-38. We, too, bathing there, offering libations of water to the manes and gods, feeding gifted Brâhmanas with excellent food, and respectfully offering[1] gifts to these worthies, shall by means of these gifts get over our sins, like crossing the sea by means of boats.

[1] *Offering*—The word in the text literally means "sowing". As seeds sown on good soil yield abundant crops, so gifts made to proper persons bear rich fruit in future life.

श्रीशुक उवाच ।

एवं भगवतादिष्टा यादवाः कुलनन्दन ।
गन्तुं कृतधियस्तीर्थं स्यन्दनान्समयूयुजन् ॥३६॥

Shuka said:

39. O scion[1] of the Kurus, being thus ordered by the Lord, the Yâdavas made ready their chariots with the object of going to the place of pilgrimage.

[1] *Scion etc.*—King Parikshit, to whom Shuka narrates the incidents described in the Bhâgavata.

UDDHAVA GITA

तन्निरीक्ष्योद्धवो राजन् श्रुत्वा भगवतोदितम् ।
दृष्ट्वाऽरिष्टानि घोराणि नित्यं कृष्णमनुव्रतः ॥४०॥
विविक्त उपसंगम्य जगतामीश्वरेश्वरम् ।
प्रणम्य शिरसा पादौ प्राञ्जलिस्तमभाषत ॥४१॥

40-41. O King, seeing this, hearing the Lord's words, and noticing dire portents, Uddhava, ever devoted to Shri Krishna, approached the Lord of the world-rulers in a retired place, and touching His feet with his head, addressed Him with folded palms.

उद्धव उवाच ।
देवदेवेश योगेश पुण्यश्रवणकीर्तन ।
संहृत्यैतत्कुलं नूनं लोकं संत्यक्ष्यते भवान् ।
विप्रशापं समर्थोऽपि प्रत्यहन्न यदीश्वरः ॥४२॥

Uddhava said:

42. O Lord of the Rulers among the gods, O Lord of Yoga, O Thou Whom[1] it is auspicious to hear and talk about, surely Thou wilt quit this world after destroying this line, since Thou didst not counteract the Brâhmanas' curse, even though Thou hadst the power to do it.

[1] *Whom etc.*—because it destroys Avidyâ or ignorance.

नाहं तवाङ्घ्रिकमलं क्षणार्धमपि केशव ।
त्यक्तुं समुत्सहे नाथ स्वधाम नय मामपि ॥४३॥

THE LAST MESSAGE OF SHRI KRISHNA   17

43.   O Keshava, not for half a second can I bear to be separated from Thy lotus-feet. Therefore, O Lord, take me also to Thy abode.[1]

[1] *Abode*—The word *dhâma* also means the *svarupa* the status or essential nature, which is its inner significance, as in Verse 47.

तव विक्रीडितं कृष्ण नृणां परममङ्गलम् ।
कर्णपीयूषमास्वाद्य त्यजत्यन्यस्पृहां जनः ॥४४॥

44.   O Krishna, tasting[1] Thy sports which are conducive to the highest good of mankind and are like nectar to the ear, men give up all other desires.

[1] *Tasting*—i.e. hearing of them.

शय्यासनाटनस्थानस्नानक्रीडाशनादिषु ।
कथं त्वां प्रियमात्मानं वयं भक्तास्त्यजेमहि ॥४५॥

45.   And how can we, Thy devotees, give up Thy company in lying, sitting, walking, staying, bathing, sport, eating, and so on, for Thou art dearly beloved of us, nay, our very Self?

त्वयोपभुक्तस्रग्गन्धवासोऽलंकारचर्चिताः ।
उच्छिष्टभोजिनो दासास्तव मायां जयेमहि ॥४६॥

46.   We, Thy servants, will surely conquer Thy Mâyâ, being decked in the garlands, perfumes, and ornaments used by Thee, and partaking of the leavings of Thy food.[1]

[1] *Food*—Teachers of Bhakti attach great importance to this as a factor contributing to devotion.

UDDHAVA GITA

वाताशना य ऋषयः श्रमणा ऊर्ध्वमन्थिनः ।
ब्रह्माख्यं धाम ते यान्ति शान्ताः संन्यासिनोऽमलाः ॥४७॥

47. Sages who[1] live on air,[2] who are ascetics and observe continence, who have pacified their senses, renounced the world and are pure, reach Thy status known as Brahman.

[1] *Who etc.*—They may undergo all these troubles to realise Brahman, but ours is a much safer and easier way—says Uddhava.

[2] *Live on air*—Another reading is वातरशना: which means "clothed with air" i.e. nude.

वयं त्विह महायोगिन्भ्रमन्तः कर्मवर्त्मसु ।
त्वद्वार्तया तरिष्यामस्तावकैर्दुस्तरं तमः ॥४८॥

48. But we, O great Yogin, who wander in the world through the by-ways of work,[1] will transcend its darkness, so difficult to wade through, by conversing about Thee with Thy devotees:

[1] *Work*—We are not so advanced people; consequently ours is the path of work; we cannot ignore our duties in life.

स्मरन्तः कीर्तयन्तस्ते कृतानि गदितानि च ।
गत्युत्स्मितेक्षणक्ष्वेलि यन्नृलोकविडम्बनम् ॥४९॥

49. Remembering and reciting Thy deeds and words, Thy movements, smiles, glances, and pleasantries in imitation of human beings.

THE LAST MESSAGE OF SHRI KRISHNA

श्रीशुक उवाच ।

एवं विज्ञापितो राजन्भगवान्देवकीसुतः ।

एकान्तिनं प्रियं भृत्यमुद्धवं समभाषत ॥५०॥

Shuka said:

50. Being thus appealed to, O King, Bhagavân Shri Krishna spoke to His beloved servant, Uddhava, who was all attention.

CHAPTER II

श्रीभगवानुवाच ।

यदात्थ मां महाभाग तच्चिकीर्षितमेव मे ।

ब्रह्मा भवो लोकपालाः स्वर्वासं मेऽभिकाङ्क्षणः ॥१॥

The Lord said:

1. What thou sayest to Me, O blessed one, is indeed what I have wished to do. Brahmâ, Shiva, and the Lords of beings desire My going back to heaven.

मया निष्पादितं ह्यत्र देवकार्यमशेषतः ।

यदर्थमवतीर्णोऽहमंशेन ब्रह्मणार्थितः ॥२॥

2. Indeed, I have entirely finished the task[1] of the gods for which, at the request of Brahmâ, I incarnated Myself with My partial Manifestation.[2]

[1] *Task*—viz. the destruction of the forces of evil on earth. See Chapter I, Verse 21.

[2] *Partial Manifestation*—He means Balarâma, his elder brother, considered as the Incarnation of Anantadeva, who supports the universe. This interpretation (supplying सह, "with", after अंशेन) is in keeping with the accepted view, viz. that "Krishna is the Lord Himself." (Bhâgavata, I. iii. 28.

कुलं वै शापनिर्दग्धं नङ्क्ष्यत्यन्योन्यविग्रहात् ।

समुद्रः सप्तमेऽह्न्येतां पुरीं च प्लावयिष्यति ॥३॥

THE LAST MESSAGE OF SHRI KRISHNA

3. This line, which is thoroughly burnt, by the curse, will come to destruction through mutual fight, and the sea will submerge this city on the seventh day.

यद्वै वायं मया त्यक्तो लोकोऽयं नष्टमङ्गलः ।

भविष्यत्यचिरात्साधो कलिनाऽपि निराकृतः ॥४॥

4. O noble soul, as soon as I leave this world, it will be shorn of its well-being and will soon be overtaken by Kali—the spirit of the Dark Age.

न वस्तव्यं त्वयैवेह मया त्यक्ते महीतले ।

जनोऽधर्मरुचिर्भद्र भविष्यति कलौ युगे ॥५॥

5. Thou, too, shouldst not stay here after I leave the earth; for, O good soul, men will be addicted to evil in the Iron Age.

त्वं तु सर्वं परित्यज्य स्नेहं स्वजनबन्धुषु ।

मय्यावेश्य मनः सम्यक् समदृग्विचरस्व गाम् ॥६॥

6. Giving up thy love for thy kinsmen and friends, and renouncing everything, roam thou over the world, with evenness of vision, fixing thy mind wholly in Me.

यदिदं मनसा वाचा चक्षुर्म्यां श्रवणादिभिः ।

नश्वरं गृह्यमाणं च विद्धि मायामनोमयम् ॥७॥

7. Whatever is cognised by the mind, speech, eyes, ears, and the rest—know it all to be a figment of the mind, a phantasmagoria, and withal doomed to pass away.

UDDHAVA GITA

पूंसोऽयुक्तस्य नानार्थो भ्रमः स गुणदोषभाक् ।
कर्माकर्मविकर्मेति गुणदोषधियो भिदा ॥८॥

8. The man of uncontrolled mind falls into the error that there is a plurality of objects, and this error leads to merit or demerit.[1] The differences of action, inaction, and evil action concern only the man[2] who has ideas of merit and demerit.

[1] *Merit or demerit*—i.e. good and evil.

[2] *Only the man etc.*—Because they are within the domain of Avidyâ or ignorance.

तस्माद्युक्तेन्द्रियग्रामो युक्तचित्त इदं जगत् ।
आत्मनीक्षस्व विततमात्मानं मय्यधीश्वरे ॥९॥

9. Therefore, controlling thy senses and thy mind, behold this universe as spread out[1] in the self[2] and behold the self as resting in Me, the Supreme Lord.

[1] *Spread out*—manifested.

[2] *Self*—the individual aspect of the Âtman. The universe depends on the Jiva and the Jiva has Brahman as its background.

ज्ञानविज्ञानसंयुक्त आत्मभूतः शरीरिणाम् ।
आत्मानुभवतुष्टात्मा नान्तरायैर्विहन्यसे ॥१०॥

10. Possessed of knowledge[1] and realisation,[2] with thy mind satisfied with the realisation of the Self, and being the very Self of all embodied beings, thou wilt not[3] be thwarted by obstacles.

[1] *Knowledge*—of the purport of the scriptures.

[2] *Realisation*—of the oneness of the Self.

THE LAST MESSAGE OF SHRI KRISHNA

[3] *Thou wilt not etc.*—The idea is that prior to realisation one should observe the duties of life, but after that one becomes the Self of all, including the gods, who naturally therefore cannot hurt the man of realisation. Compare Brihadâranyaka Upanishad I. iv. 10.

दोषबुद्धयोभयातीतो निषेधान्न निवर्तते ।
गुणबुद्धया च विहितं न करोति यथार्भकः ॥११॥

11. Beyond the reach of both merit and demerit, (such a man)[1] will, like a child,[2] desist from prohibited actions, but not through a sense of evil, and perform enjoined actions, but not through an idea that it will conduce to merit.

[1] *Such a man etc.*—He acts on the momentum of his past good impressions or Samskâras, and never deviates, even unconsciously, from the strictly moral path. It is now his *nature* to do good acts and avoid evil actions. So there is no chance of his behaving according to caprice.

[2] *Like a child*—i.e. mechanically.

सर्वभूतसुहृच्छान्तो ज्ञानविज्ञाननिश्चयः ।
पश्यन्मदात्मकं विश्वं न विपद्येत वै पुनः ॥१२॥

12. Friend of all beings, with the settled conviction due to knowledge and realisation, and beholding the universe as consisting of nothing but Me, (he) no more comes to grief.[1]

[2] *Comes to grief*—transmigrates.

श्रीशुक उवाच ।
इत्यादिष्टो भगवता महाभागवतो नृप ।
उद्धवः प्रणिपत्याह तत्त्वजिज्ञासुरच्युतम् ॥१३॥

24   **UDDHAVA GITA**

Shuka said:

13. O King, being thus commanded by the Lord, the great devotee Uddhava, desirous to know the truth, prostrated himself before Shri Krishna and said:

उद्धव उवाच ।

योगेश योगविन्न्यास योगात्मन्योगसंभव ।
निःश्रेयसाय मे प्रोक्तस्त्यागः संन्यासलक्षणः ॥१४॥

Uddhava said:

14. O Lord of Yoga, O Thou Treasure[1] of the Yogis, Thou Embodiment of Yoga, from whom Yoga emanates, for my liberation Thou hast recommended to me the path of renunciation known as Sannyâsa.

[1] *Treasure etc.*—A slightly different reading— योग-विन्यास —would give the meaning, "Thou on whom Yoga is concentrated."

त्यागोऽयं दुष्करो भूमन् कामानां विषयात्मभिः ।
सुतरां त्वयि सर्वात्मन्नभक्तैरिति मे मतिः ॥१५॥

15. O Infinite, I consider this renunciation of desires as difficult for worldly-minded people, and the more so for those who are not devoted to Thee, who art the Self of all.

सोऽहं ममाहमिति मूढमतिर्विगाढ-
स्वन्मायया विरचितात्मनि सानुबन्धे ।
तत्त्वञ्जसा निगदितं भवता यथाऽहं
संसाधयामि भगवन्ननुशाधि भृत्यम् ॥१६॥

THE LAST MESSAGE OF SHRI KRISHNA 25

16. I[1] am but a fool, being passionately attached
to this body[2] and its appurtenances—which are the
creation of Thy Mâyâ[3]—and considering these as "I
and mine"; gently so, instruct Thy servant, O Lord,
so that I can faithfully carry out what Thou hast
taught me.

[1] *I am etc.—The* स: in the text means: "Whom Thou
dost consider as fit for Sannyâsa."

[2] *Body etc.*—The body is erroneously considered as "I"
and children and property, etc., as "mine."

[3] *Mâyâ*—The inscrutable Power of the Lord—nay, the
Lord Himself in action.

सत्यस्य ते स्वदृश आत्मन आत्मनोऽन्यं
वक्तारमीश विबुधेष्वपि नानुचक्षे ।
सर्वे विमोहितधियस्तव माययेमे
ब्रह्मादयस्तनुभृतो बहिरर्थभावाः ॥१७॥

17. O Lord, even among the gods I find no other
teacher of the Self than Thee who art Self-effulgent,
the Truth, the Âtman; for Brahmâ[1] and all other
embodied beings (whom we know of) are deluded by
Thy Mâyâ, and consider the objective world a reality.

[1] *Brahmâ etc.*—Their illumination is no doubt very great,
but still they are nothing compared with Thee.

तस्माद्भवन्तमनवद्यमनन्तपारं
सर्वज्ञमीश्वरमकुण्ठविकुण्ठधिष्ण्यम् ।
निर्विण्णधीरहमु ह वृजिनाभितप्तो
नारायणं नरसखं शरणं प्रपद्ये ॥१८॥

UDDHAVA GITA

18. Therefore, afflicted by sins and dispirited, do I take my refuge in Thee who art[1] unimpeachable, infinite and eternal, omniscient, the Lord of the Universe, who dwellest in the changeless Vaikuntha, who art the Supreme Being Nârâyana,[2] and the Friend of man.

[1] *Who art etc.*—In every respect Thou art my best Refuge.

[2] Narayana—In whom Brahmâ and all finally merge.

श्रीभगवानुवाच ।

प्रायेण मनुजा लोके लोकतत्त्वविचक्षणाः ।

समुद्धरन्ति ह्यात्मानमात्मनैवाशुभाशयात् ॥१६॥

The Lord said:

19. Very often in the world men who have truly discerned the truth about the universe deliver themselves from evil inclinations through their own exertions.

In this and the following verses the Lord encourages Uddhava to exert for Self-knowledge, specially as he was fortunate enough to get such a perfect Guru.

आत्मनो गुरुरात्मैव पुरुषस्य विशेषतः ।

यत्प्रत्यक्षानुमानाभ्यां श्रेयोऽसावनुविन्दते ॥२०॥

20. The Self alone is the teacher of all beings, and specially of men, for It conduces to well-being through direct perception and inference.

पुरुषत्वे च मां धीराः सांख्ययोगविशारदाः ।

आविस्तरां प्रपश्यन्ति सर्वशक्त्युपबृं'हितम् ॥२१॥

THE LAST MESSAGE OF SHRI KRISHNA 27

21. Those who are of a balanced mind and are skilled in knowledge and Yoga behold Me in the human body as fully manifest[1] and endowed with all powers.

[1] *Fully manifest etc.*—An echo of the Shruti passage: **पुरुषत्वे च आविस्तरामात्मा** etc.—"In the human body the Ātman is most manifest. There, being most endowed with illumination, It speaks cogent words and sees approved conduct; knows present duties, and heaven and hell; wishes immortality through this mortal frame; thus is It pre-eminently gifted. While the inferior animals have knowledge of hunger and thirst merely."

एकद्वित्रिचतुष्पादो बहुपादस्तथाऽपदः ।
बहव: सन्ति पुर: सृष्टास्तासां मे पौरुषी प्रिया ॥२२॥

22. There are many created cities[1] such as those with one, two, three, four, or many legs, as well as without legs; of these the human body is My favourite city.

[1] *Cities*—i.e. bodies.

अत्र मां मार्गयन्त्यद्धा युक्ता हेतुभिरीश्वरम् ।
गृह्यमाणैर्गुणैर्लिङ्गैरग्राह्यमनुमानतः ॥२३॥

23. In this, men who have controlled their senses directly seek Me, the inscrutable Lord, through attributes[1] such as the intellect etc., that are perceived, and by means of inference[2] through those indications.

[1] *Through attributes etc.*—This method is known as *Arthâpatti* or implication. The intellect etc. are inert, and must have some Self-effulgent unit principle behind them to make them active. This is the Ātman.

UDDHAVA GITA

[2] *Inference etc.*—The intellect etc. are instruments of knowledge and as such require some intelligent agent to use them.

It should be noted that these processes simply clear our notion about the Âtman, of which we hear from the Shruti.

अत्राप्युदाहरन्तीममितिहासं पुरातनम् ।

अवधूतस्य संवादं यदोरमिततेजसः ॥२४॥

24. Regarding this they also cite an old tale comprising the dialogue between Yadu,[1] of matchless valour, and an Avadhuta.

[1] *Yadu*—was the son of Yayâti and grandson of Nahusha, powerful kings of the Lunar Race, and ancestors of Shri Krishna.

अवधूतं द्विजं कंचिच्चरन्तमकुतोभयम् ।

कविं निरीक्ष्य तरुणं यदुः पप्रच्छ धर्मवित् ॥२५॥

25. Seeing a learned and young Brahmin Avadhuta[1] roaming fearlessly, Yadu who was versed in religion asked him:

[1] *Avadhuta*—a class of liberated saints who wear no external badge, and whose realisation of sameness in everything lifts them above the ordinary duties of life.

यदुरुवाच ।

कुतो बुद्धिरियं ब्रह्मन्नकर्तुः सुविशारदा ।

यामासाद्य भवाँल्लोकं विद्वाँश्चरति बालवत् ॥२६॥

THE LAST MESSAGE OF SHRI KRISHNA

Yadu said:

26. O Brahmin, free from action as you are, whence have you got this excellent discernment attaining which you roam over the world like a child, although you are a sage?

प्रायो धर्मार्थकामेषु विवित्सायां च मानवा: ।
हेतुनैव समीहन्ते आयुषो यशसः श्रियः ॥२७॥

27. Most often men exert themselves for virtue, wealth, desire, and enquiry about Âtman, and that too with the motive of gaining longevity, fame, and prosperity.

The king tries to show how far removed the saint was from ordinary men.

त्वं तु कल्पः कविर्दक्षः सुभगोऽमृतभाषण: ।
न कर्ता नेहसे किंचिज्जडोन्मत्तपिशाचवत् ॥२८॥

28. But you, in spite of your being able, learned, dexterous, well-formed, and possessed of mellifluous speech, neither work nor exert in the least, as if you were an idiot, or a lunatic, or a ghoul.

There is nothing to prevent you from asserting your rightful position in the world.

जनेषु दह्यमानेषु कामलोभदवाग्निना ।
न तप्यसेऽग्निना मुक्तो गङ्गाम्भस्थ इव द्विपः ॥२९॥

29. While people are being scorched by the forest-fire of lust and greed, you are not heated by

UDDHAVA GITA

the fire, being free from its influence like an elephant in the midst of Ganga water.

त्वं हि नः पृच्छतां ब्रह्मन्नात्मन्यानन्दकारणम् ।
ब्रूहि स्पर्शविहीनस्य भवतः केवलात्मनः ॥३०॥

30. O Brahmin, do tell us who ask you, how you derive bliss in your Self alone, untouched by sense-objects, and living a solitary life.

Please tell me the secret of your strength.

श्रीभगवानुवाच ।
यदुनैवं महाभागो ब्रह्मण्येन सुमेधसा ।
पृष्टः सभाजितः प्राह प्रश्रयावनतं द्विजः ॥३१॥

The Lord said:

31. Being thus asked and honoured by the intelligent Yadu who was devoted to Brahmins, the noble Brâhmana addressed the king who had bent himself low in reverence:

ब्राह्मण उवाच ।
सन्ति मे गुरवो राजन् बहवो बुद्ध्य पाश्रिताः ।
यतो बुद्धिमुपादाय मुक्तोऽटामीह तान् श्रृणु ॥३२॥

The Brâhmana said:

32. I have many teachers, O King, whom I resorted to through the intellect,[1] receiving wisdom from whom I roam on earth at large. Listen who they are.

THE LAST MESSAGE OF SHRI KRISHNA

31

[1] *Through the intellect*—Not that they actually instructed me but I derived these lessons from their way of living.

पृथिवी वायुराकाशमापोऽग्निश्चन्द्रमा रविः ।
कपोतोऽजगरः सिन्धुः पतङ्गो मधुकृद्गजः ॥३३॥

33. The earth, air, sky, water, fire, the moon, the sun, the pigeon, the python, the sea, the moth, the bee, the elephant;

मधुहा हरिणो मीनः पिङ्गला कुररोऽर्भकः ।
कुमारी शरकृत् सर्प ऊर्णनाभिः सुपेशकृत् ॥३४॥

34. The honey-gatherer, the deer, the fish, the courtesan Pingalâ, the osprey, the child, the maiden, the arrow-maker, the snake, the spider, and a particular insect known as Bhramara-kita.[1]

[1] *Bhramara-kita*—When it catches a cockroach, the latter through fright is almost metamorphosed into the likeness of this insect.

एते मे गुरवो राजंश्चतुर्विंशतिराश्रिताः ।
शिक्षा वृत्तिभिरेतेषामन्वशिक्षमिहात्मनः ॥३५॥

35. These, O King, are the twenty-four teachers whom I have resorted to; from the characteristic traits of these I have gathered all my lessons.

यतो यदनुशिक्षामि यथा वा नाहुषात्मज ।
तत् तथा पुरुषव्याघ्र निबोध कथयामि ते ॥३६॥

32 UDDHAVA GITA

36. O grandson of Nahusha, I am going to relate to you which lesson I have learnt from whom, and how; listen.

भूतैराक्रम्यमाणोऽपि धीरो दैववशानुगैः ।
तद्विद्वान्न चलेन्मार्गादन्वशिक्षं क्षितेर्व्रतम् ॥३७॥

37. The man of steady intellect should not, even though oppressed[1] by creatures that are themselves under the sway of destiny,[2] swerve from his path,[3] being conversant with this fact—this is the trait I have learnt from the earth.

[1] *Oppressed etc.*—The earth is called "all-forbearing". So should the saint also be. Hills and trees also are cited in the next verse as forming part of the earth and giving their own lessons.

[2] *Destiny*—or God's dispensation.

[3] *Path*—of sameness of vision.

शश्वत्परार्थसर्वेहः परार्थैकान्तसंभवः ।
साधुः शिक्षेत भूभृत्तो नगशिष्यः परात्मताम् ॥३८॥

38. The good man should learn from the hill[1] how one should always direct one's entire actions to the good of others and one's very birth should be absolutely for the sake of others; while, as a disciple of trees, he should learn how to be at the disposal[2] of others.

[1] *The hill*—produces vegetation, streams, etc., which contribute to others' good.

[2] *Disposal etc.*—Even if you hew it down, it will not

THE LAST MESSAGE OF SHRI KRISHNA

murmur. Pelt at it, and it will give you luscious fruits. It calmly bears the ravages of the seasons, and so on.

प्राणवृत्त्यैव संतुष्येन्मुनिर्नेवेन्द्रियप्रियैः ।
ज्ञानं यथा न नश्येत नावकीर्येत वाङ्मनः ॥३९॥

39. The sage should be satisfied with merely ministering[1] to the vital functions and not with things pleasing to the senses, so that knowledge may not be destroyed and the mind and speech frittered away.

Verses 39-41 set forth the lessons to be derived from Vâyu, ordinarily rendered as "wind", but having also the broader and inner significance of "vibration" or "life-function" (*Prâna*). Verse 39 deals with the latter phase of the principle, and the other two verses with external air.

[1] *Ministering* etc.—i.e. just as the Prâna-Vâyu merely requires food to sustain the body, so the Yogi also must eat to live, not live to eat.

विषयेष्वाविशन् योगी नानाधर्मेषु सर्वतः ।
गुणदोषव्यपेतात्मा न विषज्जेत वायुवत् ॥४०॥

40. The Yogi, moving amid sense-objects possessed of diverse characters, should not be attached to them, keeping his mind absolutely free from their virtues and shortcomings, like the wind.[1]

[1] *Wind*—which remains unaffected by the good or bad odour of things over which it blows.

पार्थिवेष्विह देहेषु प्रविष्टस्तद्गुणाश्रयः ।
गुणैर्न युज्यते योगी गन्धैर्वायुरिवात्मदृक् ॥४१॥

41. Even though entering material bodies on earth and associating with their attributes, the Yogi

with his eyes always on the Self, is not affected by those attributes, like the wind by odours.

अन्तर्हितश्च स्थिरजङ्गमेषु
ब्रह्मात्मभावेन समन्वयेन ।
व्याप्त्याऽऽव्यवच्छेदमसङ्गमात्मनो
मुनिर्नभस्त्वं विततस्य भावयेत् ॥४२॥

42. Even though living in the body, the sage, through his identity with the Self, should reflect on the unity, non-attachment, and sky-like trait of the omnipresent Âtman, which runs as a substratum through all movable and immovable things.

Verses 42 and 43 bring out the resemblance of the Yogi with the Âkâsha, commonly translated as sky or ether. According to Hindu philosophy, Âkâsha is the first and finest of the primordial elements (*Mahâbhutas*), is indivisible and present everywhere. So it is a fit exemplar for the absolute omnipresence of the Âtman. The sage should reflect on this.

तेजोऽबन्नमयैर्भावैर्मेघाद्यै र्वायुनेरितैः ।
न स्पृश्यते नभस्तद्वत् कालसृष्टैर्गुणैः पुमान् ॥४३॥

43. As the sky is not touched by things which are the products of fire,[1] water, and earth, nor by clouds driven by the wind, so a man[2] should not be touched by things which are the creations of time.

[1] *Fire, water, and earth*—With Âkâsha and Vâyu these form the five successive Mahâbhutas in the initial creative process. We have used here the common English equivalents of the Sanskrit terms *Tejas, Ap,* and *Kshiti,*

THE LAST MESSAGE OF SHRI KRISHNA

which are highly open to criticism. Fire, water, and earth are only types or convenient gross manifestations of the subtle principles or states which may roughly be rendered as heat, liquidity, and solidity. The reader should remember this inner significance of all these terms to really understand in which sense a particular word occurs in a certain passage.

[2] *A man etc.*—i.e. realising his identity with the Âtman.

स्वच्छः प्रकृतितः स्त्रिग्धो माधुर्यस्तीर्थभूर्नृणाम् ।
मुनिः पुनात्यपां मित्रमीक्षोपस्पर्शकीर्तनैः ॥४४॥

44. Pure,[1] genial by nature, sweet, and a source of imparting holiness[2] to men, the sage—resembling water—purifies all, being seen,[3] touched, and praised by them.

[1] *Pure etc.*—It should be noticed how these adjectives apply both to water and the sage.

[2] *Holiness etc.*—e.g. the sacred rivers, lakes, etc.

[3] *Seen etc.*—One becomes pure by seeing, touching, and singing praises to the sacred waters as well as the saint.

तेजस्वी तपसा दीप्तो दुर्धर्षोदरभाजनः ।
सर्वभक्ष्योऽपि युक्तात्मा नादत्ते मलमग्निवत् ॥४५॥

45. Bright,[1] resplendent with Tapas, powerful, with no receptacle[2] for food except the belly, and eating everything—the man of self-control, like fire, is not polluted (thereby).

Verses 45 to 47 relate the similarity between the sage and the fire.

[1] *Bright etc.*—The adjectives in this and the next verse are applicable alike to fire and the sage.

UDDHAVA GITA

²*Receptacle etc.*—The fire consumes only what is put into it; so does the all-renouncing sage accept only what is offered to him.

कचिच्छन्नः कचित्स्पष्ट उपास्यः श्रेय इच्छताम् ।
भुंक्ते सर्वत्र दातॄणां दहन्प्रागुत्तराशुभम् ॥४६॥

46. Sometimes disguised,[1] sometimes patent, being resorted[2] to by those who desire welfare, he eats everywhere from donors, burning their past and future evils.

[1]*Disguised*—the fire by ashes, and the Jnâni by assumed madness and the like.

[2]*Resorted etc.*—People make sacrifice in the sacred fire, and entertain the Jnâni, and are thereby ennobled in spirit. This explains the last line.

ख्मायया सृष्टमिदं सदसल्लक्षणं विभुः ।
प्रविष्ट ईयते तत्तत्सरूपोऽग्निरिवैधसि ॥४७॥

47. The omnipresent Lord, pervading this gross and subtle[1] universe created by His own Mâyâ,[2] acts in the shape of different things, like fire[3] in combustible things.

[1]*Gross and subtle*—*Sat* and *Asat* may also mean higher and lower beings.

[2]*Mâyâ*—See note 3 on verse 16, Ch. II.

[3]*Fire etc.*—Fire has no form of its own. As the principle of Tejas it is present in everything. But when a piece of wood burns, fire also seems to have that shape. So all the apparent activity of the Âtman is due to the supervening adjuncts (Upâdhis) through which It manifests Itself.

THE LAST MESSAGE OF SHRI KRISHNA

विसर्गांद्याः शमशानान्ता भावा देहस्य नात्मनः ।
कलानामिव चन्द्रस्य कालेनाव्यक्तवर्त्मना ॥४८॥

48. The states[1] from birth to death belong to the body, not to the Âtman, like the digits of the moon[2] occasioned by Time whose march is inscrutable.

The illustration of the moon is explained in this verse. [1] *States etc.*—all the stages of a corporeal being's life. [2] *Moon etc.*—The moon remains as it is; only there is an apparent change over it due to astronomical motions.

कालेन ह्योघवेगेन भूतानां प्रभवाप्ययौ ।
नित्यावपि न दृश्येते आत्मनोऽग्नेर्यथार्चिषाम् ॥४९॥

49. Birth and death, though ever assailing bodies through the massive velocity of Time, are never witnessed of the Self, as in the case of the flames[1] of fire.

This is a return, in passing, to the topic of fire to emphasise the transitoriness of things and thus stimulate a spirit of renunciation. [1] *Flames etc.*—The flames are subject to change, but not the fire.

गुणैर्गुणानुपादत्ते यथाकालं विमुञ्चति ।
न तेषु युज्यते योगी गोभिर्गा इव गोपतिः ॥५०॥

50. The Yogi accepts sense-objects through the sense-organs and returns them at the due season,[1] without being attached to them, like the sun[2] (giving back) the water (it sucked) through its rays.

The analogy of the sun is made explicit in this and the next verse.

UDDHAVA GITA

[1]*Due season*—wherever there is a needy person.
[2]*The sun etc.*—The reference is to the circulation of water between the earth and the sky.

बुध्यते स्वे न भेदेन व्यक्तिस्थ इव तद्गतः ।
लक्ष्यते स्थूलमतिभिरात्मा चावस्थितोऽर्कवत् ॥५१॥

51. Like the sun,[1] the Âtman, established in[2] Itself, is not perceived as admitting of varieties, but when manifesting[3] Itself through an adjunct, is looked upon by dull-witted people as becoming identified with that.

[1]*The sun etc.*—The sun, as it is, is one, but when reflected in water etc., it appears to be many and seems to be small or distorted and so forth.
[2]*Established etc.*—ever the same.
[3]*Manifesting etc.*—See note 3 on verse 47.

नातिस्नेहः प्रसङ्गो वा कर्तव्यः क्वापि केनचित् ।
कुर्बन्निन्देत संतापं कपोत इव दीनधीः ॥५२॥

52. One should not cherish too much affection or attachment for anyone. If one does so, one is smitten with affliction like the poor pigeon.

The lesson which the pigeon taught is graphically set forth from this verse to the end of the chapter.

कपोतः कश्चनारण्ये कृतनीडो वनस्पतौ ।
कपोत्या भार्यया सार्धमुवास कतिचित्समाः ॥५३॥

53. A pigeon built his nest on a certain tree in a forest and lived there for some years with his partner.

THE LAST MESSAGE OF SHRI KRISHNA

कपोतौ स्नेहगुणितहृदयौ गृहधर्मिणौ ।
दृष्टि दृष्ट्याङ्गमङ्गेन बुद्धि बुद्ध्या बबन्धतुः ॥५४॥

54. The pigeons, with their hearts tied in a bond
of love, lived a family life, fixing their gaze on each
other, in close companionship, each intent on the
other.

शय्यासनाटनस्थानवार्ताक्रीडाशनादिकम् ।
मिथुनीभूय विस्रब्धौ चेरतुर्वनराजिषु ॥५५॥

55. In that forest they together went through
such acts as lying, sitting, roaming, resting, talk, sport,
and eating—without any fear.

यं यं वाञ्छति सा राजंस्तर्पयन्त्यनुकम्पिता ।
तं तं समनयत्कामं कृच्छ्रेणाप्यजितेन्द्रियः ॥५६॥

56. Whatever the female bird, who pleased her
partner and was agreeably treated by him, wished
for, the other, O King,[1] fulfilled those wants, even at
the cost of much trouble, for he was a slave to his
senses.

[1] King—Yadu.

कपोती प्रथमं गर्भं गृह्णति काल आगते ।
अण्डानि सुषुवे नीडे स्वपत्युः संनिधौ सती ॥५७॥

57. In course of time the good female bird had
her first conception and laid (some) eggs in that nest
in the presence of her mate.

UDDHAVA GITA

तेषु काले व्यजायन्त रचितावयवा हरेः ।
शक्तिभिर्दुर्विभाव्याभिः कोमलाङ्गतनूरुहाः ॥५८॥

58. In due season some young birds with tender limbs and feathers grew out of those eggs, the inscrutable Power of the Lord fashioning their features.

प्रजाः पुपुषतुः प्रीतौ दम्पती पुत्रवत्सलौ ।
शृण्वन्तौ कूजितं तासां निर्वृतौ कलभाषितैः ॥५९॥

59. The happy pair, devoted to their offspring, reared the young ones, listening to their chirping and delighted by their sweet accents.

तासां पतत्रैः सुस्पर्शैः कूजितैर्मुग्धचेष्टितैः ।
प्रत्युद्गमैरदीनानां पितरौ मुदमापतुः ॥६०॥

60. They were cheerful, and their wings soft to the touch, their warblings and graceful movements, and their going out to meet their parents,[1] gladdened the latter.

[1] *Parents*—when they returned from their search for food.

स्नेहानुबद्धहृदयावन्योन्यं विष्णुमायया ।
विमोहितौ दीनधियौ शिशून्पुपुषतुः प्रजाः ॥६१॥

61. The two birds, with their hearts attached to each other in love, beguiled by the Lord's Mâyâ, reared their young ones, with no higher outlook on life.

THE LAST MESSAGE OF SHRI KRISHNA

एकदा जग्मतुस्तासामन्नार्थं तौ कुटुम्बिनौ ।
परितः कानने तस्मिन्नर्थिनौ चेरतुश्चिरम् ॥६२॥

62. One day, the pair went in search of food for them, and roamed about for a long time in that forest, with this object.

दृष्ट्वा ताँल्लुब्धकः कश्चिद्यदृच्छातो वनेचरः ।
जगृहे जालमातत्य चरतः खालयान्तिके ॥६३॥

63. A fowler rambling in the woods at will saw them[1] flying near their nest, and caught them by spreading a trap.

[1] *Them*—the young ones.

कपोतश्च कपोती च प्रजापोषे सदोत्सुकौ ।
गतौ पोषणमादाय खनीडमुपजग्मतुः ॥६४॥

64. The parent birds who were always eager to bring up their young ones and had been out (for that end) returned to their nest with food.

कपोती खात्मजान्वीक्ष्य बालकाञ्जाल्संवृतान् ।
तानभ्यधावत्क्रोशन्ती क्रोशतो भृशदुःखिता ॥६५॥

65. The female pigeon, finding her young off-spring caught in the trap and weeping, rushed at them, crying and much aggrieved.

साऽसकृत्स्नेहगुणिता दीनचित्ताऽजमायया ।
खयं चाबध्यत शिचा बद्धान्पश्यन्त्यपस्मृतिः ॥६६॥

UDDHAVA GITA

66. The poor mother-bird, fettered by many a tie of love through the Lord's Mâyâ, herself fell into the trap, even though seeing the young ones caught in it; for she was beside herself (with grief).

कपोतश्चात्मजान्बद्धानात्मनोऽप्यधिकान्प्रियान् ।
भार्यां चात्मसमां दीनो विललापातिदुःखितः ॥६७॥

67. The poor male-pigeon, too, finding his young ones who were more to him than his own self, as well as his beloved partner who was a (fit) match for him, caught in the trap, wept, sorely afflicted.

अहो मे पश्यतापायमल्पपुण्यस्य दुर्मतेः ।
अतृप्तस्याकृतार्थस्य गृहस्त्रैवर्गिको हतः ॥६८॥

68. "Alas, behold my calamity—unlucky and wicked that I am; before I have been satisfied, and have attained the consummation of life, my home, which conduces to the threefold end[1] of life, is gone!

[1] *Threefold end*—Virtue, wealth, and the fulfilment of desires.

अनुरूपाऽनुकूला च यस्य मे पतिदेवता ।
शून्ये गृहे मां संत्यज्य पुत्रैः स्वर्याति साधुभिः ॥६९॥

69. "Now that my wife who was a match for me and always agreeable, who looked upon me her husband as God, has ascended to heaven with her virtuous children, leaving me behind in this lonely house—

THE LAST MESSAGE OF SHRI KRISHNA
43

सोऽहं शून्ये गृहे दीनो मृतदारो मृतप्रजः ।
जिजीविषे किमर्थं वा विधुरो दुःखजीवितः ॥७०॥

70. "For what purpose should I desire to live,
in this deserted house, miserable and afflicted, a
widower with all my children gone—to whom life
would mean nothing but woe?"

तांस्तथैवावृतान् शिग्भिर्मृत्युप्रस्तान्विचेष्टतः ।
स्वयं च कृपणः शिक्षु पश्यन्नप्यबुधोऽपतत् ॥७१॥

71. Even though seeing them caught in the
trap, almost in the jaws of death, and struggling in
that (pitiful) way, he, too, lost his senses and, woe-
begone, fell into it himself.

तं लब्ध्वा लुब्धकः क्रूरः कपोतं गृहमेधिनम् ।
कपोतकान्कपोतीं च सिद्धार्थः प्रययौ गृहम् ॥७२॥

72. The cruel fowler, getting the pigeon who
was intent on family life, with his partner and the
young ones, was satisfied and went home.

एवं कुटुम्ब्यशान्तात्मा द्वन्द्वारामः पतत्रिवत् ।
पुष्णन्कुटुम्बं कृपणः सानुबन्धोऽवसीदति ॥७३॥

73. Thus the miserable family man, with his
senses uncontrolled, and taking delight in the pairs of
opposites,[1] maintains his family and like the bird,
comes to grief together with his belongings.[2]

[1] *Opposites*—such as pleasure and pain, heat and cold,
and so on.

[2] *Belongings*—the body, children, etc.

UDDHAVA GITA

44

यः प्राप्य मानुषं लोकं मुक्तिद्वारमपावृतम् ।
गृहेषु खगवत्सक्तस्तमारूढच्युतं विदुः ।।७४।।

74. He who attaining a human birth, which
is like an open gateway to liberation, is attached, like
the bird, to the family concerns merely, is considered
as one who has fallen from his status.[1]

[1] *Status*—the high state which he already occupied.

CHAPTER III

ब्राह्मण उवाच ।

सुखमैन्द्रियकं राजन्स्वर्गे नरक एव च ।
देहिनां यद्यथा दुःखं तस्मान्नेच्छेत तद्बुधः ॥१॥

The Brâhmana said:

1. O King, the enjoyment[1] that comes to beings through the senses is met with in heaven as well as in hell, just as misery is; hence the wise man should not hanker after it.

Verses 1-4 set forth the lesson derived from the python which never moves in search of food but takes just what comes. This peculiarity has given the name to the mode of life of a class of Sâdhus who never leave their seats in quest of food. See next verse.

[1] *Enjoyment etc.*—Enjoyment like misery is inevitable in any sphere of life, being due to one's *Prârabdha* work. Hence one should not waste energy over its acquisition, but should strive after Self-realisation.

ग्रासं सुमृष्टं विरसं महान्तं स्तोकमेव बा ।
यदृच्छयैवापतितं प्रसेदाजगरोऽक्रियः ॥२॥

2. Whether food be delicious or insipid, sumptuous or scanty, the sage who lives a python's life should take just what comes of itself, without exerting for it.

शयीताहानि भूरीणि निराहारोऽनुपक्रमः ।
यदि नोपनमेद्ग्रासो महाहिरिव दिष्टभुक् ॥३॥

UDDHAVA GITA

46

3. He should lie many days without food and without exertion; and if no food presents itself, then like the great python, he should abide by what destiny[1] decrees.

[1] *Destiny etc.*—i.e. he must bear it calmly.

ओजःसहोबलयुतं बिभ्रद् हमकर्मकम् ।
शयानो वीतनिद्रश्च नेहेतेन्द्रियवानपि ॥४॥

4. Holding still the body endowed with energy,[1] fortitude, and strength, he should lie wide awake,[2] and not exert, even though having the organs intact.

[1] *Energy etc.*—These three refer respectively to the efficiency of the organs, the mind and the physical body—says Shridhara. Even possessed of full vigour the sage should not exert for food.

[2] *Wide awake*—with his mind intent upon God-realisation, the supreme goal of life.

मुनिः प्रसन्नगम्भीरो दुर्विगाह्यो दुरत्ययः ।
अनन्तपारो ह्यक्षोभ्यः स्तिमितोद इवार्णवः ॥६॥

5. The sage should be placid and profound, difficult to fathom and to cross over,[1] illimitable[2] and immovable,[3] like the ocean with its mass of waters at rest.

Verses 5-6 bring out the parallel between the ocean and the saint.

[1] *To cross over*—i.e. to slight.

[2] *Illimitable*—as the sage has realised his identity with the Âtman.

[3] *Immovable*—because he has no attachment or aversion.

THE LAST MESSAGE OF SHRI KRISHNA

47

The application of the epithets to the ocean is plain enough.

समृद्धकामो हीनो वा नारायणपरो मुनिः ।
नोत्सर्पेत न शुष्येत सरिद्भिरिव सागरः ॥६॥

6. Whether he has an abundance of enjoyable things or he has none, the sage, who has set his heart upon the Lord, neither overflows[1] nor shrinks, like the ocean on account of the waters[2] of the rivers.

[1] *Neither overflows etc.*—suffers no change. See notes 2 and 3 under verse 5.

[2] *Waters etc.*—which vary in volume according to the monsoon.

दृष्ट्वा स्त्रियं देवमायां तद्भावैरजितेन्द्रियः ।
प्रलोभितः पतत्यन्धे तमस्यग्नौ पतङ्गवत् ॥७॥

7. The man of uncontrolled senses, seeing women—the enchantment created by the Lord—and being tempted by their blandishments, falls[1] into abysmal darkness, like the moth into the fire.

Verses 7 and 8 utter a note of warning against sex-attraction and sense-gratification in general, by the illustration of the fate of the moth which is attracted by the beauty of fire.

[1] *Falls etc.*—suffers transmigration.

योषिद्धिरण्याभरणाम्बरादि-
द्रव्येषु मायारचितेषु मूढः ।
प्रलोभितात्मा ह्युपभोगबुद्ध्या
पतङ्गवन्नश्यति नष्टदृष्टिः ॥८॥

48   UDDHAVA GITA

8. The foolish man who, with his vision blinded, is tempted by such illusive creations as women, gold, ornaments, apparel, and the like, considering them as objects of enjoyment, is destroyed like the moth.

स्तोकं स्तोकं ग्रसेद्ग्रासं देहो वर्तेत यावता ।
गृहानहिंसन्नातिष्ठेद्‌वृत्तिं माधुकरीं मुनिः ॥६॥

9. The sage should live a bee-like life,[1] taking little doles of food from several houses—without taxing them—just so much as would maintain the body.

The lessons taught by the bee is given in verses 9-12.
[1] *Bee-like life*—this is actually the name given to the house-to-house begging of cooked food by Sâdhus in India.

अणुभ्यश्च महद्‌भ्यश्च शास्त्रेभ्यः कुशलो नरः ।
सर्वतः सारमादद्यात्पुष्पेभ्य इव षट्पदः ॥१०॥

10. The clever man should take the essence out of all sources, from scriptures—small as well as great—like the bee from flowers.

सायंतनं श्वस्तनं वा न संगृह्णीत भिक्षितम् ।
पाणिपात्रोदरामत्रो मक्षिकेव न संग्रही ॥११॥

11. (The sage) should not store alms for the evening or the next day; either the hands or the stomach should be his receptacle; he should not be a hoarder like the bee.

THE LAST MESSAGE OF SHRI KRISHNA

सायंतनं श्वस्तनं वा न संगृह्णीत भिक्षुकः ।
मक्षिका इव संगृह्णन्सह तेन विनश्यति ॥१२॥

12. The mendicant should not store for the evening or the next day; one who does so is destroyed[1] with his store, like the bee.

[1] *Destroyed*—by robbers.

पदापि युवतीं भिक्षुर्न स्पृशेद्दारवीमपि ।
स्पृशन्करीव बध्येत करिण्या अङ्गसङ्गतः ॥१३॥

13. The Sannyâsin should not touch even the wooden figure of a young woman—no, not with his feet even. If he does so, he would be caught, as is the elephant through his attachment for the touch[1] of the she-elephant.

The lesson to be learnt from the elephant is described in verses 13-14. Attachment to the sense of touch is deprecated.

[1] *Touch etc.*—The reference is to the well-known device adopted in *Khedâ* operations, of bringing in a tame she-elephant to decoy the wild intruders.

नाधिगच्छेत्स्त्रियं प्राज्ञः कर्हिचिन्मृत्युमात्मनः ।
बलाधिकैः स हन्येत गजैरन्यैर्गजो यथा ॥१४॥

14. The wise man should never court the company of women as if it were death to him; for he would be killed by more powerful (rivals) as is the elephant by other (rival) elephants.

न देयं नोपभोग्यं च लुब्धैर्यद्दुःखसंचितम् ।
भुङ्क्ते तदपि तच्चान्यो मधुहेवार्थविन्मधु ॥१५॥

UDDHAVA GITA

15. What avaricious people hoard with pains and would neither[1] give away nor enjoy, another, who knows his business,[2] seizes, that again another, and so on, as the honey-gatherer collects honey.[3]

The parallel of the honey-gatherer is explained in this and the next verse.

[1] *Neither give away etc.*—Poet Bhartrihari aptly says, that there are only three ways in which wealth can be spent: It must either be given away in charity, or utilised personally, or—last alternative—fill the pockets of the robber!

[2] *Knows his business*—scents out the treasure and finds out means to seize it.

[3] *Collects honey*—by depriving the poor bees.

सुदुःखोपार्जितैर्वित्तैराशासानां गृहाशिषः ।
मधुहेवाग्रतो भुङ्क्ते यतिर्वे गृहमेधिनाम् ॥१६॥

16. Like the honey-gatherer, the Sannyâsin first partakes[1] of the good things which householders, with a view to enjoy, collect through money earned with great pains.

[1] *First partakes*—The custom in India gives the Sannyâsin this privilege. So even without exertion the subsistences of life may be had by simply thinking on the Lord—this is the idea.

ग्राम्यगीतं न श्रृणुयाद्यतिर्वनचरः क्वचित् ।
शिक्षेत हरिणाद्बद्धान्मृगयोर्गीतमोहितात् ॥१७॥

17. The Sannyâsin who roams about in the woods should never listen to sensuous music,[1] but should take a lesson from the deer that was caught, being enamoured by the fowler's music.

THE LAST MESSAGE OF SHRI KRISHNA

In this and the next verse the evils of attachment to the sense of hearing are suggested by a reference to the proneness of deer for music, and to the case of Rishyashringa, who is fabled to have been born of a deer, and—so the illustration suggests—could not wholly get rid of the evils of heredity!

[1] *Sensuous music*—No restriction is made against devotional music.

नृत्यवादित्रगीतानि जुषन्ग्राम्याणि योषिताम् ।
आसां क्रीडनको वशय ऋष्यशृंगो मृगीसुतः ॥१८॥

18. Rishyashringa, the offspring of deer, listening to the sensuous music of women, became their docile plaything.

जिह्वयातिप्रमाथिन्या जनो रसविमोहितः ।
मृत्युमृच्छत्यसद्बुद्धिर्मीनस्तु बडिशैर्यथा ॥१९॥

19. The foolish man infatuated with delicacies by an over-greedy tongue meets with death, like the fish by means of the hook.[1]

The dangers of pandering to the sense of taste are pointed out through the example of the fish in verses 19-21.

[1] *Hook*—The bait hides the hook which the fish fails to notice. Behind every sense-pleasure enjoyed as such, there also lurks a reaction.

इन्द्रियाणि जयन्त्याशु निराहारा मनीषिणः ।
वर्जयित्वा तु रसनं तन्निरन्नस्य वर्धते ॥२०॥

20. Great men, who give up food, easily control the sense-organs excepting the organ of taste, which

UDDHAVA GITA

becomes more troublesome[1] to one who does not take food.

[1] *More troublesome*—hence the secret of controlling it is to take little quantities of food just enough to maintain life, without being attached to taste.

तावज्जितेन्द्रियो न स्याद्विजितान्येन्द्रियः पुमान् ।
न जयेद्रसनं यावज्जितं सर्वं जिते रसे ॥२१॥

21. A man who has overcome the other organs cannot be a master of his senses until he controls the organ of taste; when the organ of taste is controlled, everything is controlled.

पिङ्गला नाम वेश्यासीद्विदेहनगरे पुरा ।
तस्या मे शिक्षितं किंचिन्निबोध नृपनन्दन ॥२२॥

22. In days of yore, there was a courtesan named Pingalâ in the city of Videha. I have learnt something from her. Listen to it, O King.

The lesson of satiety or disgust for worldly things received from Pingalâ is narrated in these verses up to the end of the chapter.

सा स्वैरिण्येकदा कान्तं संकेत उपनेष्यती ।
अभूत्काले बहिर्द्वारि बिभ्रती रूपमुत्तमम् ॥२३॥

23. One day that courtesan, with a view to conduct some lover to the trysting-place, took her stand at the door in the evening, beautifully dressed.

मार्ग आगच्छतो वीक्ष्य पुरुषान्पुरुषर्षभ ।
तान् शुल्कदान्वित्तवतः कान्तान्मेनेऽर्थकामुका ॥२४॥

THE LAST MESSAGE OF SHRI KRISHNA

24. O best of men, seeing men coming along the way, she, who was greedy after money, considered them to be rich, and persons likely to yield her some income.

आगतेष्वपयातेषु सा संकेतोपजीविनी ।
अप्यन्यो वित्तवान्कोऽपि मामुपैष्यति भूरिदः ॥२५॥

25. As they came and passed by (one by one), she who lived upon the proceeds of such a life, thought that some other rich man would approach her and bring her a lot of money.

एवं दुराशया ध्वस्तनिद्रा द्वार्यवलम्बती ।
निर्गच्छन्ती प्रविशती निशीथं समपद्यत ॥२६॥

26. Thus she kept at the door—now going in, now coming out—with her sleep upset by this fond expectation, till it was midnight.

तस्या वित्ताशया शुष्यद्वक्त्राया दीनचेतसः ।
निर्वेदः परमो जज्ञे चिन्ताहेतुः सुखावहः ॥२७॥

27. When through this expectation of money her countenance sank and she was very much down in spirits, then as a result of this brooding an utter disgust came to her, that made her happy.

तस्या निर्विण्णचित्ताया गीतं श्रृणु यथा मम ।
निर्वेद आशापाशानां पुरुषस्य यथा ह्वसिः ॥२८॥

54 UDDHAVA GITA

28. Hear from me how she, disgusted, sang; for disgust is like a sword to cut asunder a man's fetters of expectation.

नह्यंगाऽजातनिर्वेदो देहबन्धं जिहासति ।

यथा विज्ञानरहितो मनुजो ममतां नृप ॥२९॥

29. One, my dear, does not desire to get rid of the bondage of the body until one has become disgusted, as a man without illumination, O King, the clinging[1] to things.

[1] *Clinging etc.*—lit. "mineness".

पिङ्गलोवाच ।

अहो मे मोहवितर्ति पश्यताऽविजितात्मनः ।

या कान्तादसतः कामं कामये येन बालिशा ॥३०॥

Pingalâ said:

30. Alas, behold the extent of my infatuation: I am a fool, whose senses are not under control! Therefore I seek the satisfaction of desires from such puny creatures as men.

सन्तं समीपे रमणं रतिप्रदं

वित्तप्रदं नित्यमिमं विहाय ।

अकामदं दुःखभयादिशोक-

मोहप्रदं तुच्छमहं भजेऽज्ञा ॥३१॥

31. I am so foolish as to neglect this eternal Âtman who lives near, who is a fit lover and can

THE LAST MESSAGE OF SHRI KRISHNA

satisfy me, and who can give me wealth; leaving
Him I am courting a puny man, who cannot satisfy
my desires, and who causes misery, fear, disease, grief,
and infatuation!

अहो मयात्मा परितापितो वृथा
सांकेत्यवृत्त्याऽतिविगर्ह्य वार्तया ।
स्त्रैणान्नराद्याऽर्थतृषोऽनुशोच्या-
क्रीतेन वित्तं रतिमात्मनेच्छती ॥३२॥

32. Oh, in vain have I afflicted my soul by
this despicable mode of living, viz. that of a
courtesan; I have sought wealth and pleasure from
pitiable men who are greedy and slaves to women,
after selling my body to them!

यदस्थिभिर्निर्मितवंशवंश्य-
स्थूणं त्वचा रोमनखैः पिनद्धम् ।
क्षरन्नवद्वारमगारमेतद्
विण्मूत्रपूर्णं मदुपैति कान्या ॥३३॥

33. Who but myself should make much of this
body[1] which consists of bony structures such as the
spine, ribs, and limbs (like the ridge-pole, rafters, and
posts of a house), and is covered ever with skin, hair
and nails, with its nine doors for secretion, and full
of filthy stuff?

[1] *This body*—the human body which she looks upon
as "lover". The body which is so full of impurities cannot
be a source of enjoyment. It is the Âtman from which all
enjoyment comes.

UDDHAVA GITA

विदेहानां पुरे ह्यस्मिन्नहमेकैव मूढधीः ।
याऽन्यमिच्छन्त्यसत्यस्मादात्मदात्काममच्युतात् ॥३४॥

34. In this city of Videha, verily I am the only foolish person who, of wicked heart, seeks any other source of enjoyment than the Lord who confers (the realisation of) the Self.

सुहृद्श्रेष्ठतमो नाथ आत्मा चायं शरीरिणाम् ।
तं विक्रीयात्मनैवाहं रमेऽनेन यथा रमा ॥३५॥

35. He is the friend, the dearest of the dear, the Master, nay, the very Self of all embodied beings; winning Him over by giving up the body (to Him), I shall enjoy His company, like Lakshmi.

कियत्प्रियं ते व्यभजन्कामा ये कामदा नराः ।
आद्यन्तवन्तो भार्याया देवा वा कालविद्रुताः ॥३६॥

36. How much[1] enjoyment have these ever conferred on women who depend upon them—your sense-objects; or men who pose as fulfilling desires; or your gods either, having a beginning and end and being overrun by Time?

[1] *How much etc.*—None but God can give us lasting bliss. He is the only Refuge of all beings.

नूनं मे भगवान्प्रीतो विष्णुः केनापि कर्मणा ।
निर्वेदोऽयं दुराशाया यन्मे जातः सुखावहः ॥३७॥

THE LAST MESSAGE OF SHRI KRISHNA   57

37. Surely I have pleased the Lord Vishnu by some deed or other, since out of a vain expectation this happy disgust has come to me.

मैवं स्युर्मन्दभाग्यायाः क्लेशा निर्वेदहेतवः ।
येनानुबन्धं निर्हृत्य पुरुषः शममृच्छति ॥३८॥

38. Otherwise, unhappy that I am, these miseries would not have fallen to my lot, bringing on disgust, by means of which man getting rid of trammels[1] attains to peace.

[1] *Trammels*—e.g. the house and chattels etc.

तेनोपकृतमादाय शिरसा ग्राम्यसंगताः ।
त्यक्त्वा दुराशाः शरणं व्रजामि तमधीश्वरम् ॥३९॥

39. Accepting this gift of the Lord on my head,[1] I give up my vain expectations that pertain only to sense-objects, and take refuge in the Supreme Lord.

[1] *On my head*—i.e. reverentially.

संतुष्टा श्रद्धधत्येतदथालाभेन जीवती ।
विहराम्यमुनैवाहमात्मना रमणेन वै ॥४०॥

40. Putting my faith in this (gift of the Lord) I shall live content on what comes to me, and shall enjoy the company of that Lover—the Âtman.

संसारकूपे पतितं विषयैर्मु षितेक्षणम् ।
ग्रस्तं कालाहिनाऽऽत्मानं कोऽन्यस्त्रातुमधीश्वरः ॥४१॥

UDDHAVA GITA

41. Who else can save the Jiva fallen into the pit of transmigration, robbed of his vision by the senses[1] and swallowed up by the serpent of Time?

[1] *Senses*—i.e. the clinging to the senses.

आत्मैव ह्यात्मनो गोप्ता निर्विद्येत यदाखिलात् ।
अप्रमत्त इदं पश्येद्ग्रस्तं कालाहिना जगत् ।।४२।।

42. When one beholds this universe swallowed up by the serpent of Time, becomes watchful and turns oneself away from everything, then the Self alone[1] is the saviour of oneself.

[1] *Self alone etc.*—This suggests that Pingalâ, having now attained this state of dispassion, is not anxious for Mukti and wishes to serve the Lord from no selfish motive but simply for love.

ब्राह्मण उवाच ।
एवं व्यवसितमतिर्दुराशां कान्ततर्षजाम् ।
छित्त्वोपशममास्थाय शय्यामुपविवेश सा ।।४३।।

The Brâhmana said:

43. Having thus determined in her mind, she broke loose from the vain expectations due to a hankering for lovers, and sat on her bed, attaining composure.

आशा हि परमं दुःखं नैराश्यं परमं सुखम् ।
यथा संछिद्य कान्ताशां सुखं सुष्वाप पिङ्गला ।।४४।।

44. Expectation is surely the greatest misery, and the giving up of all expectations is the greatest bliss—as Pingalâ slept happily, getting rid of the hankering for lovers.

CHAPTER IV

ब्राह्मण उवाच ।

परिग्रहो हि दुःखाय यद्यत्प्रियतमं नृणाम् ।
अनन्तं सुखमाप्नोति तद्विद्वान्यस्त्वकिंचनः ॥१॥

The Brâhmana said:

1. The acquisition[1] of anything whatsoever that men hold as dearest leads to misery. But he who knows this and gives up all possession attains to endless bliss.

[1] *Acquisition etc.*—Verses 1 and 2 set forth the lesson derived from the osprey—viz. that one must have no possession, that is, attachment for it.

सामिषं कुररं जघ्नुर्बलिनो ये निरामिषाः ।
तदामिषं परित्यज्य स सुखं समविन्दत ॥२॥

2. An osprey with a piece of flesh was tormented by others, stronger than itself, that had no flesh. It gave that flesh up and became happy.

न मे मानावमानौ स्तो न चिन्ता गेहपुत्रिणाम् ।
आत्मक्रीड आत्मरतिर्विचराम्यीह बालवत् ॥३॥

3. I do not care for honour or dishonour, nor have I any anxiety such as men with houses and children have. I sport with the Self,[1] take pleasure in the Self and roam on earth like a child.

UDDHAVA GITA

Verses 3 and 4 deal with the child.
[1] *With the Self*—realising himself as the Self.

द्वावेव चिन्तया मुक्तौ परमानन्द आप्लुतौ ।
यो विमुग्धो जडो बालो यो गुणेभ्यः परं गतः ॥४॥

4. Two people only are free from anxiety and immersed in supreme bliss—the child that knows nothing and never works, and the man who has realised the Being above the Gunas.[1]

[1] *Gunas*—Sattva, Rajas, and Tamas—or balance, activity, and inertia—which comprise the Prakriti or sentient and insentient nature.

कचित्कुमारी त्वात्मानं वृणानान्गृहमागतान् ।
स्वयं तानर्हयामास कापि यातेषु बन्धुषु ॥५॥

5. Once upon a time a maiden, in the absence of her relatives elsewhere, herself had to receive a party who came to her house to ask her in marriage.

Verses 5 to 10 describe the lesson derived from the maiden.

तेषामभ्यवहारार्थं शालीन् रहसि पार्थिव ।
अवघ्नन्त्याः प्रकोष्ठस्थाश्चक्रुः शङ्खाः स्वनं महत् ॥६॥

6. As she was husking paddy for their meal in a retired corner, O King, the conch bracelets in her wrist made a great noise.

सा तज्जुगुप्सितं मत्वा महती व्रीडिता ततः ।
बभञ्जैकैकशः शङ्खान्द्वौ द्वौ पाण्योरशेषयत् ॥७॥

THE LAST MESSAGE OF SHRI KRISHNA

7. The intelligent girl, considering this as disgraceful,[1] was ashamed and broke[2] the bracelets one by one till only two were left in each arm.

[1] *Disgraceful*—as betraying their poverty.

[2] *Broke*—The commentator takes it to mean "removed".

उभयोरप्यभूद्घोषो ह्वघ्नन्त्याः स्म शङ्ख्योः ।
तत्राप्येकं निरभिददेकस्मान्नाभवद्ध्वनिः ॥८॥

8. As she went on husking, even those two bracelets produced a sound. So she removed one of these also. From the single bracelet there was no more sound.

अन्वशिक्षमिमं तस्या उपदेशमरिन्दम ।
लोकाननुचरन्नेताँल्लोकतत्त्वविवित्सया ॥६॥

9. Roaming[1] over the world with a view to know the ways of men, I learnt this lesson from her, O queller of foes:

[1] *Roaming etc.*—This explains how he met that girl.

वासे बहूनां कलहो भवेद्वार्ता द्वयोरपि ।
एक एव चरेत्तस्मात्कुमार्या इव कङ्कणः ॥१०॥

10. Where many dwell there is quarrel, and even between two people there is a chance for talk. Therefore one should live alone, like the bracelet of the maiden.

मन एकत्र संयुज्याज्जितश्वासो जितासनः ।
वैराग्याभ्यासयोगेन ध्रियमाणमतन्द्रितः ॥११॥

UDDHAVA GITA

11.   Conquering posture and (through that) controlling the breath, one, ever alert should collect the mind together, and hold it steady through renunciation[1] and systematic practice.

Verses 11-13 set forth the lesson of concentration derived from the arrow-maker.

[1] *Renunciation etc.*—Compare Gitâ VI. 35.

यस्मिन्मनो लब्धपदं यदेत-
व्छनैः शनैमुर्च्छति कर्मरेणून् ।
सत्त्वेन वृद्धेन रजस्तमश्च
विधूय निर्वाणमुपैत्यनिन्धनम् ॥१२॥

12.   Where,[1] being steady, this collected mind gradually gives up the impulsions to work, and winnowing off Rajas (activity) and Tamas (inertia), through increased Sattva (balance), becomes pacified,[2] having no fuel (of sense-impressions) to feed it.

[1] *Where*—i.e. in God.
[2] *Pacified*—lit. extinguished.

तदैवमात्मन्यवरुद्धचित्तो
न वेद किंचिद्बहिरन्तरं वा ।
यथेषुकारो नृपतिं व्रजन्त-
मिषौ गतात्मा न ददर्श पार्श्वे ॥१३॥

13.   Having the mind thus controlled within himself, the man, at that time, knows nothing external[1] or internal,[2] just as the arrow-maker, with

THE LAST MESSAGE OF SHRI KRISHNA

his mind absorbed in (making) the arrow, did not notice the king passing by his side.

[1] *External*—outside objects.
[2] *Internal*—his ideas and feelings.

एकचार्यनिकेतः स्यादप्रमत्तो गुहाशयः ।
अलक्ष्यमाण आचारैर्मु निरेकोऽल्पभाषणः ॥१४॥

14. The sage should wander alone, be homeless, ever alert, and resorting to caves,[1] he should not betray[2] his real worth by his actions, and be without companions and reticent of speech.

The resemblance between the life of a snake and that of a saint is brought out in this and the next verse.

[1] *Caves*—i.e. solitudes.
[2] *Betray etc.*—just as one cannot tell by the mere sight of a snake whether it is venomous or not.

गृहारम्भोऽतिदुःखाय विफलश्चाध्रुवात्मनः ।
सर्पः परकृतं वेश्म प्रविश्य सुखमेधते ॥१५॥

15. It is extremely troublesome, and useless, for a man to build a house, since his body is so frail; the snake enters a house[1] made by others and is happy and prosperous.

[1] *House etc.*—e.g. a rat-hole.

एको नारायणो देवः पूर्वसृष्टं स्वमायया ।
संहृत्य कालकलया कल्पान्त इदमीश्वरः ॥१६॥

16. Through the Energy of Time, the Lord Nârâyana, who is One, draws back, at the end of a

UDDHAVA GITA

64

cycle, this universe which He created before through His Mâyâ;[1]

The analogy of the spider and its web, to explain the evolution and involution of the world, is delineated in verses 16-21.

[1] *Mâyâ*—the inscrutable Power of the Lord through which He projects, maintains, and dissolves this universe, Himself remaining unchanged all the while. This has led the Advaitic philosophers to conclude that this universe is merely an *appearance*—it is Brahman seen through the prism of ignorance.

एक एवाद्वितीयोऽभूदात्माधारोऽखिलाश्रयः ।
कालेनात्मानुभावेन साम्यं नीतासु शक्तिषु ।
सत्त्वादिष्वादिपुरुषः प्रधानपुरुषेश्वरः ॥१७॥

17. The principles of Sattva[1] etc. being put into equilibrium by Time—which is His own Shakti (Power)—the Primeval Being,[2] the Lord of Prakriti and Purusha, then remains One without a second, Himself His own support—though supporting the whole universe.

[1] *Sattva etc.*—the three component forces of Prakriti.
[2] *Primeval Being*—Brahman, the substratum of the soul and matter.

परावराणां परम आस्ते कैवल्यसंज्ञितः ।
केवलानुभवानन्दसन्दोहो निरुपाधिकः ॥१८॥

18. He, the Supreme Lord of the high and low,[1] remains as a mass of transcendent Knowledge and Bliss, known as the Absolute, and without attributes.

THE LAST MESSAGE OF SHRI KRISHNA   65

[1] *High and low*—all beings and things from Brahmâ down to grossest matter.

केवलात्मानुभावेन स्वमायां त्रिगुणात्मिकाम् ।
संक्षोभयन्सृजत्यादौ तया सूत्रमरिन्दम ॥१९॥

19. O queller[1] of foes, He through His transcendent power (of Time) stirs into activity His Mâyâ consisting of the three Gunas, and through that projects first the Sutra.[2]

[1] *Queller etc.*—King Yadu.

[2] *Sutra*—The Cosmic Energy variously known as Prâna, Hiranyagarbha, Sutrâtmâ, Mahat, or even Vâyu. In the Purânas this is called Brahmâ who projects the world. It is the next link after Prakriti in the creative process and is subtler than both mind and matter, which evolve later on from this.

तामाहुस्त्रिगुणव्यक्तिं सृजन्तीं विश्वतोमुखम् ।
यस्मिन्प्रोतमिदं विश्वं येन संसरते पुमान् ॥२०॥

20. (Sages describe) this manifestation of the Prakriti (viz. the Sutra) as projecting[1] the universe—in which the universe is strung,[2] and through which[3] the Jiva transmigrates.[4]

[1] *Projecting*—through the Ahamkâra or Egoism—its next step.

[2] *Strung etc.*—The reference is to the Brihadâranyaka Upanishad III. vii. 2.

[3] *Through which etc.*—i.e. as Prâna.

[4] *Transmigrates*—from one body or sphere to another.

यथोर्णनाभिर्हृदयादूर्णां संतत्य वक्त्रतः ।
तया विहृत्य भूयस्तां ग्रसत्येवं महेश्वरः ॥२१॥

5

UDDHAVA GITA

21. As the spider spreads its web from its heart through the mouth, and after playing with it, swallows it again, so[1] the Lord also does (with the universe).

[1] *So etc.*—Ishvara projects the universe out of Himself, maintains it and reabsorbs it at the end of a cycle into Himself. Hence the universe is not essentially different from Brahman whose real (according to Dualists) or apparent (according to Advaitists) projection it is.

यत्र यत्र मनो देही धारयेत्सकलं धिया ।
स्नेहाद्द्वेषाद्भयाद्वापि याति तत्तत्स्वरूपताम् ॥२२॥

22. On whatever object a corporeal being may concentrate his whole mind with his intellect, either through love or through hate or through fear, he attains the form of that very object.

Verses 22 and 23 give out the lesson derived from the Bhramara-kita.

कीटः पेशस्कृतं ध्यायन्कुड्यां तेन प्रवेशितः ।
याति तत्सात्मतां राजन्पूर्वरूपमसंत्यजन् ॥२३॥

23. O King, the cockroach being confined by a Bhramara-kita within a wall, thinks and thinks of that till it attains a form[1] partly resembling that of the insect, without discarding[2] its own.

[1] *Form etc.*—such is the popular notion.

[2] *Without discarding etc.*—The case is therefore stronger for those who die with a settled impression upon their mind.

THE LAST MESSAGE OF SHRI KRISHNA

एवं गुरुभ्य एतेभ्य एषा मे शिक्षिता मतिः ।
स्वात्मोपशिक्षितां बुद्धि श्रृणु मे वदतः प्रभो ॥२४॥

24. Thus have I learnt these things from all these teachers. Now listen, O King, to what I have learnt from my own body, as I relate it to you.

देहो गुरुर्मम विरक्तिविवेकहेतु-
    बिभ्रत्स्म सत्त्वनिधनं सततात्युर्दर्कम् ।
तत्त्वान्यनेन विमृशामि यथा तथापि
    पारक्यमित्यवसितो विचराम्यसङ्गः ॥२५॥

25. The body is a teacher of mine, being the cause of dispassion and discrimination, and being subject[1] to birth and death which always bring pain in their wake. With its help[2] I adequately reflect on the ultimate principles,[3] yet I have known for a certainty that it belongs to others,[4] and hence I wander without attachment.

The lesson which the body teaches is set forth in verses 25-27.

[1] *Subject etc.*—this is the cause of "dispassion".

[2] *With its help etc.*—The body and the mind help us to realisation, by rousing our "discrimination".

[3] *Ultimate principles*—i.e. Truth and its phases.

[4] *Others*—e.g. the animals that devour it after death.

जायात्मजार्थपशुभृत्यगृहाप्तवर्गान्
    पुष्णाति यत्प्रियचिकीर्षया वितन्वन् ।
स्वान्ते सकृच्छ्रमवरुद्धधनः स देहः
    सृष्ट्वास्य बीजमवसीदति वृक्षधर्मा ॥२६॥

UDDHAVA GITA

68

26. That very body for the sake of whose welfare a man adds unto himself and maintains a wife, children, sense-objects, domestic animals, servants, home, and relatives, and painfully amasses wealth, withers at the end of its term like a tree, creating the seed[1] of a fresh body for the man.

[1] *Seed etc.*—viz. fresh Karma which prolongs the chain of transmigration.

जिह्वैकतोऽमुमवकर्षति कर्हि तर्षा
शिश्नोऽन्यतस्त्वगुदरं श्रवणं कुतश्चित् ।
घ्राणोऽन्यतश्चपलदृक् क्व च कर्मशक्ति-
र्बह्व्यः सपत्न्य इव गेहपतिं लुनन्ति ॥२७॥

27. The tongue[1] attracts the man to one direction and thirst to another; the sex-impulse draws somewhere and skin, stomach, and ears to other quarters; the nose attracts in one direction, the restive eyes elsewhere, while the tendency for work draws to something else—all these undermine the man like so many wives of a householder.

[1] *Tongue etc.*—The verse gives a graphic warning to a man attached to the senses. He must utilise the body for the sole purpose of realisation.

सृष्ट्वा पुराणि विविधान्यजयाऽऽत्मशक्त्या
वृक्षान्सरीसृपपशून्खगदंशमत्स्यान् ।
तैस्तैरतुष्टहृदयः पुरुषं विधाय
ब्रह्मावलोकधिषणं मुदमाप देवः ॥२८॥

THE LAST MESSAGE OF SHRI KRISHNA

69

28.   The Lord through His eternal Power created various abodes[1] such as trees, reptiles, and beasts, birds, insects, and fish, but was not satisfied in His heart with these. Then He made the human body which is endowed with the desire to realise Brahman, and He was delighted.

[1] *Abodes etc.*—the various bodies are meant. Compare Aitareya Upanishad I. ii. 2-3. See also note on verse 21, Ch. II.

लब्ध्वा सुदुर्लभमिदं बहुसंभवान्ते
मानुष्यमर्थदमनित्यमपीह धीरः ।
तूर्णं यतेत न पतेदनुमृत्यु याव-
न्निःश्रेयसाय विषयः खलु सर्वतः स्यात् ॥२९॥

29.   The wise man having after many births obtained this extremely rare human body, which though frail is yet conducive to man's supreme welfare,[1] should quickly strive for liberation, before the body, which is always subject to death, chances to fall; for sense-enjoyment is obtainable in any body.[2]

[1] *Welfare*—Moksha.
[2] *Any body*—but not realisation.

एवं संजातवैराग्यो विज्ञानालोक आत्मनि ।
विचरामि महीमेतां मुक्तसङ्गोऽनहंकृतिः ॥३०॥

30.   With my dispassion roused thus and with Illumination as my light, I roam over this world, established in myself, free from attachment and egoism.

70 UDDHAVA GITA

नहोकस्माद्गुरोर्ज्ञानं सुस्थिरं स्यात्सुपुष्कलम् ।
ब्रह्मैतद्द्वितीयं वै गीयते बहुधर्षिभिः ॥३१॥

31. Verily knowledge from a single teacher[1] is neither very steady nor very ample. Well, Brahman, though One without a second, is nevertheless sung of variously by sages.

[1] *Single teacher etc.*—The teacher who imparts the ultimate truth is one, but there may be various teachers to help the student to assimilate that truth. Compare verse 5, Ch. V.

श्रीभगवानुवाच ।

इत्युक्त्वा स यदुं विप्रस्तमामन्त्र्य गभीरधीः ।
वन्दितोऽभ्यर्थितो राज्ञा ययौ प्रीतो यथागतम् ॥३२॥

The Lord said:

32. Saying this to Yadu the highly gifted Brâhmana begged his leave, and being saluted and duly worshipped by the king joyously went his way, just as he had come.

अवधूतवचः श्रुत्वा पूर्वेषां नः स पूर्वजः ।
सर्वसङ्गविनिर्मुक्तः समचित्तो बभूव ह ॥३३॥

33. Hearing the words of the Avadhuta that progenitor of our forefathers was rid of all attachment and became of an even mind.

CHAPTER V

श्रीभगवानुवाच ।

मयोदितेष्ववहितः स्वधर्मेषु मदाश्रयः ।
वर्णाश्रमकुलाचारमकामात्मा समाचरेत् ॥१॥

The Lord said:

1. The man who has taken refuge in Me will attend to his particular duties as inculcated[1] by Me and perform the rites of his caste, order of life, or family, with an unattached mind.

[1] *Inculcated*—in the scriptures.

अन्वीक्षेत विशुद्धात्मा देहिनां विषयात्मनाम् ।
गुणेषु तत्त्वध्यानेन सर्वारम्भविपर्ययम् ॥२॥

2. With a purified mind he should notice[1] the reverses that befall all undertakings of people who are attached to sense-objects, considering them as real.

[1] *Notice etc.*—and hence work without attachment.

सुप्तस्य विषयालोको ध्यायतो वा मनोरथः ।
नानात्मकत्वाद्विफलस्तथा भेदात्मधीर्गुणैः ॥३॥

3. As the vision of sense-objects by a sleeping man, or the fancies of a man absorbed in reverie are unreal, since they are ever-changing by their very nature, so is the notion[1] of a diversity of objects outside, by means of the sense-organs.

[1] *Notion etc.*—There is only Brahman.

UDDHAVA GITA

निवृत्तं कर्म सेवेत प्रवृत्तं मत्परस्त्यजेत् ।
जिज्ञासायां संप्रवृत्तो नाद्रियेत्कर्मचोदनाम् ॥४॥

4. Intent on Me, one should give up actions[1]
that continue transmigration, and perform those
actions that conduce to a cessation[2] of it. Being
thoroughly launched on the quest for Truth, he should
pay no attention to the injunctions of work.[3]

[1] *Actions etc.*—i.e. those undertaken with selfish
motives.

[2] *Cessation etc.*—the "obligatory" and "occasional"
works.

[3] *Work*—he should go beyond the latter class of work
even.

यमानभीक्ष्णं सेवेत नियमान्मत्परः कचित् ।
मदभिज्ञं गुरुं शान्तमुपासीत मदात्मकम् ॥५॥

5. Intent on Me, he should always attend to
the Yamas,[1] and occasionally to the Niyamas.[2] He
should serve[3] the pacified Teacher who has known Me
and has thus become one with Me.

[1] *Yamas*—universal moral principles, such as non-injury
etc.

[2] *Niyamas*—subsidiary rules of conduct, such as cleanliness etc.

[3] *Serve etc.*—without caring much for the Yamas even.

अमान्यमत्सरो दक्षो निर्ममो दृढसौहृदः ।
असत्वरोऽर्थजिज्ञासुरनसूयुरमोघवाक् ॥६॥

6. He should be free from pride and jealousy,
be able, without attachment, firmly devoted to the

THE LAST MESSAGE OF SHRI KRISHNA 73

Guru, not hasty, eager to know the Truth, free from envy, and not given to unnecessary talk.

जायापत्यगृहक्षेत्रस्वजनद्रविणादिषु ।
उदासीनः समं पश्यन्सर्वेष्वर्थमिवात्मनः ॥७॥

7. He should be indifferent to his wife, children, house, fields, relatives, wealth, etc., considering everything whatsoever as equally[1] subserving his interest.

[1] *Equally etc.*—Through everything the Âtman shines, so he need not be particularly attached to anything.

विलक्षणः स्थूलसूक्ष्मादेहादात्मेक्षिता स्वदृक् ।
यथाग्निर्दारुणो दाह्यादाहकोऽन्यः प्रकाशकः ॥८॥

8. The Âtman, the Self-effulgent Witness, is distinct from the gross and subtle bodies, as a blazing fire that burns and illumines is other than the combustible wood.

निरोधोत्पत्त्यणुबृहन्नानात्वं तत्कृतान्गुणान् ।
अन्तः प्रविष्ट आधत्त एवं देहगुणान्परः ॥९॥

9. (As fire) entering (into the wood) imbibes[1] the attributes due to it, such as destruction and origin, minuteness, hugeness, and diversity, so also does the Âtman the attributes of the body.

[1] *Imbibes etc.*—The principle of fire is without form and omnipresent. But we wrongly identify it with the fuel.

UDDHAVA GITA

योऽसौ गुणैर्विरचितो देहोऽयं पुरुषस्य हि ।
संसारस्तन्निबन्धोऽयं पुंसो विद्याच्छिदात्मनः ॥१०॥

10. This body which is created by the Lord's attribute known as Mâyâ, is verily the cause of man's transmigration. And the knowledge of the Self serves to destroy this.

तस्माज्जिज्ञासयात्मानमात्मस्थं केवलं परम् ।
संगम्य निरसेदेतद्वस्तुबुद्धिं यथाक्रमम् ॥११॥

11. Therefore, by means of discrimination one should unite the soul to the Absolute Self which is[1] in the body, and remove the idea of reality in the body etc., in order.[2]

[1] *Is etc.*—i.e. manifests Itself through it.
[2] *In order*—first the gross, and then the subtle.

आचार्योऽरणिराद्यः स्यादन्तेवास्युत्तरारणिः ।
तत्संधानं प्रवचनं विद्या संधिः सुखावहः ॥१२॥

12. The teacher should be looked upon as the first or lower churning piece,[1] and the student the upper one; instruction is the piece connecting them; and knowledge is the union that conduces to happiness.

[1] *Churning piece*—The allusion is to the ancient method of generating fire by rubbing a piece of wood pressed between two other pieces. As fire destroys impurities so the knowledge derived by a fit disciple from a competent Guru dispels ignorance that veils his true nature. An echo of Taittiriya Upanishad. I. ii—"The teacher is the first form" etc.

THE LAST MESSAGE OF SHRI KRISHNA

वैशारदी साऽतिविशुद्धबुद्धि-
धुर्नोति मायां गुणसंप्रसूताम् ।
गुणांश्च संदह्य यदात्ममेतत्
स्वयं च शाम्यत्यसमिद्यथाग्निः ॥१३॥

13. That highly refined wisdom which comes to (or of) a competent person removes the delusion which is the product of the Gunas,[1] and completely burning the Gunas, of which this universe consists, is itself extinguished[2] also, like fire without fuel.

[1] *Gunas*—Sattva, Rajas, and Tamas, the components of Mâyâ.

[2] *Extinguished etc.*—There is no more knower, knowledge, and known—there is only Brahman.

अथैषां कर्मकर्तॄणां भोक्तॄणां सुखदुःखयोः ।
नानात्वमथ नित्यत्वं लोककालागमात्मनाम् ॥१४॥
मन्यसे सर्वभावानां संस्था हौत्पत्तिकी यथा ।
तत्तदाकृतिभेदेन जायते भिद्यते च धीः ॥१५॥

14-15. If you suppose[1] that these doers of action and experiencers of happiness and misery are many in number, or that the heavenly spheres, time, scriptures,[2] and souls are eternal, or that the existence of all things is eternal as a series and is real, and that knowledge originates and is diverse according to the form of things cognised—

[2] *Suppose etc.*—Here the view of the Mimâmsakas who are upholders of work with motive, is put forward, which is refuted in verses 16-21, and 31-34. According to this school, the souls are real and many in number; they

actually experience happiness and misery, do work and go to various spheres as the result of their deeds. The Mimâmsakas do not believe in Ishvara or God; and heaven is their goal—not Moksha. They, of course, do not believe in the One Existence-Knowledge-Bliss Absolute—the Brahman or Âtman of the Vedantists—whose *apparent* manifestation is everything, internal and external.

[2] *Scriptures*—enjoining selfish work.

एवमप्यङ्ग सर्वेषां देहिनां देहयोगतः ।
कालावयवतः सन्ति भावा जन्मादयोऽसकृत् ॥१६॥

16. Even then, my friend, all corporeal beings repeatedly undergo such states as birth and the like, owing to their connection with the body and owing to time having parts.[1]

[1] *Parts*—such as year, months, etc.

अत्रापि कर्मणां कर्तुरस्वातन्त्र्यं च लक्ष्यते ।
भोक्तुश्च दुःखसुखयोः कोऽन्वर्थो विवशं भजेत् ॥१७॥

17. Even in this case one notices the want of freedom on the part of the doers of action and the experiencers of happiness and misery; and what fruition[1] ever attends one who is not independent?

[1] *Fruition etc.*—The subordinate being is always unhappy.

न देहिनां सुखं किंचिद्विद्यते विदुषामपि ।
तथा च दुःखं मूढानां वृथाहंकरणं परम् ॥१८॥

18. Sometimes even wise men have not the least

THE LAST MESSAGE OF SHRI KRISHNA

happiness, and ignorant people are sometimes without the least misery. So bragging[1] is simply useless.

[1] *Bragging*—about the efficacy of work.

यदि प्राप्ति विघातं च जानन्ति सुखदुःखयोः ।
तेऽप्यद्धा न विदुर्योगं मृत्युनं प्रभवेद्यथा ॥१६॥

19. If they at all know how to attain happiness and destroy misery, they certainly do not know the contrivance[1] by which death can be made powerless.

[1] *Contrivance etc.*—Only realisation of one's eternal identity with Brahman can do this.

को न्वर्थः सुखयत्येनं कामो वा मृत्युरन्तिके ।
आघातं नीयमानस्य वध्यस्येव न तुष्टिदः ॥२०॥

20. While death is near, what acquisition, or enjoyment, can please a man? It cannot please him, like an animal which is being dragged for slaughter.

श्रुतं च दृष्टवद् दुष्टं स्पर्धाऽसूयात्ययव्ययैः ।
बह्वन्तरायकामत्वात्कृषिवच्चापि निष्फलम् ॥२१॥

21. The happiness (of heaven etc.) that we hear of from the scriptures, is also vitiated,[1] like that we experience here, by rivalry, jealousy, destruction, and waste. And because the desire for it is attended by many obstacles, it is sometimes fruitless[2] like agriculture.

[1] *Vitiated*—It is just like an earthly pleasure, only keener. The loss of it, therefore, is all the more poignant.

[2] *Fruitless*—Therefore so much labour is often wasted. Only a perfect work will lead to heaven.

UDDHAVA GITA

अन्तरायैरविहतो यदि धर्मः स्वनुष्ठितः ।
तेनापि निर्जितं स्थानं यथा गच्छति तच्छृणु ॥२२॥

22. If duty is properly performed and is un-impeded by obstacles, then one attains to heavenly spheres through it. Listen also how it happens.

इष्ट्वे ह देवता यज्ञैः स्वर्लोकं याति याज्ञिकः ।
भुञ्जीत देववत्तत्र भोगान्दिव्यान्निजार्जितान् ॥२३॥

23. The man of sacrifices goes to heaven, wor-shipping the gods through sacrifices here below. Like a god he enjoys there celestial pleasures which he has himself acquired.

The fruits of good work done with selfish motive are described in verses 23-26.

स्वपुण्योपचिते शुभ्रे विमान उपगीयते ।
गन्धर्वैर्विहरन्मध्ये देवीनां हृद्यवेषभृक् ॥२४॥

24. In the aerial car acquired by his own good actions, he enjoys, dressed in beautiful attire, in the company of nymphs, and is eulogised by Gandharvas.

स्त्रीभिः कामगयानेन किंकिणीजालमालिना ।
क्रीडन्न वेदात्मपातं सुराक्रीडेषु निर्वृतः ॥२५॥

25. Dallying with women, with a car decked with little bells, that goes to any place desired, he is happy in the gardens of the gods, and thinks not of his fall.[1]

[1] *Fall*—which is inevitable.

THE LAST MESSAGE OF SHRI KRISHNA

तावत्रमोदते स्वर्गे यावत्पुण्यं समाप्यते ।
क्षीणपुण्यः पतत्यर्वाग्निच्छन्कालचालितः ॥२६॥

26. He enjoys in heaven till the merits of his good deeds are exhausted. Then on the expiry of his merits he falls down, against his will, being propelled by time.

यद्यधर्मरतः सङ्गादसतां वाऽजितेन्द्रियः ।
कामात्मा कृपणो लुब्धः स्त्रैणो भूतविहिंसकः ॥२७॥
पशूनविधिनाऽऽलभ्य प्रेतभूतगणान्यजन् ।
नरकानवशो जन्तुर्गत्वा यात्युल्बणं तमः ॥२८॥

27-28. Or if he, owing to the company of wicked people, is addicted to sin; if he is not a master of his senses, is lustful, servile, avaricious, under the sway of women and causing injury to beings; if he slaughters animals against the sanction of scriptures, and worships ghosts and demons, then he goes helpless to various hells, and enters dreadfully Tâmasika bodies.

The fruits of evil work are set forth in verses 27-29.

कर्माणि दुःखोदर्काणि कुर्वन्देहेन तैः पुनः ।
देहमाभजते तत्र किं सुखं मर्त्यधर्मिणः ॥२६॥

29. Doing through those bodies deeds that but result in grief, they again get new bodies. What happiness[1] comes to mortals in this process?

[1] *Happiness etc.*—so one should try for realisation.

UDDHAVA GITA

लोकानां लोकपालानां मद्भयं कल्पजीविनाम् ।
ब्रह्मणोऽपि भयं मत्तो द्विपरार्धपरायुषः ॥३०॥

30. The heavenly spheres and the lords of those spheres who live up to a cycle, have apprehensions from Me.[1] Even Brahmâ who has a longevity of two Parârdhas,[2] has to be afraid of Me.

[1] *Me*—as the All-destroyer.
[2] *Parârdha*—a fabulously large number equal to ten thousand billions. Brahmâ also has to expire after so many human years.

Compare the Katha Upanishad II. iii. 3.

गुणाः सृजन्ति कर्माणि गुणोऽनुसृजते गुणान् ।
जीवस्तु गुणसंयुक्तो भुङ्क्ते कर्मफलान्यसौ ॥३१॥

31. The organs create actions, and the Gunas[1] direct the organs. And this Jiva experiences the fruits of actions, being mixed up[2] with the organs etc.

[1] *Gunas*—Sattva, Rajas, and Tamas. So the Âtman is inactive. It should be noted that the word Guna admits of several meanings.
[2] *Mixed up*—through his false identification with them.

यावत्स्याद्गुणवैषम्यं तावन्नानात्वमात्मनः ।
नानात्वमात्मनो यावत्पारतन्त्र्यं तदैव हि ॥३२॥

32. As long as there is rupture[1] of the equilibrium of Gunas, so long is the diversity[2] of the soul. And so long as the diversity of the soul lasts, it is verily at the mercy of others.

[1] *Rupture etc.*—leading to manifestation of the universe.

THE LAST MESSAGE OF SHRI KRISHNA 81

²Diversity etc.—The Âtman, through Avidyâ or ignorance which is without beginning, *imagines* Itself divided into the subject and the infinite variety of objects. Realisation puts an end to this self-hypnotism.

यावदस्यास्वतन्त्रत्वं तावदीश्वरतो भयम् ।
य एतत्समुपासीरंस्ते मुह्यन्ति शुचार्पिताः ॥३३॥

33. So long as it is not independent it has apprehensions from the Lord. And they who uphold this doctrine of enjoyment are smitten with grief[1] and are stupefied.

¹Grief—They find no way out of this maze of Karma and rebirth.

काल आत्मागमो लोकः स्वभावो धर्म एव च ।
इति मां बहुधा प्राहुर्गुणव्यतिकरे सति ॥३४॥

34. When the equilibrium of the Gunas is disturbed, it is I[1] whom sages call variously as time,[2] soul, scripture, heavenly spheres, temperament, and virtue.

¹I etc.—Sages know that the universe, though appearing as various through delusion, is nothing but Brahman.

²Time etc.—all these are auxiliaries of Karma. "Time" is the period of enjoyment. "Soul" is the enjoyer. "Temperament" causes the transformation into gods and other beings. "Virtue" is the Apurva or the unseen result of good actions which later on fructifies as the enjoyment of heaven.

उद्धव उवाच ।
गुणेषु वर्तमानोऽपि देहजेष्वनपावृतः ।
गुणैर्न बध्यते देही बध्यते वा कथं विभो ॥३५॥

6

UDDHAVA GITA

Uddhava said:

35. O Lord, so long as the Jiva is mixed up with the attributes[1] that spring from the body, how can he help being bound by those attributes? And if he is not enveloped[2] by them how does he come to be bound?

[1] *Attributes*—such as work and its consequent happiness etc.

[2] *Not enveloped etc.*—as the Âtman, the eternal subject.

कथं वर्तेत विहरेत्कैर्वा ज्ञायेत लक्षणैः ।
किं भुञ्जीतोत विसृजेच्छयीतासीत याति वा ॥३६॥

36. How do the free and bound souls live and enjoy? By what signs[1] can they be distinguished? What or how do they eat, and how attend to other bodily functions? How do they lie, or sit, or go?

[1] *What signs etc.*—Since the outward actions of both are so similar.

एतदच्युत मे ब्रूहि प्रश्नं प्रश्नविदां वर ।
नित्यमुक्तो नित्यबद्ध एक एवेति मे भ्रमः ॥३७॥

37. O Thou best of the knowers of (answers to) questions, answer me these questions. My doubt is this: Is the same soul eternally bound and eternally free?

CHAPTER VI

श्रीभगवानुवाच ।

बद्धो मुक्त इति व्याख्या गुणतो मे न वस्तुतः ।
गुणस्य मायामूलत्वान्न मे मोक्षो न बन्धनम् ॥१॥

The Lord said:

1. The soul is described as bound or free from the point of view of My Gunas,[1] but it is not so in reality. And since the Gunas are the creation of Mâyâ,[2] there is, in my opinion, neither bondage nor liberation.

Verses 1 and 2 show how bondage and freedom cannot really exist.

[1] *My Gunas*—Sattva, Rajas, and Tamas which comprise My Prakriti.

[2] *Creation of Mâyâ*—the effects of ignorance, hence having no reality of their own.

शोकमोहौ सुखं दुःखं देहापत्तिश्च मायया ।

स्वप्नो यथात्मनः ख्यातिः संसृतिर्न तु वास्तवी ॥२॥

2. Grief and infatuation, happiness and misery, as well as taking on a body are all due to Mâyâ. Just as a dream is a fiction[1] of the mind, so transmigration also is not a reality.[2]

[1] *Fiction etc.*—The mind creates them out of impressions of the waking state.

[2] *Not a reality*—but conjured up by ignorance.

UDDHAVA GITA

विद्याविद्ये मम तनू विद्धय् उद्धव शरीरिणाम् ।
मोक्षबन्धकरी आद्ये मायया मे विनिर्मिते ॥३॥

3. Know knowledge and ignorance to be My Powers, O Uddhava, which are (respectively) the cause of liberation and bondage of beings; they are primordial[1] and created by My Mâyâ.

[1] *Primordial*—being functions of Mâyâ or the Lord's eternal inscrutable power, they also are without beginning.

एकस्यैव ममांशस्य जीवस्यैव महामते ।
बन्धोऽस्याविद्ययाऽनादिर्विद्यया च तथेतरः ॥४॥

4. O talented one, for the selfsame Jiva, who is My part,[1] there is bondage without beginning owing to ignorance, and liberation through knowledge.

This verse divides the scope of bondage and freedom.

[1] *Part etc.*—To take an illustration. The sun is separate from its reflection in water, and any motion in the water causes the reflection also to move; also the reflection in one vessel may differ from that in another; and when one vessel is broken, that particular reflection is one with the sun, but not the others. Similar is the case with the Jiva, who is a reflection of the Brahman in nescience which causes the appearance of diversity, and that Jiva from whom nescience has vanished is one with the Brahman. This is the Advaitist view. The Dualists consider the relation between the Lord and Jivas as that between the sun and its rays.

अथ बद्धस्य मुक्तस्य वैलक्षण्यं वदामि ते ।
विरुद्धधर्मिणोस्तात स्थितयोरेकधर्मिणि ॥५॥

THE LAST MESSAGE OF SHRI KRISHNA

85

5. Now I am relating to thee the difference between the bound and the free soul, endowed with opposite qualities and living in the same abode, the body.

The answer to the other questions is now taken up. The difference is twofold—that between the Jiva and the Lord, and that among the Jivas themselves. Verses 5-7 set forth the former kind of difference, and verses 8-17 the latter kind.

सुपर्णावेतौ सदृशौ सखायौ
यदृच्छयैतौ कृतनीडौ च वृक्षे ।
एकस्तयोः खादति पिप्पलान्न-
मन्यो निरन्नोऽपि बलेन भूयान् ॥६॥

6. Two birds which look alike[1] and are friends[2] have casually[3] come and built their nest in a tree.[4] One[5] of these eats the fruits[6] of that tree, while the other,[7] though not taking any fruit, is greater[8] in strength.

This is an echo of Mundaka III. i. 1-2.

[1] *Alike*—both being Chit or Knowledge Absolute.

[2] *Friends*—they are ever together and are apparently of the same opinion.

[3] *Casually*—through inscrutable Mâyâ.

[4] *Tree*—the body. Compare Katha Upanishad II. iii. 1. Also Gitâ XV. 1-3.

[5] *One*—the Jiva.

[6] *Fruits, etc.*—the results of one's action reaped in the body. "Pippala" (peepul tree) has another synonym, "Ashvattha", which literally means "not lasting till the next day". Hence the term refers to the body which is also transient.

[7] *Other*—Brahman who is but the Witness.
[8] *Greater etc.*—Having infinite knowledge and all.

आत्मानमन्यं च स वेद विद्वान-
पिप्पलादो न तु पिप्पलादः ।
योऽविद्यया युक् स तु नित्यबद्धो
विद्यामयो यः स तु नित्यमुक्तः ॥७॥

7. That[1] which does not partake of the fruits is wise and knows itself as well as the other; but not so the one that eats the fruits. That which is tied to ignorance is always bound, while that which is full of knowledge is eternally free.

[1] *That etc.*—i.e. Brahman.

देहस्थोऽपि न देहस्थो विद्वान्स्वप्नाद्यथोत्थितः ।
अदेहस्थोऽपि देहस्थः कुमतिः स्वप्नदृग्यथा ॥८॥

8. The wise one, even though in the body,[1] is not of it,[2] like a man awakened from dream. But the foolish one, even though not[3] in the body, is yet[4] of it like one seeing a dream.

[1] *In the body*—apparently. This and the next two verses suggest that the wise man should live without caring for pleasure or pain and without identification with the body and mind.

[2] *Of it*—affected by its shortcomings.
[3] *Not etc.*—in reality.
[4] *Yet etc.*—owing to ignorance.

इन्द्रियैरिन्द्रियार्थेषु गुणैरपि गुणेषु च ।
गृह्यमाणेष्वहंकुर्यान्न विद्वान्यस्त्वविक्रियः ॥९॥

THE LAST MESSAGE OF SHRI KRISHNA
87

9. When the organs cognise sense-objects—or, in other words, Gunas[1] perceive Gunas—he who is wise does not identify himself with such phenomena, being unaffected by them.

[1] *Gunas etc.*—The term has a number of meanings. Here it stands for organs and sense-objects, as in Gitâ III. 28.

देवाधीने शरीरेऽस्मिन्गुणभाव्येन कर्मणा ।
वर्तमानोऽबुधस्तत्र कर्तास्मीति निबध्यते ॥१०॥

10. Living in the body which is under the sway of the resultant of past actions, the foolish one, on account of work done by the organs, becomes bound by identifying himself with them.

Compare Gitâ III. 27.

एवं विरक्तः शयन आसनाटनमज्जने ।
दर्शनस्पर्शनघ्राणभोजनश्रवणादिषु ॥११॥
न तथा बध्यते विद्वांस्तत्र तत्रादयन्गुणान् ।
प्रकृतिस्थोऽप्यसंसक्तो यथा खं सवितानिळः ॥१२॥

11-12. The wise one, being thus free from attachment in such acts as lying, sitting, walking, bathing, seeing, touching, smelling, eating, hearing, etc., is not bound like the other man, because in such cases he is but watching[1] the organs experience the sense-objects. Even living in the midst of Prakriti, he is unattached, like the sky, the sun, and the wind.

[1] *Watching etc.*—i.e. not identifying himself with them.

UDDHAVA GITA

वैशारद्ये क्षयाऽसङ्गशितया छिन्नसंशयः ।
प्रतिबुद्ध इव स्वप्नान्नानात्वाद्विनिवर्तते ॥१३॥

13. With his doubts dispelled by a clear vision sharpened by non-attachment, he turns away[1] from multiplicity, like an awakened man from his dreams.

[1] *Turns away etc.*—sees the one Brahman amid the unreality of the universe.

यस्य स्युर्वीतसंकल्पाः प्राणेन्द्रियमनोधियाम् ।
वृत्तयः स विनिर्मुक्तो देहस्थोऽपि हि तद्गुणैः ॥१४॥

14. He, the functions of whose Prânas, organs, Manas, and intellect are free from plans, is indeed free from the attributes of the body even though he may be in it.

यस्यात्मा हिंस्यते हिंस्रैर्येन किंचिद्यदृच्छया ।
अर्च्यते वा क्वचित्तत्र न व्यतिक्रियते बुधः ॥१५॥

15. He who is not affected when his body, without any ostensible cause, is tortured by the cruel, or at another time somewhat worshipped by anybody, is a wise man.

न स्तुवीत न निन्देत कुर्वतः साध्वसाधु वा ।
वदतो गुणदोषाभ्यां वर्जितः समदृङ्मुनिः ॥१६॥

16. The saint, with an even eye to all, and free from merits or demerits, should not praise or blame anybody who may do or say anything good or evil.

THE LAST MESSAGE OF SHRI KRISHNA

न कुर्यान्न वदेत्किंचिन्न ध्यायेत्साध्वसाधु वा ।

आत्मारामोऽनया वृत्त्या विचरेज्जडवन्मुनिः ॥१७॥

17. The saint should not do, or say, or think of, anything good or evil; taking pleasure in the Self, he should wander in this manner[1] like an idiot.

[1] *In this manner*—indifferent to all bodily functions. All these are preparations for one seeking liberation.

शब्दब्रह्मणि निष्णातो न निष्णायात्परे यदि ।

श्रमस्तस्य श्रमफलो ह्यधेनुमिव रक्षतः ॥१८॥

18. If one versed in the Vedas be not versed[1] also in Brahman, his labour[2] is the only result of his exertions, as in the case of one who maintains a cow that no more calves.

[1] *Versed etc.*—i.e. a man of realisation.
[2] *Labour etc.*—i.e. it is in vain.

गां दुग्धदोहामसतीं च भार्यां

देहं पराधीनमसत्प्रजां च ।

वित्तं त्वतीर्थीकृतमङ्ग वाचं

हीनां मया रक्षति दुःखदुःखी ॥१६॥

19. My friend, he who maintains a cow that no more gives milk, an unchaste wife, a body under the control of another, a wicked child, wealth not bestowed on deserving people, and speech devoid of references to Me, is one who suffers misery after misery.

UDDHAVA GITA

यस्यां न मे पावनमङ्ग कर्म
स्थित्युद्भवप्राणनिरोधमस्य ।
लीळावतारेप्सितजन्म वा स्याद्-
बन्ध्यां गिरं तां बिभृयात्र धीरः ॥२०॥

20. The wise man, my dear, should not entertain that futile speech in which there is no mention of My sanctifying deeds comprising the origin, maintenance, and dissolution of this universe, or of My births— dear[1] to the world—when I incarnate Myself at will.

[1] *Dear etc.*—which people so much like.

एवं जिज्ञासयाऽपोह्य नानात्वभ्रममात्मनि ।
उपारमेत विरजं मनो मय्यर्प्य सर्वगे ॥२१॥

21. Removing the delusion of manifoldness in the Âtman through such discrimination, one should cease from activities, holding the purified mind on Me, the Omnipresent One.

यद्यनीशो धारयितुं मनो ब्रह्मणि निश्चलम् ।
मयि सर्वाणि कर्माणि निरपेक्षः समाचर ॥२२॥

22. If thou art unable to hold the mind steady on the Brahman, then perform all actions without caring for results, giving them up unto Me.

Finishing the topic of Jnâna, the Lord proceeds to inculcate Bhakti which is an easier and surer path.

THE LAST MESSAGE OF SHRI KRISHNA

श्रद्धालुर्मे कथाः शृण्वन्सुभद्रा लोकपावनीः ।
गायन्ननुस्मरन्कर्म जन्म चाभिनयन्मुहुः ॥२३॥
मदर्थे धर्मकामार्थानाचरन्मदपाश्रयः ।
लभते निश्चलां भक्तिं मय्युद्धव सनातने ॥२४॥

23-24. O Uddhava, listening to, singing, and reflecting on tales about Me that are highly conducive to
the well-being and purity of the worlds, repeatedly
imitating[1] My deeds and lives, having Me as their
refuge, and pursuing duty, desire, and wealth for My
sake, the man of faith attains steadfast devotion for
Me, the Eternal One.

[1] *Imitating etc.*—playing these wonderful dramas.

सत्सङ्गलब्धया भक्त्या मयि मां स उपासिता ।
स वै मे दर्शितं सद्धिरञ्जसा विन्दते पदम् ॥२५॥

25. He worships Me attaining devotion for Me
through association with sages. He indeed easily
realises[1] My state inculcated by the sages.

[1] *Realises etc.*—realises his Brahmanhood.

उद्धव उवाच ।

साधुस्तवोत्तमश्लोक मतः कीदृग्विधः प्रभो ।
भक्तिस्त्वय्युपयुज्येत कीदृशी सद्धिराहृता ॥२६॥

Uddhava said:

26. O Thou of surpassing glory, O Lord, what
sort of a sage dost Thou prefer most? What kind of
devotion approved by sages[1] is most acceptable to
Thee?

[1] *Sages*—such as Nârada and others.

UDDHAVA GITA

एतन्मे पुरुषाध्यक्ष लोकाध्यक्ष जगत्प्रभो ।
प्रणतायानुरक्ताय प्रपन्नाय च कथ्यताम् ॥२७॥

27. O Lord of men, O Lord of the spheres, O Lord of the Universe, say this to me, for I have[1] prostrated myself to Thee, am devoted to Thee, and have surrendered myself to Thee.

[1] *I have etc.*—Hence Thou shouldst not make it a secret from me.

त्वं ब्रह्म परमं व्योम पुरुषः प्रकृतेः परः ।
अवतीर्णोऽसि भगवन्स्वेच्छोपात्तपृथग्वपुः ॥२८॥

28. O Lord, Thou art the Supreme Brahman, infinite like the sky, the Purusha[1] who is beyond the Prakriti; Thou art incarnated (on earth) assuming a separate body, of Thy own accord.[2]

[1] *The Purusha etc.*—the Spirit that is beyond nature.
[2] *Own accord*—Thy birth is not due to Karma as with others.

श्रीभगवानुवाच ।

कृपालुरकृतद्रोहस्तितिक्षुः सर्वदेहिनाम् ।
सत्यसारोऽनवद्यात्मा समः सर्वोपकारकः ॥२९॥

The Lord said:

29. Compassionate, with enmity to no creature, forbearing, with truth as his strength, of an unimpeachable mind, same to all, benefactor of all beings;

Thirty characteristics of a Sâdhu are enumerated in verses 29-33.

THE LAST MESSAGE OF SHRI KRISHNA

कामैरहतधीर्दान्तो मृदुः शुचिरकिंचनः ।
अनीहो मितभुक् शान्तः स्थिरो मच्छरणो मुनिः ॥३०॥

30. With his intellect unsullied by desires, a master of his organs, mild, pure, without possessions, without outward activity, with measured diet, a master of his mind, steady, having Me as his refuge, and meditative;

अप्रमत्तो गभीरात्मा धृतिमाञ्जितषड्गुणः ।
अमानी मानदः कल्पो मैत्रः कारुणिकः कविः ॥३१॥

31. Ever alert, of a balanced mind, with fortitude, mastering the sixfold evil,[1] seeking no name, yet giving honour to others, expert, friendly,[2] merciful,[3] and illumined;

[1] *Sixfold evil*—viz. hunger and thirst, grief and infatuation, and decay and death.

[2] *Friendly*—to those who are happy.

[3] *Merciful*—to those that are in misery.

आज्ञायैवं गुणान्दोषान्मयादिष्टानपि स्वकान् ।
धर्मान्संत्यज्य यः सर्वान्मां भजेत स सत्तमः ॥३२॥

32. He who knowing the merits and demerits (of duty and its opposite) gives up[1] all his formal duties even as sanctioned[2] by Me, and worships Me, is also the best among sages.

[1] *Gives up etc.*—transcends the preparatory or formal (*Gauni* or *Vaidhi*) stages to pursue that higher form characterised by spontaneous, selfless love (*Parâ* or *Râgânuga Bhakti*).

[2] *Sanctioned*—in the scriptures.

UDDHAVA GITA

ज्ञात्वाज्ञात्वाऽथ ये वे मां यावान्यश्चास्मि याद्दशः ।
भजन्त्यनन्यभावेन ते मे भक्ततमा मताः ॥३३॥

33. Those who knowing or not knowing how much,[1] what,[2] and of what sort[3] I am, worship Me with their whole soul given up to Me[4] are in My opinion the best of My devotees.

[1] *How much*—that I am unlimited by time or space.
[2] *What*—that I am the Self of all.
[3] *Of what sort*—that I am the embodiment of Existence-Knowledge-Bliss, and so on.
[4] *Whole soul etc.*—This is the *sine qua non* of religion.
Pure (*Shuddhâ*) Bhakti, as distinct from Bhakti with reason (*Jnânamishrâ*), is extolled in this verse. In Shri Ramakrishna's language, it is that form of devotion which remains when one is beyond both knowledge and ignorance.

मल्लिङ्गमद्भक्तजनदर्शनस्पर्शनार्चनम् ।
परिचर्या स्तुतिः प्रह्वगुणकर्मानुकीर्तनम् ॥३४॥

34. Seeing, touching, worshipping, serving, praising, and saluting My images as well as My devotees and reciting the glories and deeds of both;

Some characteristics of devotion are pointed out in verses 34-41.

मत्कथाश्रवणे श्रद्धा मदनुध्यानमुद्धव ।
सर्वलाभोपहरणं दास्येनात्मनिवेदनम् ॥३५॥

35. Faith in listening to tales about Me, O Uddhava, meditating on Me, offering everything received unto Me, and surrendering oneself in service to Me;

THE LAST MESSAGE OF SHRI KRISHNA

मज्जन्मकर्मकथनं मम पर्वानुमोदनम् ।
गीतताण्डवबादित्रगोष्ठीभिर्मद्गृहोत्सवः ॥३६॥

36. The recounting of My lives and deeds, observance of My special days, festivities in My temples with songs, dance, and instrumental music in company;

यात्रा बलिविधानं च सर्ववार्षिकपर्वसु ।
वैदिकी तान्त्रिकी दीक्षा मदीयव्रतधारणम् ॥३७॥

37. Processions to sacred sites and making offerings of worship on all special days of the year, initiation according to Vedic and other scriptural rites, and taking up vows in My honour;

ममार्चास्थापने श्रद्धा स्वतः संहत्य चोद्यमः ।
उद्यानोपवनाक्रीडपुरमन्दिरकर्मणि ॥३८॥

38. Eagerness to instal My images, and endeavour, either single-handed or jointly, to construct gardens, orchards, play-grounds, compound walls, and temples dedicated to me;

संमार्जनोपलेपाभ्यां सेकमण्डलवर्तनैः ।
गृहशुश्रूषणं मह्यं दासवद्यदमायया ॥३९॥

39. Taking care of My temples without deceit, like a servant, through sweeping, plastering, watering, and drawing[1] sacred designs;

[1] *Drawing etc.*—The word in the text may also mean "circumambulating".

UDDHAVA GITA

अमानित्वमदम्भित्वं कृतस्यापरिकीर्तनम् ।
अपि दीपावलोकं मे नोपयुञ्ज्यान्निवेदितम् ॥४०॥

40. Disregard for fame, absence of haughtiness, and not trumpeting one's good deeds, not using for selfish ends the light of the lamp[1] offered to Me;

[1] *The lamp*—Suggesting that other things offered are also to be held sacred. Commentators have explained the passage variously.

यद्यदिष्टतमं लोके यच्चातिप्रियमात्मनः ।
तत्तन्निवेद्येन्मह्यं तदानन्त्याय कल्पते ॥४१॥

41. What is most covetable to people in general and whatever is specially dear to oneself should be offered unto Me. That offering produces infinite results.

सूर्योऽग्निर्ब्राह्मणो गावो वैष्णवः खं मरुज्जलम् ।
भूरात्मा सर्वभूतानि भद्र पूजापदानि मे ॥४२॥

42. The sun, fire, a Brâhmana, cows, a devotee, the sky, air, water, earth, the body, and all beings— these, O friend, are the objects wherein to worship Me.

Eleven symbols of worship are mentioned in this verse, the details being given in the next few verses.

सूर्ये तु विद्यया त्रय्या हविषाग्नौ यजेत माम् ।
आतिथ्येन तु विप्राग्र्ये गोष्वङ्ग यवसादिना ॥४३॥

43. One should worship Me in the sun through Vedic hymns, in the fire through oblations of ghee,

THE LAST MESSAGE OF SHRI KRISHNA 97

in the best of Brâhmanas through hospitality, and in cows with grass etc., My friend.

वैष्णवे बन्धुसत्कृत्या हृदि खे ध्याननिष्ठया ।
वायौ मुख्यधिया तोये द्रव्यैस्तोयपुरस्कृतैः ॥४४॥

44. In the devotee through cordial reception, in the sky of the heart through regular meditation, in the air by looking upon it as Prâna, in water with things such as water etc.

स्थण्डिले मन्त्रहृदयैर्भोगैरात्मानमात्मनि ।
क्षेत्रज्ञं सर्वभूतेषु समत्वेन यजेत माम् ॥४५॥

45. In the consecrated ground through secret[1] Mantras; in the body one should worship the Âtman with eatables[2] etc., and in all beings one should worship Me, the Kshetrajna,[3] with an evenness of vision.

[1] *Secret*—because sacred.
[2] *Eatables*—Considering them as offerings to the Lord, not for satisfying the palate.
[3] *Kshetrajna*—The Lord as the indwelling Spirit of the universe—the Eternal Subject.

धिष्ण्येष्वेष्विति मद्रूपं शङ्खचक्रगदाम्बुजैः ।
युक्तं चतुर्भुजं शान्तं ध्यायन्नर्चेत्समाहितः ॥४६॥

46. In all these abodes one should meditate on My benign form with four hands, in which are the conch, disc, mace, and lotus, and should worship it with concentration.

7

UDDHAVA GITA

इष्टापूर्तेन मामेवं यो यजेत समाहितः ।
ऌभते मयि सद्भक्तिं मत्स्मृतिः साधुसेवया ॥४७॥

47. He who thus worships Me through Ishta[1]
and Purta[2] with concentration, remembers Me and
through the service of sages attains to perfect devotion for Me.

[1] *Ishta*—making sacrifices.

[2] *Purta*—constructing tanks, gardens, temples, etc.

Some of the forms of devotion mentioned in verses
34-41 may come under these heads.

प्रायेण भक्तियोगेन सत्सङ्गेन विनोद्धव ।
नोपायो विद्यते सभ्रथङ् प्रायणं हि सतामहम् ॥४८॥

48. O Uddhava, there is almost no other efficient way[1] except the Bhakti-Yoga due to the
association of sages, for I am the goal of the sages.

[1] *Way*—out of this world.

अथैतत्परमं गुह्यं शृण्वतो यदुनन्दन ।
सुगोप्यमपि वक्ष्यामि त्वं मे भृत्यः सुहृत्सखा ॥४९॥

49. Now I am going to tell thee this profound
secret, even though most confidential, for thou art
My servant, companion, and friend.

CHAPTER VII

श्रीभगवानुवाच ।

न रोधयति मां योगो न सांख्यं धर्म एव च ।
न स्वाध्यायस्तपस्त्यागो नेष्टापूर्तं न दक्षिणा ॥१॥
व्रतानि यज्ञश्छन्दांसि तीर्थानि नियमा यमाः ।
यथावरुन्धे सत्सङ्गः सर्वसङ्गापहो हि माम् ॥२॥

The Lord said:

1-2. Yoga, discrimination, piety, study of the Vedas, austerities, renunciation, rites such as Agnihotra, and works[1] of public utility, charity, vows, sacrifices, secret Mantras, places of pilgrimage, and moral rules[2] particular as well as universal—none of these, I say, binds Me so much as the association of saints that roots out all attachment.

[1] *Works etc.*—constructing wells, tanks, parks, etc.

[2] *Rules etc.*—For the Niyamas and Yamas see Patanjali's Yoga Aphorisms II. 30-32.

The association of perfected souls is extolled here above everything else, as it imperceptibly cleanses the mind. Shri Ramakrishna's comparing it to a soap solution is characteristic enough.

सत्सङ्गेन हि दैतेया यातुधाना मृगाः खगाः ।
गन्धर्वाप्सरसो नागाः सिद्धाश्चारणगुह्यकाः ॥३॥
विद्याधरा मनुष्येषु वैश्याः शूद्राः स्त्रियोऽन्त्यजाः ।
रजस्तमःप्रकृतयस्तस्मिंस्तस्मिन्युगेऽनघ ॥४॥
बहवो मत्पदं प्राप्तास्त्वाष्ट्रकायाधवादयः ॥५॥

UDDHAVA GITA

3-5. It was through the association of saints, O sinless one, that many who were of a Râjasika or Tâmasika nature—such as Vritra,[1] Prahlâda,[2] and others[3]—attained Me in different ages: Daityas and Râkshasas, beasts and birds, Gandharvas, Apsarâs Nâgas, Siddhas, Châranas, Guhyakas, and Vidyâdharas, and among mankind—Vaishyas and Shudras, women and outcasts.

[1] *Vritra*—son of the sage Tvashtri. Vritra in his previous life had the association of the sages Nârada and Angirâ.

[2] *Prahlâda*—son of Kayâdhu, a daughter of the Devas whom Nârada instructed and the child listened from its mother's womb.

[3] *Others*—some of these are enumerated in the next verse.

वृषपर्वा बलिर्वाणो मयश्चाथ विभीषण: ।

सुग्रीवो हनुमानृक्षो गजो गृध्रो वणिक्पथ: ।

व्याधः कुब्जा व्रजे गोप्यो यज्ञपत्न्यस्तथापरे ॥६॥

6. Vrishaparvâ,[1] Bali, Bâna, Maya, Vibhishana, Sugriva, Hanumân, the bear Jâmbavân, the elephant Gajendra, the vulture Jatâyu, the merchant Tulâdhâra, the fowler Dharmavyâdha, the hunchbacked (perfume-vendor) Kubjâ, the Gopis as well as the wives of the Brâhmanas engaged in sacrifices, in Vrindâvana, and others.

[1] *Vrishaparvâ etc.*—Vrishaparvâ was a demon who was brought up by a saint. Bali associated with his grandfather Prahlâda. Bâna was the eldest son of Bali, and he was also blessed with the association of the Lord Shiva. Maya came in contact with the Pândavas while constructing the royal court for them, while Vibhishana and Sugriva mixed

THE LAST MESSAGE OF SHRI KRISHNA

with Hanumân, who himself as well as Jâmbavân had the blessed association of the Lord Himself as Râma and Krishna. Gajendra had in his previous life associated with Sâdhus and in his present life was rescued from his old enemy—now a crocodile—by Shri Krishna Himself. Jatâyu met Garuda, King Dasharatha, etc.; the Shudra Tulâdhâra met Nârada etc.; Dharmavyâdha had mixed with a Vaishnava king in his past life, while Kubjâ with the Gopis and Brahmanas' wives had the association of Shri Krishna.

ते नाधीतश्रुतिगणा नोपासितमहत्तमाः ।
अव्रतातप्ततपसः मत्सङ्गान्मामुपागताः ॥७॥

7. They had not studied the Vedas, nor served the great saints, nor observed any vows, nor performed any austerities, yet through their association with Me[1] they attained Me.

[1] *With Me*—as represented by the saints.

केवलेन हि भावेन गोप्यो गावो नगा मृगाः ।
येऽन्ये मूढधियो नागाः सिद्धा मामीयुरञ्जसा ॥८॥

8. The Gopis, and even the cows, trees, beasts, serpents, and others that were dull of understanding were perfected, and easily attained Me through love[1] alone.

[1] *Love*—engendered by the association of Sâdhus.

यं न योगेन सांख्येन दानव्रततपोऽध्वरैः ।
व्याख्यास्वाध्यायसंन्यासैः प्राप्नुयाद्यत्नवानपि ॥९॥

9. Whom one attains not even after struggle, through Yoga, discrimination, charity, vows, auster-

102

UDDHAVA GITA

ities, sacrifices, teaching and study of the Vedas, or renunciation.

रामेण साधं मथुरां प्रणीते
श्वाफल्किना मय्यनुरक्तचित्ताः ।
विगाढभावेन न मे वियोग-
तीव्राधयोऽन्यं दृश्शुः सुखाय ॥१०॥

10. When I was taken with Balarâma to Mathura by Akrura,[1] the Gopis with their minds attached to Me through intense love, were sorely afflicted at My bereavement and considered nothing else (but Me) as of interest to them.

Verses 10-13 describe the case of the blessed Gopis of Vrindâvana.

[1] *Akrura*—son of Shvaphalka, whom King Kamsa despatched to Vrindâvana to bring the two brothers, with a view to killing them, first by setting on his wild elephant, and failing that, by challenging the children to a duel with his famous wrestlers. His vain idea was to baffle the prophecy that Krishna would kill him.

तास्ताः क्षपाः प्रेष्ठतमेन नीता
मयैव वृन्दावनगोचरेण ।
क्षणार्धवत्ताः पुनरङ्ग तासां
हीना मया कल्पसमा बभूवुः ॥११॥

11. Those very nights, my friend, which, with Me their Beloved in their midst at Vrindâvana, they had passed like moments, became in My absence like ages to them.

THE LAST MESSAGE OF SHRI KRISHNA

ता नाविदन्मय्यनुषंगबद्ध-
धियः स्वमात्मानमदस्तथेदम् ।
यथा समाधौ मुनयोऽब्धितोये
नद्यः प्रविष्टा इव नामरूपे ॥१२॥

12. With their minds fixed on Me through attachment, they knew neither their kinsmen,[1] nor their bodies, nor things far or near—as sages in the superconscious state know not name and form—like unto rivers merging in the waters of the ocean.

[1] *Kinsmen etc.*—Their one thought was Krishna.

मत्कामा रमणं जारमस्वरूपविदोऽबलाः ।
ब्रह्म मां परमं प्रापुः संगाच्छतसहस्रशः ॥१३॥

13. Not knowing My real nature,[1] the Gopis, who were ignorant women, desired Me as their beloved sweetheart, yet they attained Me, the Supreme Brahman, by hundreds and thousands, through the power of holy association.

[1] *Real nature*—as "Supreme Brahman".

तस्मात्त्वमुद्धवोत्सृज्य चोदनां प्रतिचोदनाम् ।
प्रवृत्तं च निवृत्तं च श्रोतव्यं श्रुतमेव च ॥१४॥
मामेकमेव शरणमात्मानं सर्वदेहिनाम् ।
याहि सर्वात्मभावेन मया स्या ह्यकुतोभयः ॥१५॥

14-15. Therefore, O Uddhava, giving up injunctions and prohibitions, the paths of enjoyment[1] and renunciation, things learnt and yet to be learnt,[2] do thou whole-heartedly take refuge in Me alone,

UDDHAVA GITA

104

the Self of all beings, and be fearless through Me.

¹ *Enjoyment*—i.e. family life.
² *Learnt etc.*—about personal well-being.

उद्धव उवाच ।

संशयः शृण्वतो वाचं तव योगेश्वरेश्वर ।

न निवर्तत आत्मस्थो येन भ्राम्यति मे मनः ॥१६॥

Uddhava said:

16. O Lord of the masters of Yoga, though I am listening to Thy words, the doubts that are in my mind are not dispelled, and hence my mind is wandering.

श्रीभगवानुवाच ।

स एष जीवो विवरप्रसूतिः

प्राणेन घोषेण गुहां प्रविष्टः ।

मनोमयं सूक्ष्ममुपेत्य रूपं

मात्रा स्वरो वर्ण इति स्थविष्ठः ॥१७॥

The Lord said:

17. This¹ Paramâtman which manifests Itself in the centres² of the spinal column, has entered the Mulâdhâra³ centre with the Prâna⁴ coupled with the subtlest form⁵ of sound, and passing through less subtle forms perceptible to the mind only, is (ultimately) manifest in the grossest form as syllable,⁶ pitch, and letter-sound.

Verses 17-24 furnish the Lord's answer. The idea is this: It is the Lord who through His Mâyâ appears as this universe; the Jivas identify themselves with it through nescience without beginning, and imagine them-

THE LAST MESSAGE OF SHRI KRISHNA 105

selves as agents, enjoyers, etc. Hence they come under the injunctions and prohibitions of the Shâstras, and must work then, for the purification of their minds. When the mind has become pure, they should give up work and practise devotion for the Lord with steady faith, until they are blessed with realisation, which is the goal.

In verses 17-21 is first of all set forth how from the Lord the universe has sprung up through the organs of speech and so on, causing the transmigration of the Jivas.

[1] *This*—with which we are ever identified, though we may not be aware of the fact.

[2] *Centres etc.*—In the Yogis' parlance, the six "lotuses" that are distributed along the Sushumnâ canal.

[3] *Mulâdhâra*—corresponding probably to the lowest or sacral plexus.

[4] *Prâna*—the source of all energy, microcosmic as well as macrocosmic.

[5] *Subtlest form etc.*—viz. Parâ or superfine, also called Nâda. The intermediate and slightly more developed stages of sound are called Pashyanti and Madhyamâ, which have their respective seats in the Manipura and Anâhata centres, i.e. those about the region of the navel and the heart, and the last is Vaikhari or articulate speech. These three forms of sound are related respectively to Prâna, Manas, and Buddhi.

[6] *Syllable etc.*—Syllable—as short or long etc.; *pitch*—as high or low etc.; *letter-sound*—as 'ka,' 'kha,' etc.

यथाऽनलः खेऽनिलबन्धुरूष्मा
बलेन दारुण्यधिमथ्यमानः ।
अणुः प्रजातो हविषा समिध्यते
तथैव मे व्यक्तिरियं हि वाणी ॥१८॥

18. As fire exists in the pores of wood as (latent) heat,[1] which through vigorous friction aided by wind manifests itself in the wood (first) as a spark,

UDDHAVA GITA

then as tangible fire, and is (finally) set ablaze by ghee, similarly is speech My manifestation.

[1] *Heat etc.*—The heat typifies the Parâ, the spark the Pashyanti, the tangible fire the Madhyamâ, and the blazing fire the Vaikhari form of sound.

एवं गदिः कर्मगतिर्विसर्गो
घ्राणो रसो टक् स्पर्शः श्रुतिश्च ।
संकल्पविज्ञानमथाभिमानः
सूत्रं रजः सत्त्वतमोविकारः ॥१६॥

19. And so also are articulation,[1] action, motion, and expulsion; smelling, tasting, seeing, touching, and hearing; cogitating, knowledge, identification, and the Sutra,[2] as also the modifications[3] of Sattva, Rajas, and Tamas.

[1] *Articulation etc.*—The first four (the last covering two) are the functions of the five organs of action; the next five, of the five organs of perception; cogitation, of the Manas; knowledge, of the Buddhi and Chitta; and identification, of the Ahamkâra.

[2] *Sutra*—Cosmic Energy or Intelligence, which is an effect of the Pradhâna. See note 2 on verse 19, Ch. IV.

[3] *Modifications etc.*—comprising the Âdhidaivika Âdhyâtmika, and Âdhibhautika divisions, i.e. those pertaining to the gods, the body, and other animals, respectively.

All the foregoing are manifestations of the Lord.

अयं हि जीवस्त्रिवृद्ब्जयोनि-
र्व्यक्त एको वयसा स आद्यः ।
विशिष्टशक्तिर्बहुधेव भाति
बीजानि योनिं प्रतिपद्य यद्वत् ॥२०॥

THE LAST MESSAGE OF SHRI KRISHNA   107

20. This Ishvara,[1] one and undifferentiated (at first), has His powers[2] differentiated by time, and appears to be of diverse forms, like seeds[3] reaching (proper) fields; for He is the Primeval One, the substratum of Mâyâ—the component of the three Gunas—and the cause of the cosmic lotus.[4]

The universe being an emanation of the Lord is not different from Him—this is the idea.

[1] *Ishvara*—"Jiva" in the text means "That which causes everything to live", the life-principle, hence God.

[2] *Powers*—such as the organs of speech etc.

[3] *Seeds etc.*—Just as a tiny seed develops into a big tree with so many subdivisions.

[4] *Cosmic lotus*—the universe conceived of as a lotus.

यस्मिन्निदं प्रोतमशेषमोतं
पटो यथा तन्तुवितानसंस्थः ।
य एषं संसारतरुः पुराणः
कर्मात्मकः पुष्पफले प्रसूते ॥२१॥

21. On whom, as Its warp and woof, this entire universe rests, as a cloth on the network of threads. And this tree of Samsâra[1] is ancient,[2] activity[3] is its nature, and it produces flowers[4] and fruits.

[1] *Samsâra*—The word means both universe and transmigration. Hence there is a natural transition to the second meaning. The metaphor of the tree in this connection is quite familiar in the scriptures.

[2] *Ancient*—for nobody knows its beginning.

[3] *Activity etc.*—It is ever moving forward.

[4] *Flowers etc.*—experience and emancipation, or work and its results.

UDDHAVA GITA

द्वे अस्य बीजे शतमूलत्रिनालः
पञ्चस्कन्धः पञ्चरसप्रसूतिः ।
दशैकशाखो द्विसुपर्णनीड-
स्त्रिवल्कलो द्विफलोऽर्कं प्रविष्टः ॥२२॥

22. It has got two seeds,[1] a hundred roots, three trunks, five main branches, and eleven minor branches; it exudes five saps; it has got two birds' nests on it, three layers of bark, and two fruits, and reaches[2] up to the sun.

[1] *Seeds etc.*—The seeds are virtue and vice. The roots are the innumerable desires. The trunks are Sattva, Rajas, and Tamas. The main branches are the five elements, viz. earth, water, etc., and the minor branches are the ten organs and Manas. The saps are the five sense objects, viz. touch, taste, etc. The birds are the Jiva and Paramâtman. The bark refers to the nervous, bilious, and lymphatic temperaments. The fruits are happiness and misery.

[2] *Reaches...sun*—and no further, since one who goes beyond the solar sphere, is no more subject to transmigration.

अदन्ति चैकं फलमस्य गृध्रा
ग्रामेचरा एकमरण्यवासाः ।
हंसा य एकं बहुरूपमिज्यै-
र्मायामयं वेद स वेद वेदम् ॥२३॥

23. Vultures[1] frequenting villages[2] eat one[3] of the fruits, while swans[4] living in forests eat the other. He who with the help of his Gurus knows the One Lord—whose attribute is Mâyâ—assuming diverse forms, understands the Vedas.

THE LAST MESSAGE OF SHRI KRISHNA   109

[1] *Vultures etc.*—"Gridhra" literally means "greedy". Hence the epithet refers to the householders.

[2] *Villages*—"Grâma" also means the senses, which is the suggested meaning.

[3] *One etc.*—viz. misery. The enjoyment of heaven etc. is also no better.

[4] *Swans etc.*—refer to the Sannyâsins, who enjoy *bliss*.

एवं गुरूपासनयैकभक्त्या
विद्याकुठारेण शितेन धीरः ।
विवृश्चथ जीवाशयमप्रमत्तः
संपद्य चात्मानमथ त्यजास्त्रम् ॥२४॥

24. Thus, being steady and watchful, with the axe of knowledge sharpened by the service of the Guru with one-pointed devotion, cut asunder this tree[1] of Samsâra rooted in the soul, and then, being identified with thy Self, lay down[2] thy weapon.

[1] *Tree...soul*—"Jivâshayâ" means the "subtle body"—the storehouse of all our experiences—which being the cause of transmigration is here identified with the "tree of Samsâra".

[2] *Lay down etc.*—i.e. cease from the struggle for realisation.

CHAPTER VIII

श्रीभगवानुवाच ।
सत्त्वं रजस्तम इति गुणा बुद्धेर्नं चात्मनः ।
सत्त्वेनान्यतमौ हन्यात्सत्त्वं सत्त्वेन चैव हि ॥१॥

The Lord said:

1. The Gunas[1] Sattva, Rajas, and Tamas belong to the intellect and not to the Self. Through Sattva[2] one should subdue the other two, and (subdue) Sattva[3] also by means of Sattva itself.

Verses 1-7 describe how knowledge may arise through the destruction of the three Gunas.

[1] *Gunas*—the components of Prakriti or sentient and insentient nature. Tamas is inertia, Rajas is activity, and Sattva is the equilibrium or balance between these two. For their respective functions in different spheres, see Gitâ XVIII.

[2] *Through Sattva*—i.e. by developing it.

[3] *Sattva...itself*—one should control the functions of truthfulness, compassion, etc. through that of absorption in Brahman. Compare Vivekachudâmani, verse 278.

सत्त्वाद्धर्मो भवेद्वृद्धात्पुं सो मद्भक्तिलक्षणः ।
सात्त्विकोपासया सत्त्वं ततो धर्मः प्रवर्तते ॥२॥

2. Through developed Sattva a man attains to that form of spirituality which consists in devotion to Me. Through the use of Sâttvika[1] things Sattva is developed; this leads to spirituality.

[1] *Sâttvika things*—i.e. those that tend to purity, illumination and so on. See note on verse 6.

THE LAST MESSAGE OF SHRI KRISHNA

111

धर्मो रजस्तमो हन्यात्सत्त्ववृद्धिरनुत्तमः ।
आशु नश्यति तन्मूलो ह्यधर्म उभये हते ॥३॥

3. That superior form of spirituality which is brought on by an increase of Sattva destroys Rajas and Tamas. And when both of these are destroyed, iniquity, which has its rise in them, is also quickly destroyed.

आगमोऽपः प्रजा देशः कालः कर्म च जन्म च ।
ध्यानं मन्त्रोऽथ संस्कारो दशैते गुणहेतवः ॥४॥

4. Scripture,[1] water, people, place, time, work, birth,[2] meditation, Mantra, and purification—these are the ten causes which develop the Gunas.

[1] *Scripture etc.*—each of these has its Sâttvika, Râjasika, and Tâmasika counterparts; the first conducing to purity, illumination, and bliss; the second to temporary pleasure followed by a painful reaction; and the last leading to ignorance and increasing bondage. See note on verse 6.

[2] *Birth*—here means spiritual rebirth, i.e. taking initiation etc.

तत्तत्सात्त्विकमेवैषां यद्यद्वृद्धाः प्रचक्षते ।
निन्दन्ति तामसं तत्तद्राजसं तदुपेक्षितम् ॥५॥

5. Of these, those alone are Sâttvika which the sages praise; the Tâmasa are what they condemn; while those are Râjasa about which they are indifferent.

सात्त्विकान्येव सेवेत पुमान् सत्त्वविवृद्धये ।
ततो धर्मस्ततो ज्ञानं यावत्स्मृतिरपोहनम् ॥६॥

UDDHAVA GITA

6. For the increase of Sattva a man should concern himself with Sâttvika[1] things alone. Thence comes spirituality, and from this again knowledge—pending[2] the realisation of one's independence and the removal of the superimposition of gross and subtle bodies.

[1] *Sâttvika etc.*—e.g. only those scriptures are to be followed which teach Nivritti or the march back to the oneness of Brahman, not those that teach Pravritti or continuing the multiplicity (*Râjasika*) or those that teach downright injurious tenets (*Tâmasika*); similarly—holy water only is to be used, not scented water or wine etc.; one should mix only with spiritual people, not with worldly-minded or wicked people; a solitary place is to be preferred, not a public thoroughfare or a gaming house; early morning or some such time is to be selected for meditation in preference to hours likely to cause distraction or dullness; the obligatory and unselfish works alone should be done, not selfish or dreadful ones; initiation into pure and non-injurious forms of religion is needed, not those that require much ado or those that are impure and harmful; meditation should be on the Lord, not on sense-objects or on enemies with a view to revenge; Mantras such as Om are to be preferred, not those bringing worldly prosperity or causing injury to others; purification of the mind is what we should care for, not trimming of the body merely, or places like slaughter-houses.

[2] *Pending etc.*—i.e. devotion first purifies the mind and in that purified mind flashes knowledge characterised by these two symptoms.

वेणुसंघर्षजो वह्निर्दग्ध्वा शाम्यति तद्वनम् ।
एवं गुणव्यत्ययजो देहः शाम्यति तत्क्रियः ॥७॥

7. The fire that springs from the friction of bamboos in a forest burns that forest and is (itself)

THE LAST MESSAGE OF SHRI KRISHNA   113

quenched. Similarly[1] the body which is the outcome of an intermixture of the Gunas is destroyed in the manner of the fire.

[1] *Similarly etc.*—The fire burns the whole forest by means of its flames. Similarly the body destroys the Gunas through knowledge manifested in it.

उद्धव उवाच ।

विदन्ति मर्त्याः प्रायेण विषयान्पदमापदाम् ।
तथापि भुञ्जते कृष्ण तत्कथं श्वखराजवत् ॥८॥

Uddhava said:

8. O Krishna, mortals generally know the sense-objects to be sources of danger. Still how do they run after them like a dog, an ass, or a goat?

श्रीभगवानुवाच ।

अहमित्यन्यथाबुद्धिः प्रमत्तस्य यथा हृदि ।
उत्सर्पति रजो घोरं ततो वैकारिकं मनः ॥९॥

The Lord said:

9. In the heart of an undiscriminating man the wrong idea[1] of "I (and mine)" naturally arises; then dire Rajas overtakes the mind which is (originally) Sâttvika.

[1] *Idea etc.*—in things that are not the Self.

रजोयुक्तस्य मनसः संकल्पः सविकल्पकः ।
ततः कामो गुणध्यानादुःसहः स्याद्धि दुर्मतेः ॥१०॥

10. A mind under the influence of Rajas cherishes desires with all sorts of cogitation.[1] Then

8

114   UDDHAVA GITA

from a dwelling on the good points[2] (of a thing) the foolish man gets an inordinate hankering (for it).

For the idea compare Gitâ II. 62-63.

[1] *Cogitation*—that this thing is to be enjoyed thus, that thing in such and such a way and so on.

[2] *Good points*—e.g. Oh the beauty of it!—how expressive are the gestures!—and so on.

करोति कामवशगः कर्माण्यविजितेन्द्रियः ।
दुःखोदर्काणि संपश्यन्नूजोवेगविमोहितः ॥११॥

11. Under the sway of hankering, the man devoid of self-control wilfully commits deeds[1] fraught with future misery, being infatuated by violent Rajas.

[1] *Deeds*—Here is Rajas in action.

रजस्तमोभ्यां यदपि विद्वान्विक्षिप्तधीः पुनः ।
अतन्द्रितो मनो युञ्जन्दोषदृष्टिर्न सज्जते ॥१२॥

12. Even though distracted by Rajas and Tamas, the man of discrimination,[1] conscious of their evils, again concentrates his mind, without giving way to inadvertence and is not attached to them.

[1] *Discrimination*—this saves him.

अप्रमत्तोऽनुयुञ्जीत मनो मय्यर्पयन् शनैः ।
अनिर्विण्णो यथाकालं जितश्वासो जितासनः ॥१३॥

13. Being alert and diligent one should at the right time[1] control one's posture and breath, and

THE LAST MESSAGE OF SHRI KRISHNA 115

resigning the mind unto Me slowly practise concentration.

¹ *Right time*—morning, noon, and evening.

एतावान्योग आदिष्टो मच्छिष्यैः सनकादिभिः ।
सर्वतो मन आकृष्य मय्यद्धावेश्यते यथा ॥१४॥

14. In order that the mind, being withdrawn from everything, may be truly absorbed in Me, the above process of Yoga has been taught by My disciples, Sanaka and the rest.

उद्धव उवाच ।
यदा त्वं सनकादिभ्यो येन रूपेण केशव ।
योगमादिष्टवानेतद्रूपमिच्छामि वेदितुम् ॥१५॥

Uddhava said:

15. O Keshava, I wish to know the time when Thou taughtst this Yoga to Sanaka and others, and the form in which Thou didst do so.

श्रीभगवानुवाच ।
पुत्रा हिरण्यगर्भस्य मानसाः सनकादयः ।
पप्रच्छुः पितरं सूक्ष्मां योगस्यैकान्तिकीं गतिम् ॥१६॥

The Lord said:

16. Sanaka and others, the spiritual¹ sons of Brahmâ, asked their father the subtle and ultimate goal of Yoga.

¹ *Spiritual*—lit. created by will.

UDDHAVA GITA

सनकादय ऊचुः ।

गुणेष्वाविशते चेतो गुणाश्चेतसि च प्रभो ।

कथमन्योन्यसंत्यागो मुमुक्षोरतितितीर्षोः ॥१७॥

Sanaka and others said:

17. O Lord, the mind is attached to the sense-objects, and the sense-objects influence the mind. So for the man who seeks liberation and wants to go beyond them, how do they cease to act and react upon each other?

श्रीभगवानुवाच ।

एवं पृष्टो महादेवः स्वयंभूर्भूतभावनः ।

ध्यायमानः प्रश्नबीजं नाभ्यपद्यत कर्मधीः ॥१८॥

The Lord said:

18. Being thus asked, the great Lord Brahmâ who is uncreate[1] but the originator of all beings, thought and thought over it but could not get to the root[2] of the question, because his mind was on work.

[1] *Uncreate etc.*—This shows the difficulty of the problem—it baffled the understanding of so great a personage.

[2] *Root etc.*—what exactly troubled them.

स मामचिन्तयद्देवः प्रश्नपारतितीर्षया ।

तस्याहं हंसरूपेण सकाशमगमं तदा ॥१९॥

19. The god, with a view to answering the question effectively, reflected on Me. I then repaired to him in the form of a swan.[1]

[1] *Swan*—which is believed to have the potency of separating the milk from a mixture of milk and water.

THE LAST MESSAGE OF SHRI KRISHNA   117

दृष्ट्वा मां त उपव्रज्य कृत्वा पादाभिवन्दनम् ।
ब्रह्माणमग्रतः कृत्वा पप्रच्छुः को भवानिति ॥२०॥

20. Seeing Me they came forward, touched My feet, and making Brahmâ their leader asked Me, "Who art Thou?"

इत्यहं मुनिभिः पृष्टस्तत्त्वजिज्ञासुभिस्तदा ।
यदवोचमहं तेभ्यस्तदुद्धव निबोध मे ॥२१॥

21. Being thus asked by the sages, all eager to know the truth, I answered them. Learn from Me, O Uddhava, what I said on that occasion.

वस्तुनो यद्यनानात्त्वमात्मनः प्रश्न ईदृशः ।
कथं घटेत वो विप्रा वक्तुर्वा मे क आश्रयः ॥२२॥

22. O sages, if your question refers to the Âtman, then that Reality being one and undivided, such a question is inadmissible. On what grounds[1] also shall I, the speaker, stand?

In verses 22-25 the Lord teaches them to discriminate between the Self and non-Self. If they have this supreme knowledge, they will naturally be free from all attachment, and the dissociation of mind and sense-objects will follow as a matter of course. He begins by showing the incongruity of the question itself.

[1] *Grounds etc.*—Since there is but one Âtman, what differentiation as to species or attributes etc. is there to make the answer possible?

पञ्चात्मकेषु भूतेषु समानेषु च वस्तुतः ।
को भवानिति वः प्रश्नो वाचारम्भो ह्यनर्थकः ॥२३॥

118   UDDHAVA GITA

23. Since the bodies[1] of all beings are composed of the five elements, and since they are the same in reality,[2] your question, "Who art Thou", is a mere effort[3] of speech and is altogether meaningless.

[1] *Bodies etc.*—If the question refers to the body, then also the question is absurd, because here also there is no ground for differentiation.

[2] *In reality*—i.e. as Âtman.

[3] *Effort etc.*—an echo of Chhândogya VI. 1. 4-5.

मनसा वचसा दृष्ट्वा गृह्यतेऽन्यैरपीन्द्रियैः ।
अहमेव न मत्तोऽन्यदिति बुध्यध्वमञ्जसा ॥२४॥

24. Understand this rightly[1] that by mind, speech, sight, and the other organs I alone[2] am cognised, and nothing else.

[1] *Rightly*—i.e. by discrimination.

[2] *I alone etc.*—The Universe is Brahman *plus* mind. The mind and the senses may misread Brahman, but that does not affect Its nature. This indirectly furnishes the answer, "I am the All".

गुणेष्वाविशते चेतो गुणाश्चेतसि च प्रजाः ।
जीवस्य देह उभयं गुणाश्चेतो मदात्मनः ॥२५॥

25. Yes, My sons, the mind is attached to the sense-objects and the sense-objects influence the mind. Thus the sense-objects and the mind both (inter-twined) form the body[1] of the Jiva, who is ever identified with Me.

From this verse up to the end of the chapter the answer to the problem is given. The idea is this: If the mind, which is connected with the sense-objects as agent and enjoyer etc. and is variously named as intellect,

THE LAST MESSAGE OF SHRI KRISHNA

egoism and so forth, were the reality of the Jiva, then there might not be a dissolution of the connection between the Jiva and the sense-objects. But the Jiva is eternally identified with Brahman, and his *apparent* connection with the sense-objects is due to the superimposition of the mind on him. Hence by considering oneself as Brahman and reflecting on the unreality of the sense-objects, one should turn away from them and worship the Lord, whereby one can remain in one's true nature as the Infinite Self.

[1] *Body*—a superimposition, not the reality about him.

गुणेषु चाविशच्चित्त मभीक्ष्णं गुणसेवया ।
गुणाश्च चित्तप्रभवा मद्रूप उभयं त्यजेत् ॥२६॥

26. The mind which through constant dwelling on sense-objects is attached to them, and the sense-objects which influence[1] the mind, one should give up both, being identified with Me.

[1] *Influence*—as desires.

जाग्रत्स्वप्नः सुषुप्तं च गुणतो बुद्धिवृत्तयः ।
तासां विलक्षणो जीवः साक्षित्वेन विनिश्चितः ॥२७॥

27. Wakefulness, dream, and profound sleep are attributes of the intellect, being due to the Gunas.[1] The Self is distinct from them, since It is conclusively proved to be their Witness.[2]

[1] *Gunas*—Sattva, Rajas, and Tamas respectively.
[2] *Witness*—as the Eternal Subject.

यर्हि संसृतिबन्धोऽयमात्मनो गुणवृत्तिदः ।
मयि तुर्ये स्थितो जह्यात्त्यागस्तद्गुणचेतसाम् ॥२८॥

28. Because the entanglement with the intellect[1] sets the Gunas in motion in the Jiva, therefore one

UDDHAVA GITA

should give it up resting on Me, the Transcendent. Then the sense-objects and mind come to be dissociated.

[1] *Intellect*—The commentator Shridhara Swami takes the word *Samsriti* (*Samsâra* of verse 29) or transmigration to mean that which causes it; hence it refers to the Buddhi.

अहंकारकृतं बन्धमात्मनोऽर्थविपर्ययम् ।
विद्वान्निर्विद्य संसारचिन्तां तुर्ये स्थितस्त्यजेत् ॥२९॥

29. Knowing the bondage due to egoism to be the source of all trouble[1] for the Jiva, one should be averse to it and give up one's identification with the intellect—resting on the Transcendent.

[1] *Trouble*—by veiling his blissful nature and so on.

यावन्नानार्थधीः पुंसो न निवर्तेत युक्तिभिः ।
जागर्त्यपि स्वपन्नज्ञः स्वप्ने जागरणं यथा ॥३०॥

30. Till a man's notion of multiplicity is put a stop to by reasoning, he is as good as asleep even though awake—for he is ignorant—as one fancies oneself awake in dream.

असत्त्वादात्मनोऽन्येषां भावानां तत्कृता भिदा ।
गतयो हेतवश्चास्य मृषा स्वप्नदृशो यथा ॥३१॥

31. As objects[1] other than the Âtman are unreal, diversity[2] caused by them is false, as

THE LAST MESSAGE OF SHRI KRISHNA 121

also Its passage to other spheres with its causes,[3] as in the case of a man seeing dreams.

[1] *Objects etc.*—i.e. the body etc.
[2] *Diversity*—of caste and order of life etc.
[3] *Causes*—viz. works.

यो जागरे बहिरनुक्षणधर्मिणोऽर्थान्
भुङ्क्ते समस्तकरणैर्हृदि तत्सदृक्षान् ।
स्वप्ने सुषुप्त उपसंहरते स एकः
स्मृत्यन्वयात्त्रिगुणवृत्तिदृगिन्द्रियेशः ॥३२॥

32. He who in the waking state enjoys, through all his organs, objects with ever-changing attributes in the outside world, who in dream has experiences similar to them in his heart, and who withdraws them in profound sleep, are one[1] and the same Âtman—the Witness—of the three states and the Ruler of the organs. This is proved from the persistence of memory in all these states.

[1] *One etc.*—They are not separate, since a man remembers his experiences of the waking and dream states as also his ignorance of anything in dreamless sleep, and the one unchanging Witness of these is the Âtman.

एवं विमृश्य गुणतो मनसस्त्र्यवस्था
मन्मायया मयि कृता इति निश्चितार्थाः ।
संछिद्य हार्दमनुमानसदुक्तितीक्ष्ण-
ज्ञानासिना भजत माऽखिलसंशयाधिम् ॥३३॥

33. Thus reflecting that the three states of the mind due to Gunas are created[1] in Me by My Mâyâ,

UDDHAVA GITA

and being thus sure about the Reality, destroy egoism which is the receptacle of doubts with the sword of knowledge sharpened by inference and competent testimony,[2] and worship Me who is seated in the heart.

[1] *Created*—i.e. imagined.
[2] *Competent testimony*—including Shrutis.

ईक्षेत विभ्रममिदं मनसो विलासं
दृष्टं विनष्टमतिलोलमलातचक्रम् ।
विज्ञानमेकमुरुधेव विभाति माया
स्वप्नस्त्रिधा गुणविसर्गकृतो विकल्पः ॥३४॥

34. One should look upon this universe as a hallucination, being a phantasm of the mind, now seen and the next moment destroyed—like a dream, and extremely shifting like a circle[1] of fire. It is the One Consciousness that appears as multiple in form. The threefold distinction[2] due to the transformation of Gunas is Mâyâ.[3]

[1] *Circle etc.*—producing an appearance of a connected whole.
[2] *—Distinction*—of the states of waking, dream, and profound sleep.
[3] *Mâyâ*—i.e. unreal though appearing to be real.

दृष्टिं ततः प्रतिनिवर्त्य निवृत्ततृष्ण-
स्तूष्णीं भवेन्निजसुखानुभवो निरीहः ।
सन्दृश्यते क्व च यदीदमवस्तुबुद्ध्या
त्यक्तं भ्रमाय न भवेत्स्मृतिरानिपातात् ॥३५॥

THE LAST MESSAGE OF SHRI KRISHNA   123

35. Withdrawing the organs from the universe one should be immersed in one's own Bliss; one should give up desires, be silent and free from action. If ever[1] the universe is experienced, it will not lead to error, being one discarded as unreal,[2] but will linger as a memory only, till death.[3]

[1] *If ever etc.*—For a man must needs come down to the sense-plane.

[2] *Unreal*—like water in a mirage.

[3] *Death*—when there will be Videha-Mukti or absolute emancipation.

देहं च नश्वरमवस्थितमुत्थितं वा
    सिद्धो न पश्यति यतोऽध्यगमत्स्वरूपम् ।
दैवादपेतमुत देववशादुपेतं
    वासो यथा परिकृतं मदिरामदान्धः ॥३६॥

36. The perfect man does not behold[1] the evanescent body, sitting or standing, removed[2] by chance or restored by chance—for he has realised his true nature—as man[3] dead drunk does not care about the cloth he wears.

[1] *Behold*—i.e. treat as real.

[2] *Removed etc.*—i.e. whether it goes out or comes back.

[3] *Man etc.*—The drunkard is the one extreme (that of ignorance) and the man of realisation the other extreme (that of perfect illumination).

देहोऽपि दैववशगः खलु कर्म यावत्
    स्वारम्भकं प्रतिसमीक्षत एव सासुः ।
तं सप्रपञ्चमधिरूढसमाधियोगः
    स्वाप्नं पुनर्न भजते प्रतिबुद्धवस्तुः ॥३७॥

124 UDDHAVA GITA

37. The body is verily under the sway of destiny, and must remain,[1] together with the Prânas, so long as the work that originated it has not spent itself. The man who has attained Samâdhi in Yoga and realised the Truth no more attaches himself to the body and its appurtenances,[2] which are all like dreams.

[1] *Remain*—so one need not be particularly anxious about its preservation.

[2] *Appurtenances*—such as the sense-objects.

मयैतदुक्तं वो विप्रा गुह्यं यत्सांख्ययोगयोः ।
जानीतमागतं यज्ञं युष्मद्धर्मविवक्षया ॥३८॥

38. O sages, I have told you what is the inmost secret of Sânkhya[1] and Yoga.[2] Know Me to be Vishnu, come here to enlighten you on religion.

[1] *Sânkhya*—the science which discriminates between Self and non-Self.

[2] *Yoga*—the science which teaches how to attain the complete independence of the Self.

अहं योगस्य सांख्यस्य सत्यस्यर्तस्य तेजसः ।
परायणं द्विजश्रेष्ठाः श्रियः कीर्तेर्दमस्य च ॥३९॥

39. O best of sages, I am the supreme goal[1] of Yoga and Sânkhya, of Truth in practice and theory, of valour and opulence, of glory and self-control.

[1] *Goal*—All these are of value if only they lead to God.

THE LAST MESSAGE OF SHRI KRISHNA 125

मां भजन्ति गुणाः सर्वे निर्गुणं निरपेक्षकम् ।
सुहृदं प्रियमात्मानं साम्यासङ्गादयोऽगुणाः ॥४०॥

40. All the eternal[1] virtues, such as sameness of vision, non-attachment, etc., wait on Me who is beyond attributes and Absolute, the beloved Friend, the Self.

[1] *Eternal virtues*—lit. "Virtues that are not virtues"—because they lead us out of this network of Mâyâ.

इति मे छिन्नसंदेहा मुनयः सनकादयः ।
सभाजयित्वा परया भक्त्याऽगृणत संस्तवैः ॥४१॥

41. Having their doubts thus removed by Me, the sages, Sanaka and the rest, worshipped Me with great devotion and sang My praises.

तैरहं पूजितः सम्यक् संस्तुतः परमर्षिभिः ।
प्रत्येयाय स्वकं धाम पश्यतः परमेष्ठिनः ॥४२॥

42. Being duly worshipped and praised by those great sages, I returned to My abode, before the very eyes of Brahmâ.

CHAPTER IX

उद्धव उवाच ।

वदन्ति कृष्ण श्रेयांसि बहूनि ब्रह्मवादिनः ।
तेषां विकल्पप्राधान्यमुताहो एकमुख्यता ॥१॥

Uddhava said:

1. O Krishna, the teachers of Brahman speak of various means of attaining well-being. Are all of them equally important, or only one is the foremost of them?

भवतोदाहृतः स्वामिन्भक्तियोगोऽनपेक्षितः ।
निरस्य सर्वतः सङ्गं येन त्वय्याविशेन्मनः ॥२॥

2. Thou too hast described the path of devotion to the Lord, which is independent (of other means)—by which the mind getting rid of attachment to everything merges in Thee.

"Thou hast eulogised devotion and other sages speak of other means. What is their relative merit?"—Uddhava asks.

श्रीभगवानुवाच ।

कालेन नष्टा प्रलये वाणीयं वेदसंज्ञिता ।
मयादौ ब्रह्मणे प्रोक्ता धर्मो यस्यां मदात्मकः ॥३॥

The Lord said:

3. These words of Mine known as the Vedas, which had been destroyed by Time at the dissolution

THE LAST MESSAGE OF SHRI KRISHNA 127

of the universe, I first[1] revealed to Brahmâ. In them is set forth that religion[2] which inclines the mind to me.

"Devotion is the highest means as it directly leads to realisation; others are only of relative importance"—is the Lord's answer. Verses 3-9 give the different views of different people on this matter, all advocating minor instruments.

[1] *First*—at the beginning of the next cycle.
[2] *Religion etc.*—He means devotion.

तेन प्रोक्ता च पुत्राय मनवे पूर्वजाय सा ।
ततो भृगवादयोऽग्रृह्न्सप्तब्रह्ममहर्षयः ॥४॥

4. He declared it unto his eldest son, Manu, from whom the seven Patriarchs and sages, Bhrigu and the rest,[1] got it.

[1] *Rest*—i.e. Marichi, Atri, Angira, Pulastya, Pulaha, and Kratu.

तेभ्य. पितृभ्यस्तत्पुत्रा देवदानवगुह्यकाः ।
मनुष्याः सिद्धगन्धर्वाः सविद्याधरचारणाः ॥५॥
किंदेवाः किन्नरा नागा रक्षःकिंपुरुषादयः ।
बह्वयस्तेषां प्रकृतयो रजःसत्त्वतमोभुवः ॥६॥

5-6. From those fathers it passed on to their sons—the Devas,[1] Asuras, Guhyakas, men, Siddhas, Gandharvas, Vidyâdharas, Châranas, Kindevas, Kinnaras, Nâgas, Râkshasas, Kimpurushas, and others. Various are their natures,[2] being the outcome of Sattva, Rajas, and Tamas:

[1] *Devas etc.*—all these are different types of beings in the universe, *Kindevas* are half-gods, *Kinnaras* half-men.
[2] *Natures*—Shridhara Swami explains it as "desires".

128   UDDHAVA GITA

याभिर्भूतानि भिद्यन्ते भूतानां मतयस्तथा ।
यथाप्रकृति सर्वेषां चित्रा वाचः स्रवन्ति हि ॥७॥

7. By which[1] beings are differentiated as well as
their minds. And according to their natures their
interpretation (of the Vedas) is various.

[1] *Which*—refers to "natures" in verse 6.

एवं प्रकृतिवैचित्र्याद्भिद्यन्ते मतयो नृणाम् ।
पारंपर्येण केषांचित्पाखण्डमतयोऽपरे ॥८॥

8. Thus, owing to the difference of natures,
people differ in their ideas; while some[1] differ owing
to instructions handed down to them through a succession of teachers, and others even go against the
Vedas.

[1] *Some*—who are not learned.

मन्मायामोहितधियः पुरुषाः पुरुषर्षभ ।
श्रेयो वदन्त्यनेकान्तं यथाकर्म यथारुचि ॥९॥

9. O best of men, people deluded by My Mâyâ
describe various things as means to the highest good,
according to their occupation and taste.

धर्ममेके यशश्चान्ये कामं सत्यं दमं शमम् ।
अन्ये वदन्ति स्वार्थं वा ऐश्वर्यं त्यागभोजनम् ।
केचिद्यज्ञतपोदानं व्रतानि नियमान्यमान् ॥१०॥

10. As means to the goal some mention duty[1];
others fame, self-gratification, truth, control of the

THE LAST MESSAGE OF SHRI KRISHNA 129

senses, and control of the mind; yet others mention splendour, gifts, food; and some, again sacrifice, austerity, charity, vows, or moral rules, universal and particular.

[1] *Duty etc.*—Duty is extolled by the Mimâmsakas, fame by rhetoricians, self-gratification by Vâtsyâyana and others, the next three by the Yoga school, splendour by pragmatic politicians, the next two by materialists, and so on.

आद्यन्तवन्त एवैषां लोकाः कर्मविनिर्मिताः ।
दुःखोदर्कास्तमोनिष्ठाः क्षुद्रानन्दाः शुचार्पिताः ॥११॥

11. The results attained by these means, being the outcome of work, have a beginning and an end, produce misery, and end in infatuation. They give but transient joy and are attended with grief.

Hence they cannot compare with devotion.

मय्यर्पितात्मनः सभ्य निरपेक्षस्य सर्वतः ।
मयाऽऽत्मना सुखं यत्तत्कुतः स्याद्विषयात्मनाम् ॥१२॥

12. My friend, how can one attached to sense-objects have that bliss which a man, with his mind given up to Me and indifferent to all objects, derives[1] from Me, their (Blissful) Self?

[1] *Derives etc.*—His bliss is eternal and absolute.

अकिंचनस्य दान्तस्य शान्तस्य समचेतसः ।
मया संतुष्टमनसः सर्वाः सुखमया दिशः ॥१३॥

13. To the man who craves for nothing, who -has subdued his senses and mind, who is even-minded

9

to all, and is satisfied with Me, all[1] the quarters are full of bliss.

[1] *All etc.*—He finds bliss everywhere.

न पारमेष्ठ्यं न महेन्द्रधिष्ण्यं
न सार्वभौमं न रसाधिपत्यम् ।
न योगसिद्धीरपुनर्भवं वा
मय्यर्पितात्मेच्छति मद्विनान्यत् ॥१४॥

14. Neither the position of Brahmâ nor that of Indra, neither suzerainty nor the rulership of the nether regions, neither powers that come through Yoga nor liberation—the man who has surrendered his mind unto Me desires nothing else[1] but Me.

[1] *Nothing else etc.*—Such a devotion comes after realisation. It is love for love's sake.

न तथा मे प्रियतम आत्मयोनिर्न शंकरः ।
न च संकर्षणो न श्रीर्नैवात्मा च यथा भवान् ॥१५॥

15. Neither Brahmâ, nor Shiva, nor Balarâma, nor Lakshmi, nor My own form is so very dear to Me as you.[1]

[1] *You.*—i.e. devotees like yourself.

निरपेक्षं मुनिं शान्तं निर्वैरं समदर्शनम् ।
अनुव्रजाम्यहं नित्यं पूयेयेत्यङ्घ्रिरेणुभिः ॥१६॥

16. With a view to purifying Myself[1] by the dust of his feet, I always follow the sage who cares for

THE LAST MESSAGE OF SHRI KRISHNA 131

nothing, is calm, bears enmity to none, and is even-minded.

[1] *Myself*—even though eternally pure. Such a statement fits well in the mouth of the Lord Shri Krishna whose reverence for real Brâhmanas and sages is well known.

निष्किंचना मय्यनुरक्तचेतसः
शान्ता महान्तोऽखिलजीववत्सलाः ।
कामैरनालब्धधियो जुषन्ति यत्
तन्नैरपेक्ष्यं न विदुः सुखं मम ॥१७॥

17. High-souled sages—penniless, devoted to Me, and unsmitten by desires, calm and compassionate to all creatures—derive that bliss of Mine which they[1] only know who care for no gain, and not others.

[1] *They etc.*—Their bliss is limitless. The construction is rather involved.

बाध्यमानोऽपि मद्भक्तो विषयैरजितेन्द्रियः ।
प्रायः प्रगल्भया भक्त्या विषयैर्नाभिभूयते ॥१८॥

18. Even a devotee of Mine who not being a master of his senses is troubled by sense-objects, is generally not overcome[1] by them, owing to his powerful devotion.

[1] *Not overcome*—Even ordinary Bhaktas are blessed through devotion, not to speak of saints.

यथाग्निः सुसमृद्धार्चिः करोत्येधांसि भस्मसात् ।
तथा मद्विषया भक्तिरुद्धवैनांसि कृत्स्नशः ॥१९॥

UDDHAVA GITA

132

19. As fire kindled into a blaze burns the faggots to ashes, so, O Uddhava, devotion to Me totally destroys all sins.

न साधयति मां योगो न सांख्यं धर्म उद्धव ।
न स्वाध्यायस्तपस्त्यागो यथा भक्तिर्ममोर्जिता ॥२०॥

20. O Uddhava, neither Yoga, nor knowledge, nor piety, nor study, nor austerity, nor renunciation captivates Me so much as a heightened devotion to Me.

भक्त्याहमेकया ग्राह्यः श्रद्धयाऽऽत्मा प्रियः सताम् ।
भक्तिः पुनाति मन्निष्ठा श्वपाकानपि संभवात् ॥२१॥

21. I, the dear Self of the pious,[1] am attainable by devotion alone, which is the outcome of faith. The devotion to Me purges even outcasts of their congenital impurity.

[1] *Dear ... pious*—It is the pious who realise this, whereas the worldly-minded forget Him altogether.

धर्मः सत्यदयोपेतो विद्या वा तपसान्विता ।
मद्भक्त्यापेतमात्मानं न सम्यक्प्रपुनाति हि ॥२२॥

22. Piety joined to truthfulness and compassion or learning coupled with austerity, never wholly purifies a mind which is devoid of devotion to Me.

कथं विना रोमहर्षं द्रवता चेतसा विना ।
विनानन्दाश्रुकलया शुध्येद्भक्त्या विनाशयः ॥२३॥

THE LAST MESSAGE OF SHRI KRISHNA

23. How can the mind be purified without devotion characterised by a softening of the heart, the hair standing on end and tears of joy flowing out of the eyes?

वाग्गद्गदा द्रवते यस्य चित्तं
रुदत्यभीक्ष्णं हसति क्वचिच्च ।
विलज्ज उद्गायति नृत्यते च
मद्भक्तियुक्तो भुवनं पुनाति ॥२४॥

24. A devotee of Mine whose speech is broken by sobs, whose heart melts and who, without any idea of shame, sometimes weeps profusely, or laughs, or sings aloud, or dances, purifies the whole universe.

यथाग्निना हेम मलं जहाति
ध्मातं पुनः स्वं भजते च रूपम् ।
आत्मा च कर्मानुशयं विधूय
मद्भक्तियोगेन भजत्यथो माम् ॥२५॥

25. As gold smelted by fire gives up its dross and gets back its real state, so the mind by means of a systematic devotion to Me winnows off its desire for work and attains to Me.

यथा यथात्मा परिमृज्यतेऽसौ
मत्पुण्यगाथाश्रवणाभिधानैः ।
तथा तथा पश्यति वस्तु सूक्ष्मं
चक्षुर्यथैवाञ्जनसंप्रयुक्तम् ॥२६॥

UDDHAVA GITA

26. The more this mind is cleansed by listening to and reciting the sacred tales about Me, the more it sees the subtle Reality, like eyes through an application of collyrium.[1]

[1] *Collyrium*—supposed to improve the eyesight.

विषयान्ध्यायतश्चित्तं विषयेषु विषज्जते ।
मामनुस्मरतश्चित्तं मय्येव प्रविलीयते ॥२७॥

27. The mind of a man who thinks of sense-objects is attached to them, but the mind of one who remembers Me is merged in Me alone.

तस्मादसदभिध्यानं यथा खप्नमनोरथम् ।
हित्वा मयि समाधत्स्व मनो मद्भावभावितम् ॥२८॥

28. Therefore giving up the dwelling on unreal things, which are no better than dreams or fancies, concentrate the mind, clarified by devotion to Me, on Me.

स्त्रीणां स्त्रीसङ्गिनां सङ्गं त्यक्त्वा दूरत आत्मवान् ।
क्षेमे विविक्त आसीनश्चिन्तयेन्मामतन्द्रितः ॥२९॥

29. The man of self-control should avoid from a safe distance the company of women as well as of those who associate with the latter, sit in a secluded and congenial place, and ever alert[1] think of Me.

[1] *Ever alert*—without break. This is important.

न तथास्य भवेत्क्लेशो बन्धश्चान्यप्रसङ्गतः ।
योषित्सङ्गाद्यथा पुंसो यथा तत्सङ्गिसङ्गतः ॥३०॥

THE LAST MESSAGE OF SHRI KRISHNA

30. No other association causes so much misery and bondage as that of women and those that associate with them.

उद्धव उवाच ।

यथा त्वामरविन्दाक्ष याद्दशं वा यदात्मकम् ।
ध्यायेन्मुमुक्षुरेतन्मे ध्यानं मे वक्तुमर्हसि ॥३१॥

Uddhava said:

31. O lotus-eyed Krishna, please tell me how and in what aspect, personal or impersonal, a seeker after liberation should meditate on Thee.

श्रीभगवानुवाच ।

सम आसन आसीनः समकायो यथासुखम् ।
हस्तावुत्सङ्ग आधाय स्वनासाग्रकृतेक्षणः ॥३२॥
प्राणस्य शोधयेन्मार्गं पूरकुम्भकरेचकैः ।
विपर्ययेणापि शनैरभ्यसेन्निर्जितेन्द्रियः ॥३३॥

The Lord said:

32-33. Sitting on an even seat at ease[1] with the body erect, placing the hands on the lap and with the eyes directed[2] towards the tip of the nose, one should purify the passage[3] of Prâna by means of inhalation,[4] retention, and exhalation of the breath, and should also practise slowly in the inverse order, with the senses under control.[5]

[1] *At ease*—The Lord does not prescribe any particular posture. According to Patanjali also, posture must only be "steady and pleasant".

136 UDDHAVA GITA

²*Directed etc.*—This helps concentration.

³*Passage etc.*—the *Nâdis* or nerves. Prâna is the vital principle, the very source of all motion in the body, not to be confounded with breath which is only an external manifestation.

⁴*Inhalation etc.*—This is Prânâyâma or regulating the Prânas.

⁵*Under control*—not allowing them to run to the sense-objects. This is Pratyâhâra.

हृदयविच्छिन्नमोंकारं घण्टानादं बिसोर्णवत् ।
प्राणेनोदीर्य तत्राथ पुनः संवेशयेत्स्वरम् ॥३४॥

34. Raising[1] the syllable Om to the heart by means of Prânâyâma, one should add to it the vowel. The Om is like the continuous[2] peal of a bell, and extending in a thin line like a thread in a lotus stalk.

This and the next verse recommends the repetition of the sacred syllable Om along with the Prânâyâma.

[1]*Raising etc.*—What this process actually means is known only to adepts. We leave it as it is, without trying to explain it.

[3]*Continuous etc.*—The reference is to be the Anâhata sound which is continually rising up from the region of the navel and which Yogis only hear.

एवं प्रणवसंयुक्तं प्राणमेव समभ्यसेत् ।
दशकृत्वस्त्रिषवणं मासादर्वाग्जितानिलः ॥३५॥

35. Thus one should practise the Prânâyâma coupled with Om, ten times, thrice daily. Within a month one will then control the Prâna.

हृत्पुण्डरीकमन्तस्थमूर्ध्वनालमधोमुखम् ।
ध्यात्वोर्ध्वमुखमुन्निद्रमष्टपत्रं सकर्णिकम् ॥३६॥

THE LAST MESSAGE OF SHRI KRISHNA   137

36. Within the body there is the lotus[1] of the heart, with its stalk[2] above and point below, and with eight petals and a pericarp.

This verse describes the seat of the object of meditation.

[1] *Lotus etc.*—the nerve plexus in the spine corresponding to the heart.

[2] *Stalk etc.*—this is the position of the "lotus" before meditation, and it is also a bud. When meditating, one should think of this as pointing upwards and full-blown. It is interesting to note that Shri Ramakrishna, during his Sâdhanâ period, actually saw these things taking place, and the lotus remained in its new posture. All true Yogis probably have this experience.

कर्णिकायां न्यसेत्सूर्यसोमाग्नीनुत्तरोत्तरम् ।
वह्निमध्ये स्मरेद्रूपं ममैतद्ध्यानमङ्गलम् ॥३७॥

37. One should meditate on this as inverted with the flower upwards and opened, and in the pericarp should think of the sun, moon, and fire, one within the other. In the fire, again, one should reflect on the following form of Mine which is good for meditation:

Verses 37-42 set forth the personal aspect of the Lord for meditation.

समं प्रशान्तं सुमुखं दीर्घचारुचतुर्भुजम् ।
सुचारुसुन्दरग्रीवं सुकपोलं शुचिस्मितम् ॥३८॥

38. Symmetrical, serene, of a benign face, with four long and beautiful arms, with a well-formed and beautiful neck, beautiful cheeks, and a graceful smile:

138   UDDHAVA GITA

समानकर्णविन्यस्तस्फुरन्मकरकुण्डलम् ।
हेमाम्बरं घनश्यामं श्रीवत्सश्रीनिकेतनम् ॥३९॥

39. With shining alligator-shaped pendants in the well-matched ears, with a golden cloth, dark-complexioned like a cloud and with the peculiar marks[1] known as Shrivatsa and Lakshmi on the chest:

[1] *Marks*—formed by particular curls of the hair.

शङ्खचक्रगदापद्मवनमालाविभूषितम् ।
नूपुरैर्विलसत्पादं कौस्तुभप्रभया युतम् ॥४०॥

40. Adorned with conch, disc, mace, lotus, and a garland of wild flowers, with the feet adorned with ringing anklets, and the chest resplendent with the gem Kaustubha:

द्युमत्किरीटकटककटिसूत्राङ्गदायुतम् ।
सर्वाङ्गसुन्दरं हृद्यं प्रसादसुमुखेक्षणम् ॥४१॥

41. Decked with a shining crown, bracelets, and a waist-band, beautiful in every feature, appealing, with the face and eyes beaming with graciousness, and exquisitely tender.

सुकुमारमभिध्यायेत्सर्वाङ्गेषु मनो दधत् ।
इन्द्रियाणीन्द्रियार्थेभ्यो मनसाऽऽकृष्य तन्मनः ।
बुद्ध्या सारथिना धीरः प्रणयेन्मयि सर्वतः ॥४२॥

42. One should meditate on this form, concentrating the mind on all the features. The man of self-control should withdraw the organs from the sense-

THE LAST MESSAGE OF SHRI KRISHNA

objects with the help of the mind, and with the intellect as guide, direct the mind to My whole body.

तत्सर्वव्यापकं चित्तमाकृष्यैकत्र धारयेत् ।
नान्यानि चिन्तयेद्भूयः सुस्मितं भावयेन्मुखम् ॥४३॥

43. Then one should concentrate that mind—distributed all over My body—on one part,[1] and think of the smiling countenance alone and nothing else.

Verses 43-45 describe higher and higher stages of the meditation—thinking less and less of attributes—culminating in Samâdhi.

[1] *One part*—viz. the face.

तत्र लब्धपदं चित्तमाकृष्य व्योम्नि धारयेत् ।
तच्च त्यक्त्वा मदारोहो न किंचिदपि चिन्तयेत् ॥४४॥

44. Drawing the mind which is concentrated on that, one should fix it on the Supreme Cause.[1] Then leaving that too, one should rest on Me[2] and think of nothing[3] whatsoever.

[1] *Supreme Cause*—the Lord as projecting the universe.
[2] *Me*—as the pure Brahman, divested of all attributes. This is followed by Samâdhi.
[3] *Nothing etc.*—Such as, one is meditating, this is the object of meditation, and so forth.

एवं समाहितमतिर्मामेवात्मानमात्मनि ।
विचष्टे मयि सर्वात्मञ्ज्योतिर्ज्योतिषि संयुतम् ॥४५॥

45. With one's mind thus absorbed, one sees Me alone in oneself and sees oneself united to Me, the Self of all—like light united to light.

This is the culmination of knowledge known as Vijnâna.

UDDHAVA GITA

ध्यानेनेत्थं सुतीव्रेण युञ्जतो योगिनो मनः ।
संयास्यत्याशु निर्वाणं द्रव्यज्ञानक्रियाभ्रमः ॥४६॥

46. A Yogi who thus concentrates his mind through intense meditation will soon blow out[1] the delusion about objects,[2] finite knowledge, and action.

[1] *Blow out etc.*—This is the result of the Samâdhi.

[2] *Objects etc.*—Comprising the whole range of relativity.

CHAPTER X

श्रीभगवानुवाच ।

जितेन्द्रियस्य युक्तस्य जितश्वाससय योगिनः ।
मयि धारयतश्चेत उपतिष्ठन्ति सिद्धयः ॥१॥

The Lord said:

1. To the Yogi, who has controlled his senses and Prânas, who is balanced and concentrates the mind on Me, various powers come.

The mention of the various powers in this chapter is simply to create a distaste for them in the mind of the aspirant, since they are hindrances to realisation, which alone is the goal.

उद्धव उवाच ।

कया धारणया काखित्कथंखित्सिद्धिरच्युत ।
कति वा सिद्धयो ब्रूहि योगिनां सिद्धिदो भवान् ॥२॥

Uddhava said:

2. Tell me, O Krishna, what kind of power comes by any particular kind of concentration, and how. How many are these powers? It is Thou[1] who conferrest them on the Yogis.

[1] *Thou etc.*—Hence Thou art the best authority on the subject.

श्रीभगवानुवाच ।

सिद्धयोऽष्टादश प्रोक्ता धारणायोगपारगैः ।
तासामष्टौ मत्प्रधाना दशैव गुणहेतवः ॥३॥

142   UDDHAVA GITA

The Lord said:

3. Those who are experts in concentration and Yoga call the powers eighteen in number. Eight of these are pertaining[1] to Me, and the remaining ten are due to a perfection of Sattva.[2]

    [1] *Pertaining etc.*—These are higher ones.

    [2] *Sattva*—that element of the mind which leads to illumination.

अणिमा महिमा मूर्तेर्लंघिमा प्राप्तिरिन्द्रियैः ।
प्राकाम्यं श्रुतदृष्टेषु शक्तिप्रेरणमीशिता ॥४॥

4. Minuteness,[1] immensity, and lightness of the body; the connection[2] of a being with his organs, known as attainment; capacity[3] to derive enjoyment from everything heard or seen[4]; exerting an influence on all, known as rulership.[5]

    [1] *Minuteness etc.*—These three are powers belonging to the body.

    [2] *Connection etc.*—i.e. as their presiding deity. This (Prâpti) is the fourth power.

    [3] *Capacity etc.*—Prâkâmya. This is the fifth.

    [4] *Heard or seen*—i.e. superphysical and physical. The former is known only from the scriptures.

    [5] *Rulership*—Ishitâ. This is the sixth power.

गुणेष्वसङ्गो वशिता यत्कामस्तदवस्यति ।
एता मे सिद्धयः सौम्य अष्टावौत्पत्तिका मताः ॥५॥

5. Non-attachment to sense-objects, called self-control;[1] and consummation[2] of any and every desire —these, O friend, are considered My[3] eight natural powers.

THE LAST MESSAGE OF SHRI KRISHNA   143

[1] *Self-control*—Vashitâ. This is the seventh.

[2] *Consummation etc.*—Kâmâvasâyitâ. This is the eighth.

[3] *My etc.*—These are naturally in the Lord in infinite proportions, and by Him conferred in varying degrees on the Yogi.

अनूर्मिमत्त्वं देहेऽस्मिन्दूरश्रवणदर्शनम् ।
मनोजवः कामरूपं परकायप्रवेशनम् ॥६॥

6. Being unruffled by the necessary evils[1] of the body; hearing and seeing[2] things from a distance; swiftness like that of the mind; assuming any form at will; entering into anyone's body:

Verses 6 and 7 enumerate the ten secondary powers.

[1] *Necessary evils etc.*—Such as hunger, thirst, etc.

[2] *Hearing and seeing etc.*—These constitute two powers.

स्वच्छन्दमृत्युर्देवानां सहक्रीडानुदर्शनम् ।
यथासंकल्पसंसिद्धिराज्ञाप्रतिहता गतिः ॥७॥

7. Dying according to one's wish; joining in the recreation of the gods; fulfilment[1] of the wished-for object; having one's command obeyed everywhere without fail:

[1] *Fulfilment etc.*—This requires just a little physical effort on the part of the Yogi, which distinguishes it from "Kâmâvasâyitâ".

त्रिकालज्ञत्वमद्वन्द्वं परचित्ताद्यभिज्ञता ।
अग्न्यर्काम्बुविषादीनां प्रतिष्टम्भोऽपराजयः ॥८॥

8. Knowledge of the past, present, and future; not being affected by the pairs[1] of opposites; reading

144   **UDDHAVA GITA**

others' thoughts; counteracting the influences of fire, sun, water, poison, and the like; and not being overcome by anybody:

> This verse enumerates five petty powers.
> ¹*Pairs etc.*—such as heat and cold, pleasure and pain.

एताश्चोद्दे॑शतः प्रोक्ता योगधारणसिद्धयः ।
यया धारणया या स्यायथा वा स्यान्निबोध मे ॥६॥

9. These, in brief, are the powers that come out of concentration in Yoga. Now learn from Me what powers come out of particular concentrations, and the way they come.

> From this up to the end of the chapter, details are given. In each case, it will be noted, concentration is made on a special aspect of the Lord and the resulting power is in accordance with that.

भूतसूक्ष्मात्मनि मयि तन्मात्रं धारयेन्मनः ।
अणिमानमवाप्नोति तन्मात्रोपासको मम ॥१०॥

10. The worshipper of subtle matter attains to My power of minuteness¹ by concentrating the mind, which is also a subtle matter, on Me as possessing the supervening adjunct² of subtle matter.

> ¹ *Minuteness*—So that he can easily penetrate a rock.
> ² *Supervening adjunct*—Upâdhi that is, something extraneous that is superimposed.

महत्यात्मन्मयि परे यथासंस्थं मनो दधत् ।
महिमानमवाप्नोति भूतानां च पृथक् पृथक् ॥११॥

THE LAST MESSAGE OF SHRI KRISHNA

11. Fixing on Me, as possessing the supervening adjunct of the intelligent cosmic mind, one's mind which is characterised by a similar attribute,[1] one attains the power of immensity, and concentrating on Me as possessed of the adjunct of ether and the other elements,[2] one attains[3] the respective immensities of those elements.

[1] *Similar attribute*—i.e. intelligence.
[2] *Other elements*—wind, fire, water, and earth.
[3] *Attains etc.*—One can be as vast as one likes.

परमाणुमये चित्तं भूतानां मयि रञ्जयन् ।
कालसूक्ष्मात्मतां योगी लघिमानमवाप्नुयात् ॥१२॥

12. Attaching the mind to Me as possessing the adjunct of the atomic state of the elements, the Yogi attains to the lightness of points[1] of time, so to say.

[1] *Points etc.*—Which are imponderable. He can ascend the sun along its rays.

धार्यन्मय्यहंतत्त्वे मनो वैकारिकेऽखिलम् ।
सर्वेन्द्रियाणामात्मत्वं प्राप्ति प्राप्नोति मन्मनः ॥१३॥

13. Concentrating the entire mind on Me as possessing the adjunct of pure ego, one becomes, by this absorption in Me, the presiding deity[1] of each of the organs. This is known as the power of attainment.

[1] *Presiding deity etc.*—Hence he can direct them any way he likes; e.g. he can touch the moon with his finger.

महत्यात्मनि यः सूत्रे धार्येन्मयि मानसम् ।
प्राकाम्यं पारमेष्ठ्यं मे विन्दतेऽव्यक्तजन्मनः ॥१४॥

UDDHAVA GITA

14. One who concentrates the mind on Me as possessing the adjunct of the active cosmic mind, which is born of the Undifferentiated,[1] obtains My rare power of the capacity[2] to derive enjoyment from everything.

[1] *Undifferentiated*—the Lord's inscrutable Power, out of which the universe springs.

[2] *Capacity etc.*—i.e. infallible will-power; e.g. he can swim on land.

विष्णौ त्र्यधीश्वरे चित्तं धारयेत्कालविग्रहे ।
स ईशित्वमवाप्नोति क्षेत्रक्षेत्रज्ञचोदनाम् ॥१५॥

15. One who concentrates the mind on Vishnu, the Ruler of Mâyâ, whose form is Time, obtains rulership, consisting of the power[1] to control the Jivas and their bodies and minds.

[1] *Power etc.*—not that of controlling the cosmic processes, which belongs to the Lord alone.

नारायणे तुरीयाख्ये भगवच्छब्दशब्दिते ।
मनो मय्यादधद्योगी मद्धर्मा वशितामियात् ॥१६॥

16. Fixing the mind on Nârâyana, the Transcendent one,[1] called also Bhagavân, the Yogi, like Me, attains to the power of self-control.

[1] *Transcendent One etc.*—One must concentrate on both aspects. "Bhagavân" means the repository of all lordly virtues.

निर्गुणे ब्रह्मणि मयि धारयन्विशदं मनः ।
परमानन्दमाप्नोति यत्र कामोऽवसीयते ॥१७॥

THE LAST MESSAGE OF SHRI KRISHNA 147

17. Concentrating the clean mind on Me, the Brahman beyond attributes, one attains[1] to supreme Bliss, which is the consummation of all pleasures.

[1] *Attains etc.*—by being identified with Brahman.

श्वेतद्वीपपतौ चित्तं शुद्धे धर्ममये मयि।
धारयन् श्वेततां याति षडूर्मिरहितो नरः ॥१८॥

18. Concentrating the mind on Me, the pure embodiment of virtue and the Lord of Shvetadvipa, a man becomes pure and beyond the sixfold wave.[1]

Now the ten secondary powers mentioned in verses 6 and 7 are taken up one by one.

[1] *Sixfold wave*—viz. hunger, thirst, grief, delusion, decay and death.

मय्याकाशात्मनि प्राणे मनसा घोषमुद्वहन्।
तत्रोपलब्धा भूतानां हंसो वाचः श्रृणोत्यसौ ॥१९॥

19. Reflecting with the mind on the subtle sound in Me as possessing the supervening adjunct of ether[1] and Cosmic Prâna, the Jiva hears (from a distance) the varied speeches of beings manifested in that ether.

[1] *Ether*—which has sound for its primary attribute.

चक्षुस्त्वष्टरि संयोज्य त्वष्टारमपि चक्षुषि।
मां तत्र मनसा ध्यायन्निश्वं पश्यति सूक्ष्मदृक् ॥२०॥

20. Connecting the eye with the sun and the sun with the eye, and reflecting on Me there[1] with the mind, the man of sharpened vision sees everything (from a distance).

[1] *There*—at the junction of the sun and the eye.

UDDHAVA GITA

मनो मयि सुसंयोज्य देहं तदनु वायुना ।
मद्धारणानुभावेन तत्रात्मा यत्र वै मनः ॥२१॥

21. Effectively joining to Me[1] the mind and body together with the nerve current that follows the mind, the Yogi, through the influence of this concentration on Me, can take the body (swiftly) wherever the mind goes.

[1] *Me*—the Spirit controlling the mind etc.

यदा मन उपादाय यद्यद्रूपं बुभूषति ।
तत्तद्वेन्मनोरूपं मद्योगबलमाश्रयः ॥२२॥

22. Using the mind as material,[1] whatever forms the Yogi wishes to assume, he assumes those desired forms, by resorting to the power of concentration on Me.

[1] *Material*—for forming the new bodies.

परकायं विशन्सिद्ध आत्मानं तत्र भावयेत् ।
पिण्डं हित्वा विशेत्प्राणो वायुभूतः षडंघ्रिवत् ॥२३॥

23. Wishing to enter another's body, the Yogi should imagine himself[1] there. Then leaving the gross body and betaking himself to the subtle body, he should pass through the external air, like a bee.[2]

[1] *Himself*—as possessing Prânas etc., which are presided over by Me.

[2] *Like a bee*—as a bee flies from one flower to another.

पाष्ण्र्यापीड्य गुदं प्राणं हृदुरःकण्ठमूर्धसु ।
आरोप्य ब्रह्मरन्ध्रेण ब्रह्म नीत्वोत्सृजेत्तनुम् ॥२४॥

THE LAST MESSAGE OF SHRI KRISHNA   149

24. Sitting on heel and lifting the Prâna to the heart,[1] chest, throat, and head, and taking it to Brahman[2] through the subtle orifice in the head, one should give up the body.

[1] *Heart etc.*—i.e. the corresponding nerve centres in the spinal cord.

[2] *Brahman*—or any other coveted goal.

विहरिष्यन्सुराक्रीडे मत्स्थं सत्त्वं विभावयेत् ।
विमानेनोपतिष्ठन्ति सत्त्ववृत्तीः सुरस्त्रियः ॥२५॥

25. Wishing to play in the parks of the gods, one should think of the Sattva in Me;[1] then celestial nymphs, who are the offshoots of Sattva, will come in aerial cars.

[1] *Sattva in Me*—i.e. My pure form.

यथा संकल्पयेद्बुद्ध्या यदा वा मत्परः पुमान् ।
मयि सत्ये मनो युञ्जं स्तथा तत्समुपाश्नुते ॥२६॥

26. In whatever form, at any time, a devotee of Mine may reflect on a particular thing with his intellect, concentrating the mind on Me as possessed of infallible will, he gets that very form.

यो वै मद्भावमापन्न ईशितुर्वशितुः पुमान् ।
कुतश्चिन्न विहन्येत तस्य चाज्ञा यथा मम ॥२७॥

27. He who has imbibed[1] the nature of Me, the self-contained Lord[2] never finds his command disobeyed anywhere, like Mine.

[1] *Imbibed*—through concentration.

150 UDDHAVA GITA

[2] *Self-contained Lord*—the independent Ruler of the universe.

मद्भक्त्या शुद्धसत्त्वस्य योगिनो धारणाविदः ।
तस्य त्रैकालिकी बुद्धिर्जन्ममृत्यूपबृंहिता ॥२८॥

28. The intellect of the Yogi whose mind is purified by devotion to Me and who knows how to concentrate on God,[1] encompasses the past, present, and future, unaffected by birth and death.

Now the five petty powers mentioned in verse 8 are being explained, the third being implied by the first.

[1] *God*—as fully conscious of the projection, maintenance, and dissolution of the universe.

अग्न्यादिभिर्न हन्येत मुनेर्योगमयं वपुः ।
मद्योगश्रान्तचित्तस्य यादसामुदकं यथा ॥२९॥

29. The Yogic[1] body of the sage whose mind is pacified by union with Me, is not destroyed[2] by fire and the like, as aquatic animals by water.

[1] *Yogic*—made invulnerable by Yoga.

[2] *Not destroyed etc.*—He is in his element among them. The second of the petty powers is included in this.

मद्विभूतीरभिध्यायन् श्रीवत्सास्त्रविभूषिताः ।
ध्वजातपत्रव्यजनैः स भवेदपराजितः ॥३०॥

30. One who meditates on My Manifestations[1] with their Shrivatsa, weapons, ornaments, banner, umbrella, and chowry, never suffers a defeat.

[1] *Manifestations*—any of the Incarnations, potent enough to triumph over the universe.

THE LAST MESSAGE OF SHRI KRISHNA
151

उपासकस्य मामेवं योगधारणया मुनेः ।
सिद्धयः पूर्वकथिता उपतिष्ठन्त्यशेषतः ॥३१॥

31. To the sage who worships Me in the fore-going ways through Yogic concentration, the above-mentioned powers come in their full measure.

जितेन्द्रियस्य दान्तस्य जितश्वासात्मनो मुनेः ।
मद्धारणां धारयतः का सा सिद्धिः सुदुर्लभा ॥३२॥

32. No power[1] is beyond the reach of the sage who has controlled his mind, senses, nerve currents, and disposition and concentrates on Me.

[1] *No power etc.*—What is the use of concentrating on so many forms? Concentration on the supreme form mentioned in verse 18 is sufficient—says the Lord.

अन्तरायान्वदन्त्येता युञ्जतो योगमुत्तमम् ।
मया संपद्यमानस्य कालक्षेपणहेतवः ॥३३॥

33. For one who practises the best[1] kind of Yoga and seeks union with Me, these powers have been called obstacles and things that cause waste of time.

[1] *Best etc.*—i.e. devotion for devotion's sake. This is referred to in the next verse as "that Yoga".

जन्मौषधितपोमन्त्रैर्यावतीरिह सिद्धयः ।
योगेनाप्नोति ताः सर्वा नान्यैर्योगगतिं व्रजेत् ॥३४॥

34. Through that Yoga one obtains all those powers which come to men through birth, or drugs,

UDDHAVA GITA

or austerities, or Mantras; but one cannot attain that Yoga by any other means.

An echo of Patanjali's Yoga Aphorism IV. 1. Some are born with those powers, e.g. the gods; fishes also can live in water, birds fly in the air, and so on. Certain medicines are said to confer extraordinary powers. Mortifications also develop them, as also certain Mantras. The effects of these are short-lived, but perfect concentration on the Lord ("Samâdhi" of Patanjali) through pure devotion confers liberation.

सर्वासामपि सिद्धीनां हेतुः पतिरहं प्रभुः ।
अहं योगस्य सांख्यस्य धर्मस्य ब्रह्मवादिनाम् ॥३५॥

35. I am[1] the Lord of the powers, for I am their cause and maintainer; I am also the Lord of Yoga, of knowledge, of religion, and of the teachers of Brahman.

[1] *I am etc.*—Therefore have refuge in Me alone.

अहमात्मान्तरो बाह्योऽनावृतः सर्वदेहिनाम् ।
यथा भूतानि भूतेषु बहिरन्तः स्वयं तथा ॥३६॥

36. I am the Self of all creatures, being their indwelling Spirit;[1] I am also outside them, not being enveloped by anything. As the elements[2] are both inside and outside the bodies of all creatures, so also[3] am I.

[1] *Indwelling Spirit*—an echo of Brihadâranyaka III. iv. 1.

[2] *Elements*—earth, water, etc.

[3] *So also etc.*—I am all-pervading.

CHAPTER XI

उद्धव उवाच ।

त्वं ब्रह्म परमं साक्षादनाद्यन्तमपावृतम् ।
सर्वेषामपि भावानां त्राणस्थित्यप्ययोद्धव: ॥१॥

Uddhava said:

1. Thou art the Supreme Brahman in visible form, without beginning or end and uncovered.[1] Thou art the Cause of the protection, maintenance, death, and birth of all beings.

[1] *Uncovered*—by anything; hence Absolute.

उच्चावचेषु भूतेषु दुर्ज्ञेयमकृतात्मभिः ।
उपासते त्वां भगवन्याथातथ्येन ब्राह्मणाः ॥२॥

2. O Lord, in beings high and low, the Brâhmanas[1] worship Thee as Thou art, but Thou art unknown to less fortunate people.

[1] *Brâhmanas*—those who know the real import of the Vedas.

येषु येषु च भावेषु भक्त्या त्वां परमर्षयः ।
उपासीनाः प्रपद्यन्ते संसिद्धिं तद्वदस्व मे ॥३॥

3. Tell me in what beings the highest sages worship Thee reverentially and thereby attain to perfection.

UDDHAVA GITA

गूढश्चरसि भूतात्मा भूतानां भूतभावन ।
न त्वां पश्यन्ति भूतानि पश्यन्तं मोहितानि ते ॥४॥

4. O Thou Originator of the universe, as the Self of all Thou roamest hidden in all beings. Deluded by Thee, creatures do not see Thee, but Thou seest all.

याः काश्च भूमौ दिवि वै रसायां
विभूतयो दिक्षु महाविभूते ।
ता महमाख्याह्यनुभावितास्ते
नमामि ते तीर्थपदांघ्रिपद्मम् ॥५॥

5. O Thou of wonderful forms, tell me all those manifestations that Thou hast projected on earth, in heaven, in the nether regions, and in all quarters. I bow to Thy lotus feet in which are centred all holy places.

श्रीभगवानुवाच ।
एवमेतदहं पृष्टः प्रश्नं प्रश्नविदां वर ।
युयुत्सुना विनशाने सपत्नैरर्जुनेन वै ॥६॥

The Lord said:
6. You are skilled in questioning. This very question[1] I was asked by Arjuna about to fight his enemies at Kurukshetra.

[1] *Question etc.*—The reference is to the tenth chapter of the Gitâ, which should be compared in this connection.

THE LAST MESSAGE OF SHRI KRISHNA 155

ज्ञात्वा ज्ञातिवधं गर्ह्यमधर्मं राज्यहेतुकम् ।
ततो निवृत्तो हन्ताहं हतोऽयमिति लौकिकः ॥७॥
स तदा पुरुषव्याघ्रो युक्त्या मे प्रतिबोधितः ।
अभ्यभाषत मामेवं यथा त्वं रणमूर्धनि ॥८॥

7-8. When under the popular impression, "I am the slayer and this other is slain", he considered the killing of his relatives for the sake of kingdom as a despicable sin[1] and turned away from that, then, on the eve of battle, I roused that valiant soul through reasoning; and he (then) addressed Me exactly as you have done.

[1] *Sin*—which it was not, being a vindication of justice.

अहमात्मोद्धवामीषां भूतानां सुहृदीश्वरः ।
अहं सर्वाणि भूतानि तेषां स्थित्युद्भवाप्ययः ॥६॥

9. O Uddhava, I am[1] the Self of all creatures, their friend and Lord; I am all creatures, and the cause of their birth, life, and death.

Here begins the enumeration. The various representations of the Lord are for the purpose of meditation. Each of them has some distinctive merits which raise it above the rest of that group. Of the words in the possessive case in the text, some imply qualities and others selection.

[1] *I am etc.*—I am the general object of worship of all. The details commence from the next verse.

अहं गतिर्गतिमतां कालः कलयतामहम् ।
गुणानां चाप्यहं साम्यं गुणिन्यौत्पत्तिको गुणः ॥१०॥

156 UDDHAVA GITA

10. I am the motion of the moving, and among conquerors I am Time. Of virtues I am even-mindedness, and in things possessing attributes, I am their primary attribute.

गुणिनामप्यहं सूत्रं महतां च महानहम् ।
सूक्ष्माणामप्यहं जीवो दुर्जयानामहं मनः ॥११॥

11. Among those possessed of attributes, again, I am the Cosmic Prâna, and of all vast things I am the Cosmic Intelligence. Of all subtle things I am the soul,[1] and of things difficult to subdue I am the mind.

[1] *Soul*—so called because of its subtle superimpositions, from which it is most difficult to discriminate this.

हिरण्यगर्भो वेदानां मन्त्राणां प्रणवस्त्रिवृत् ।
अक्षराणामकारोऽस्मि पदानि छन्दसामहम् ॥१२॥

12. With regard to the Vedas I am Brahmâ,[1] and among Mantras I am the Om,[2] consisting of *A, U,* and *M.* Of letters I am *A,* and of metres I am the three-footed Gâyatri.

[1] *Brahmâ*—who first taught them.
[2] *Om*—considered the most sacred of them.

इन्द्रोऽहं सर्वदेवानां वसूनामस्मि हव्यवाट् ।
आदित्यानामहं विष्णू रुद्राणां नीललोहितः ॥१३॥

13. Of all gods I am Indra, and of the Vasus I am Agni. Of the Âdityas I am Vishnu, and of the Rudras, Nilalohita.[1]

THE LAST MESSAGE OF SHRI KRISHNA 157

[1] *Nilalohita*—a name of Shiva.

ब्रह्मर्षीणां भृगुरहं राजर्षीणामहं मनुः ।
देवर्षीणां नारदोऽहं हविर्धान्यस्मि धेनुषु ॥१४॥

14. Among Maharshis (great seers) I am Bhrigu, and among Râjarshis (royal seers), Manu. Among Devarshis (divine seers) I am Nârada, and among cows, Kâmadhenu.[1]

[1] *Kâmadhenu*—which has the power of producing anything at will.

सिद्धेश्वराणां कपिलः सुपर्णोऽहं पतत्रिणाम् ।
प्रजापतीनां दक्षोऽहं पितॄणामहमर्यमा ॥१५॥

15. I am Kapila[1] among the great Siddhas, and Garuda[2] among birds. Of the Patriarchs, I am Daksha, and of the Pitris I am Aryamâ.

[1] *Kapila*—the Father of Sânkhya Philosophy.

[2] *Garuda*—the powerful king of birds, who carries the Lord Vishnu.

मां विद्ध्य् उद्धव दैत्यानां प्रह्लादमसुरेश्वरम् ।
सोमं नक्षत्रौषधीनां धनेशं यक्षरक्षसाम् ॥१६॥

16. O Uddhava, among demons know me to be Prahlâda, the king of the Asuras. To the stars and herbs I am the moon,[1] and to Yakshas and Râkshasas I am Kubera (their king).

[1] *Moon*—their king and presiding deity.

ऐरावतं गजेन्द्राणां यादसां वरुणं प्रभुम् ।
तपतां द्युमतां सूर्यं मनुष्याणां च भूपतिम् ॥१७॥

158 UDDHAVA GITA

17. I am Airâvata[1] among the high-class elephants, and of the dwellers in water I am Varuna, their Lord. Of heating and shining objects I am the sun, and I am the king of men.

[1]*Airâvata*—Indra's elephant.

उच्चे:श्रवास्तुरंगाणां धातूनामस्मि काञ्चनम् ।
यमः संयमतां चाहं सर्पाणामस्मि वासुकिः ॥१८॥

18. Among horses I am Uchchaihshravas,[1] and among metals, gold. Of those that control I am Death, and of snakes I am Vâsuki (their king).

[1]*Uchchaihshravas*—Indra's steed.

नागेन्द्राणामनन्तोऽहं मृगेन्द्रः श्रृङ्गिदंष्ट्रिणाम् ।
आश्रमाणामहं तुर्यो वर्णानां प्रथमोऽनघ ॥१९॥

19. Among the great Nâgas[1] I am Ananta, and to all beasts with horns or teeth I am the lion. Of the orders of life I am the fourth or monastic order, and of castes I am the first or Brâhmana, O sinless one!

[1]*Nâgas*—another class of snakes. Ananta is their king.

तीर्थानां स्रोतसां गङ्गा समुद्रः सरसामहम् ।
आयुधानां धनुरहं त्रिपुरघ्नो धनुष्मताम् ॥२०॥

20. Of sacred torrents I am the Ganga, and of reservoirs I am the ocean. Of weapons I am the bow, and of wielders of the bow I am Shiva, the Destroyer of the Three Cities.[1]

THE LAST MESSAGE OF SHRI KRISHNA   159

> [1] *Three Cities*—from which impregnable stronghold their owner, a demon, greatly molested the gods.

धिष्ण्यानामस्म्यहं मेरुर्गहनानां हिमालयः ।
वनस्पतीनामश्वत्थ ओषधीनामहं यवः ॥२१॥

21. I am Mount Meru[1] among abodes, and the Himalayas among inaccessible places. Of trees I am the peepul tree, and of annuals I am barley.

> [1] *Meru*—where Brahmâ and other great beings live.

पुरोधसां वसिष्ठोऽहं ब्रह्मिष्ठानां बृहस्पतिः ।
स्कन्दोऽहं सर्वसेनान्यामग्रण्यां भगवानजः ॥२२॥

22. Of priests I am Vasishtha,[1] and of the knowers of Brahman I am Brihaspati.[2] Of all generals I am Skanda,[3] and of pioneers[4] I am the Lord Brahmâ.

> [1] *Vasishtha*—the priest of Râmachandra's dynasty.
> [2] *Brihaspati*—the preceptor of the gods.
> [3] *Skanda*—Kârtikeya, the commander-in-chief of the gods.
> [4] *Pioneers*—of righteous paths.

यज्ञानां ब्रह्मयज्ञोऽहं व्रतानामविर्हिंसनम् ।
वाय्वग्न्यर्काम्बुवागात्मा शुचीनामप्यहं शुचिः ॥२३॥

23. Of sacrifices[1] I am the study of the Vedas, and of vows, non-injury. Of purifying agencies I am the wind, fire, sun, water, speech,[2] and Self, which are specially such.

160   UDDHAVA GITA

[1] *Sacrifices*—There are five of them, viz. those to the gods, Brâhmanas, Pitris, men, and lower animals. Of these the Lord gives the highest place to the second.

[2] *Speech*—which ventilates the highest thoughts.

योगानामात्मसंरोधो मन्त्रोऽस्मि विजिगीषताम् ।
आन्वीक्षिकी कौशलानां विकल्पः ख्यातिवादिनाम् ॥२४॥

24. Of Yogas I am the perfect control of mind (Samâdhi), and I am the policy of those who aspire after victory. Of all kinds of cleverness I am the discrimination between the Self and non-Self, and with regard to the different hypotheses[1] I am the faculty of doubt.[2]

[1] *Hypotheses*—put forward by different schools of philosophy as to the nature of the world.

[2] *Doubt*—the never-ending puzzle whether the world is of this or that kind.

स्त्रीणां तु शतरूपाहं पुंसां स्वायंभुवो मनुः ।
नारायणो मुनीनां च कुमारो ब्रह्मचारिणाम् ॥२५॥

25. I am Shatarupâ[1] among women, and Manu, the son of Brahmâ among men. Of saints I am (the one called) Nârâyana, and of celibates I am Sanat-kumâra.[2]

[1] *Shatarupâ*—the wife of Manu. These were the first parents of mankind.

[2] *Sanatkumâra*—one of the four first-born sons of Brahmâ, who refused to marry and be dragged into the world.

धर्माणामस्मि संन्यासः क्षेमाणामबहिर्मतिः ।
गुह्यानां सूनृतं मौनं मिथुनानामजस्त्वहम् ॥२६॥

THE LAST MESSAGE OF SHRI KRISHNA 161

26. Of religions I am monasticism,[1] and of sources of well-being I am introspection. Of secrets I am sweet words[2] and silence, and of couples I am Brahmâ.[3]

[1] *Monasticism*—characterised by the declaration of fearlessness to all beings.

[2] *Sweet words*—because they often hide the real object of the speaker.

[3] *Brahmâ*—who out of his body created the first couple —half-man and half-woman—whom he next turned into Manu and Shatarupâ.

संवत्सरोऽस्म्यनिमिषामृतूनां मधुमाधवौ ।
मासानां मार्गशीर्षोऽहं नक्षत्राणां तथाभिजित् ॥२७॥

27. Of the watchful I am the year,[1] and of seasons I am the spring. Of months I am the Agrahâyana,[2] and of stars I am Abhijit.[3]

[1] *Year*—rotating with unerring precision and slowly reducing everything.

[2] *Agrahâyana*—middle of November to middle of December.

[3] *Abhijit*—the special name for the last quarter of Uttarâshâdhâ and the first quarter of Shrâvana.

अहं युगानां च कृतं धीराणां देवलोऽसितः ।
द्वैपायनोऽस्मि व्यासानां कवीनां काव्य आत्मवान् ॥२८॥

28. Of Yugas I am the Satya Yuga, and of the steady-minded I am Devala and Asita. Of the dividers of the Vedas I am Dvaipâyana, and of the wise I am the self-contained Shukra.[1]

[1] *Shukra*—preceptor of the Asuras, who knew the art of reviving the dead.

UDDHAVA GITA

बासुदेवो भगवतां त्वं तु भागवतेष्वहम् ।
किंपुरुषाणां हनुमान्विद्याध्राणां सुदर्शनः ॥२६॥

29. Of the Lords I am Vâsudeva, and of devotees I am yourself. Of the Kimpurushas I am Hanumân; and of Vidyâdharas, Sudarshana.

रत्नानां पद्मरागोऽस्मि पद्मकोशः सुपेशसाम् ।
कुशोऽस्मि दर्भजातीनां गव्यमाज्यं हविःष्वहम् ॥३०॥

30. Of gems I am the sapphire, and of the beautiful I am the lotus-bud. Of species of grass I am the (sacred) Kusha, and of oblations I am the clarified butter of cow's milk.

व्यवसायिनामहं लक्ष्मीः कितवानां छलग्रहः ।
तितिक्षास्मि तितिक्षणां सत्त्वं सत्त्ववतामहम् ॥३१॥

31. I am the fortune of the energetic, and the fraud of the deceitful. I am the fortitude of the painstaking, and the balance of mind of the steady.

ओजः सहोबलवतां कर्माहं विद्धि सात्त्वताम् ।
सात्त्वतां नवमूर्तीनामादिमूर्तिरहं परा ॥३२॥

32. Know that I am the energy and tenacity of the strong, and the devotional work of the devout. Of the nine forms worshipped by devotees,[1] I am the supreme first form, Vâsudeva.

[1] *Devotees*—Vaishnava devotees.

THE LAST MESSAGE OF SHRI KRISHNA 163

विश्वावसुः पूर्वचित्तिर्गन्धर्वाप्सरसामहम् ।
भूधराणामहं स्थैयं गन्धमात्रमहं भुवः ॥३३॥

33. Of the Gandharvas and Apsarases I am
Vishvâvasu and Purvachitti respectively. I am the
stability of mountains and the primary[1] smell of earth.

[1] *Primary*—i.e. unadulterated.

अपां रसश्च परमस्तेजिष्ठानां बिभावसुः ।
प्रभा सूर्येन्दुताराणां शब्दोऽहं नभसः परः ॥३४॥

34. I am the sweet taste of water, and the sun
among the resplendent. I am the lustre of the sun,
moon, and stars, and the subtle sound in ether.

ब्रह्मण्यानां बलिरहं वीराणामहमर्जुनः ।
भूतानां स्थितिरुत्पत्तिरहं वै प्रतिसंक्रमः ॥३५॥

35. Among the worshippers of Brâhmanas I am
Bali,[1] and among heroes I am Arjuna. I am verily
the origin, maintenance, and dissolution of all beings.

[1] *Bali*—the king of the nether regions, who, in the teeth
of his Guru's opposition, knowingly gave away the suzerainty
of the earth and heaven and even his own body to Vishnu
disguised as a Brâhmana boy.

गत्युक्त्युत्सगोपादानमानन्दस्पर्शलक्षणम् ।
आस्वादश्रुत्यवघ्राणमहं सर्वेन्द्रियेन्द्रियम् ॥३६॥

36. I am the motion,[1] utterance, rejecting,
taking, enjoyment, touch, sight, taste, hearing, and
smelling of the organs: I constitute their functions.

164   UDDHAVA GITA

[1] *Motion etc.*—The first five are functions of the organs of action, and the last five of the organs of knowledge.

पृथिवी वायुराकाश आपो ज्योतिरहं महान् ।
विकारः पुरुषोऽव्यक्तं रजः सत्त्वं तमः परम् ।
अहमेतत्प्रसंख्यानं ज्ञानं सत्त्वविनिश्चयः ॥३७॥

37. Earth, air, ether, water, light, the ego, and Cosmic Intelligence; the sixteen[1] modifications of Prakriti; Purusha and Prakriti; Sattva, Rajas, and Tamas; and the Supreme Brahman—all these am I. I am also their enumeration, their knowledge,[2] and the realisation of Truth.

[1] *Sixteen etc.*—The five primary elements, the ten organs, and Manas or mind.

[2] *Knowledge*—theoretical knowledge of the distinctions of the above, which deepens by practice into realisation.

मयेश्वरेण जीवेन गुणेन गुणिना विना ।
सर्वात्मनापि सर्वेण न भावो विद्यते क्वचित् ॥३८॥

38. Nothing[1] whatsoever exists without Me in My twofold aspect of the Lord and the Jiva, attribute and substance, and the indwelling Spirit and gross and subtle bodies.

[1] *Nothing etc.*—i.e. the Lord is everything.

संख्यानं परमाणूनां कालेन क्रियते मया ।
न तथा मे विभूतीनां सृजतोऽण्डानि कोटिशः ॥३९॥

THE LAST MESSAGE OF SHRI KRISHNA 165

39. I can count the atoms of the (primary) elements in course of time, but not My manifestations, for I am creating crores[1] of worlds.

[1] *Crores etc.*—and in each of these there are countless manifestations of Mine.

तेजः श्रीः कीर्तिरैश्वर्यं ह्रीस्त्यागः सौभगं भगः ।
वीर्यं तितिक्षा विज्ञानं यत्र यत्र स मेंऽशकः ॥४०॥

40. Wherever[1] there is power, beauty, fame, prosperity, modesty, sacrifice, agreeableness, luck, strength, fortitude, or knowledge, there am I manifested.

[1] *Wherever etc.*—He gives a general hint.

एतास्ते कीर्तिताः सर्वाः संक्षेपेण विभूतयः ।
मनोविकारा एवैते यथा वाचाभिधीयते ॥४१॥

41. All these manifestations of Mine I have described to you in a nutshell. They are but modifications[1] of the mind, and are somehow expressed in speech, (that is all).

[1] *Modifications etc.*—Apart from Me there is no reality in them. An echo of Chhândogya VI. i. 4.

वाचं यच्छ मनो यच्छ प्राणान्यच्छेन्द्रियाणि च ।
आत्मानमात्मना यच्छ न भूयः कल्पसेऽध्वने ॥४२॥

42. Control[1] speech, control the mind, control the Prânas and organs; control also the impure intellect by the purified intellect. Then you will no more return to the world.

UDDHAVA GITA

¹*Control etc.*—He advises introspection with a view to realising Him in Samâdhi.

यो वै वाङ्मनसी सम्यगसंयच्छन्धिया यतिः ।
तस्य व्रतं तपो दानं स्रवत्यामघटाम्बुवत् ॥४३॥

43. For the monk who has not fully controlled his speech, mind, and intellect, vows, austerities, and charity leak out[1] like water from an unbaked jar.

¹*Leak out etc.*—Without introspection everything is futile.

तस्मान्मनोवचःप्राणान्नियच्छेन्मतपरायणः ।
मद्भक्तियुक्तया बुद्ध्या ततः परिसमाप्यते ॥४४॥

44. Therefore, being[1] wholly attached to Me, one should control speech, mind, and the Prânas by the intellect endowed with devotion to Me. Then one attains the goal.

¹*Being etc.*—This is important. Then the whole thing becomes easy.

CHAPTER XII

उद्धव उवाच ।

यस्त्वयाभिहितः पूर्वं धर्मस्त्वद्भक्तिलक्षणः ।

वर्णाश्रमाचारवतां सर्वेषां द्विपदामपि ॥१॥

यथानुष्ठीयमानेन त्वयि भक्तिर्नृणां भवेत् ।

स्वधर्मेणारविन्दाक्ष तत्समाख्यातुमर्हसि ॥२॥

Uddhava said:

1-2. Thou hast already[1] spoken of religion which makes for devotion to Thee, and is meant for all human beings, with or without the observances of caste and order of life; please tell me, O Lotus-eyed One, how by practising that religion for himself a man may attain to devotion to Thee.

[1] *Already*—e.g. in Chapter V.

पुरा किल महाबाहो धर्मं परमकं प्रभो ।

यत्तेन हंसरूपेण ब्रह्मणेऽभ्याथ माधव ॥३॥

स इदानीं सुमहता कालेनामित्रकर्शन ।

न प्रायो भविता मर्त्यलोके प्रागनुशासितः ॥४॥

3-4. The supreme and blissful religion which Thou, O Mighty-armed Lord, O Mâdhava, didst once[1] expound—so it is said—to Brahmâ in Thy Swan-form, has now, O Queller of foes, almost ceased to be in the

UDDHAVA GITA

mortal world, owing to the great passage of time, even though it was once inculcated.

[1] *Once*—The reference is to Chapter VIII.

वक्ता कर्ताऽविता नान्यो धर्मस्याच्युत ते भुवि ।
सभायामपि वैरिश्चथां यत्र मूर्तिधराः कलाः ॥५॥

5. O Achyuta, there is no other teacher, originator, or defender of religion on earth than Thou, no, not even in the court of Brahmâ, where the sciences[1] are present in visible forms.

[1] *Sciences*—the Vedas etc.

कर्त्राऽविन्रा प्रवक्ता च भवता मधुसूदन ।
त्यक्ते महीतले देव विनष्टं कः प्रवक्ष्यति ॥६॥

6. O Slayer of Madhu, when Thou, the Originator, Defender, and Expounder of it, wilt leave the earth, religion too will die. Who, O Lord, will, then explain it?

तत्त्वं नः सर्वधर्मज्ञ धर्मस्त्वद्भक्तिलक्षणः ।
यथा यस्य विधीयेत तथा वर्णय मे प्रभो ॥७॥

7. Therefore, O Lord, who knowest all religions, please describe to me which of us is fit for that religion which makes for devotion to Thee, and how he is to practise it.

श्रीशुक उवाच ।
इत्थं खभृत्यमुख्येन पृष्टः स भगवान्हरिः ।
प्रीतः क्षेमाय मर्त्यानां धर्मानाह सनातनान् ॥८॥

THE LAST MESSAGE OF SHRI KRISHNA 169

Shuka said:

8. Thus asked by his own foremost servant, the Lord Hari was pleased and described the time-honoured religions for the good of men.

श्रीभगवानुवाच ।
धर्म्य एष तव प्रश्नो नैःश्रेयसकरो नृणाम् ।
वर्णाश्रमाचारवतां तमुद्धव निबोध मे ।।८।।

The Lord said:

9. This question of yours, O Uddhava, is right-eous, for it will promote the highest good of men who observe the duties of caste and order of life. Learn that religion of Me.

आदौ कृतयुगे वर्णो नृणां हंस इति स्मृतः ।
कृतकृत्याः प्रजा जात्या तस्मात्कृतयुगं विदुः ।।१०।।

10. In the beginning, in the Krita or Satya Yuga, men had but one caste which was known as Hamsa. People attained the consummation of their desires from their very birth, and hence the age was called Krita ("achieved").

वेदः प्रणव एवाग्रे धर्मोऽहं वृषरूपधृक् ।
उपासते तपोनिष्ठां हंसं मां मुक्तकिल्बिषाः ।।११।।

11. In that primeval age, Om was the Veda, and I was religion in the form of a bull.[1] The people of that age, who were pure and given to contemplation, used to reflect[2] on Me, the Pure One.

UDDHAVA GITA

170

[1] *Bull*—The four legs of the bull signify that religion was then intact. In each succeeding Yuga it lost a quarter.

[2] *Reflect*—There was no external worship.

त्रेतामुखे महाभाग प्राणान्मे हृदयात्त्रयी ।
विद्या प्रादुरभूत्तस्या अहमासं त्रिवृन्मखः ॥१२॥

12. At the beginning of the Tretâ[1] Yuga, O noble soul, the science of the Veda appeared from My[2] heart, through the agency of the Prâna. Out of that I became the sacrifice with its threefold adjunct.[3]

[1] *Tretâ*—This comes immediately after the Satya Yuga.
[2] *My*—refers to the Lord's Virât aspect.
[3] *Threefold adjunct*—viz. the three priests—Hotâ, Adhvaryu, and Udgâtâ—who perform the different functions in connection with a Vedic sacrifice.

विप्रक्षत्रियविट्शूद्रा मुखबाहूरुपादजाः ।
वैराजात्पुरुषाञ्जाता य आत्माचारलक्षणाः ॥१३॥

13. From the Virât[1] sprang the Brâhmana, Kshatriya, Vaishya, and Shudra, from the mouth, arms, thighs, and feet respectively. They were distinguished by their specialised duties.

[1] *Virât*—the Lord as possessed of a cosmic body.

गृहाश्रमो जघनतो ब्रह्मचर्यं हृदो मम ।
वक्षःस्थानाद्वने वासो न्यासः शीर्षणि संस्थितः ॥१४॥

14. The householder's life sprang from My thighs, the student life[1] from My heart,[2] the life of

THE LAST MESSAGE OF SHRI KRISHNA 171

retirement into the woods from My chest, and monasticism was on My head.

[1] *Student life*—with chastity as its chief element.
[2] *Heart*—a position below the chest.

वर्णानामाश्रमाणां च जन्मभूम्यनुसारिणीः ।
आसन्प्रकृतयो नृणां नीचैर्नीचोत्तमोत्तमाः ॥१५॥

15. The tendencies of the different castes and orders of life among men were according to the place[1] of the origin: Inferior positions produced inferior tendencies and superior positions superior ones.

[1] *Place etc.*—in the body of the Virât.

शमो दमस्तपः शौचं संतोषः क्षान्तिरार्जवम् ।
मद्भक्तिश्च दया सत्यं ब्रह्मप्रकृतयस्त्विमाः ॥१६॥

16. Control of mind and the senses, contemplation, cleanliness, contentment, forbearance, straightforwardness, devotion to Me, compassion, and truthfulness—these are the tendencies of the Brâhmana.

तेजो बलं धृतिः शौर्यं तितिक्षौदार्यमुद्यमः ।
स्थैर्यं ब्रह्मण्यतैश्वर्यं क्षत्रप्रकृतयस्त्विमाः ॥१७॥

17. An indomitable spirit, strength, patience, valour, fortitude, liberality, enterprise, steadiness, devotion to Brâhmanas, and lordship—these are the tendencies of a Kshatriya.

आस्तिक्यं दाननिष्ठा च अदम्भो ब्रह्मसेवनम् ।
अतुष्टिरर्थोपचयैर्वैश्यप्रकृतयस्त्विमाः ॥१८॥

UDDHAVA GITA

18. Faith in God, charity, humility, service unto the Brâhmanas, and an insatiety from the amassing of wealth—these are the tendencies of the Vaishya.

शुश्रूषणं द्विजगवां देवानां चाप्यमायया ।
तत्र लब्धेन संतोषः शूद्रप्रकृतयस्त्विमाः ॥१९॥

19. Attending on the Brâhmanas, the cows,[1] and the gods with sincerity, and being contented with what he gets therefrom—these are the tendencies of the Shudra.

[1] *Cows*—are held sacred because of their yielding milk out of which the ghee for making sacrifices is prepared.

अशौचमनृतं स्तेयं नास्तिक्यं शुष्कविग्रहः ।
कामः क्रोधश्च तर्षश्च स्वभावोऽन्तेवसायिनाम् ॥२०॥

20. Uncleanliness, falsehood, theft, atheism, barren disputation, lust, anger, and greed—these are the tendencies of a fifth class beyond the pale of the other four.

अहिंसा सत्यमस्तेयमकामक्रोधलोभता ।
भूतप्रियहितेहा च धर्मोऽयं सार्ववर्णिकः ॥२१॥

21. Non-injury, truthfulness, freedom from theft, lust, anger and greed, and an effort to do what is agreeable and beneficial to all creatures—this is the common duty of all castes.

द्वितीयं प्राप्यानुपूर्व्याज्जन्मोपनयनं द्विजः ।
वसन् गुरुकुले दान्तो ब्रह्माधीयीत चाहुतः ॥२२॥

THE LAST MESSAGE OF SHRI KRISHNA 173

22. Receiving in order[1] the second birth[2] known as the sacred thread ceremony, a Dvija (twice-born) should live in the house of the teacher with self-control, and summoned by him, should study the Vedas.

There are two types of Brahmachârins—the Upakurvâna, who will enter the household life after the completion of his study, and the Naishthika, who will maintain lifelong celibacy. Verses 22-30 describe the duties of the former.

[1] *In order*—The Hindu Smritis recommend a number of ceremonies to be performed for the good of a child, some before its birth and some after it. This succession is meant.

[2] *Second birth*—Because it ushers him into the domain of spiritual life. Hence the Brâhmanas, Kshatriyas, and Vaishyas are called "twice-born".

मेखलाजिनदण्डाक्षब्रह्मसूत्रकमण्डलून् ।
जटिलोऽधौतदद्वासोऽरक्तपीठः कुशान्दधत् ॥२३॥

23. He should wear a girdle,[1] deer-skin,[2] rosary of Rudrâksha beads, and the holy thread, and carry a staff, water-pot and some Kusha grass. He should wear matted locks, must not[3] wash his teeth and clothes, and never use a painted seat.

[1] *Girdle*—a waist-band made of particular kinds of grass. For details of these things refer to Manu, Chap. II.

[2] *Deer-skin*—as upper garment.

[3] *Must not etc.*—The idea seems to have been to discourage attention to personal trimming.

स्नानभोजनहोमेषु जपोच्चारे च वाग्यतः ।
न छिन्द्यान्नखरोमाणि कक्षोपस्थगतान्यपि ॥२४॥

174　UDDHAVA GITA

24. He should observe silence while bathing, eating, offering oblations to the fire, repeating his Mantra, and answering the calls of nature. He must not pare his nails, nor cut his hair in any part of the body.

रेतो नावकिरेञ्जातु ब्रह्मव्रतधरः स्वयम् ।
अवकीर्णोऽवगाह्याप्सु यतासुखिपदीं जपेत् ॥२५॥

25. He should observe strict Brahmacharya (continence) and never make any conscious lapses. If he is accidentally impure, he should have a plunge-bath in water, and after making Prânâyâma,[1] repeat the Gayatri.

[1] *Prânâyâma*—regulation of the nerve-currents through that of breath.

अग्न्यर्काचार्यगोविप्रगुरुवृद्धसुरान् शुचिः ।
समाहित उपासीत सन्ध्ये च यतवाग्जपन् ॥२६॥

26. Of mornings and evenings, after attending to cleanliness, he should silently repeat his Mantra with a concentrated mind, and offer his worship to the fire, the sun, the teacher, cows, Brâhmanas, superiors, old people, and the gods.

आचार्यं मां विजानीयान्नावमन्येत कर्हिचित् ।
न मर्त्यबुद्ध्यासूयेत सर्वदेवमयो गुरुः ॥२७॥

27. He should know[1] the teacher to be My own self, and never disregard or look down upon him as a man, for the teacher represents all the gods.

THE LAST MESSAGE OF SHRI KRISHNA   175

[1] *Know etc.*—Respect for the teacher was considered essential to the development of character and the spiritual life. The teacher also generally used to be of an exemplary character.

सायं प्रातरुपानीय भैक्ष्यं तस्मै निवेदयेत् ।
यच्चान्यदप्यनुज्ञातमुपयुञ्जीत संयतः ॥२८॥

28. In the morning and evening, he should bring the doles of food, or whatever else he may have received, to his teacher, and eat what he orders him to, with moderation.

शुश्रूषमाण आचार्यं सदोपासीत नीचवत् ।
यानशय्यासनस्थानैर्नातिदूरे कृताञ्जलिः ॥२९॥

29. He should always worship the teacher, serving him as a menial, by following,[1] resting, sitting, and being near with folded palms.

[1] *Following etc.*—i.e. following him when he is going somewhere; resting near when he is asleep; sitting by to shampoo his limbs when he is tired; and being at hand ready to do any behest when he is sitting.

एवंवृत्तो गुरुकुले वसेद्भोगविवर्जितः ।
विद्या समाप्यते यावद्बिभ्रद्व्रतमखण्डितम् ॥३०॥

30. Behaving thus he should live in the house of the teacher, shunning comforts, and maintaining absolute chastity, till his study is complete.

यद्यसौ छन्दसां लोकमारोक्ष्यन् ब्रह्मविष्टपम् ।
गुरवे विन्यसेद्देहं स्वाध्यायार्थं बृहद्व्रतः ॥३१॥

176 UDDHAVA GITA

31. If he wishes to get to the Brahmaloka, where the Vedas[1] reside, he should, while observing continence, surrender his body unto the teacher as a tribute for the study.[2]

Verses 31-36 set forth the additional duties of the other type of Brahmachârin, the Naishthika.

[1] *Vedas etc.*—Refer to verse 5

[2] *Study*—for the instructions received as well as yet to be received.

अग्नौ गुरावात्मनि च सर्वभूतेषु मां परम् ।
अपृथग्धीरुपासीत ब्रह्मवर्चस्यकल्मषः ॥३२॥

32. Being sinless and possessed of the strength that comes of studying the Vedas, he should worship Me, the Supreme Being, in the fire, the teacher, his own self, and in all beings, in a spirit of identity.

स्त्रीणां निरीक्षणस्पर्शसंलापक्ष्वेलनादिकम् ।
प्राणिनो मिथुनीभूतानगृहस्थोऽप्रतस्त्यजेत् ॥३३॥

33. Persons other than householders should forbear to look at, touch, converse, and cut jokes, etc., with women, and avoid seeing animals pair.

शौचमाचमनं स्नानं संध्योपासनमार्जवम् ।
तीर्थसेवा जपोऽस्पृश्याभक्ष्यासंभाष्यवर्जनम् ॥३४॥

सर्वाश्रमप्रयुक्तोऽयं नियमः कुलनन्दन ।
मद्भावः सर्वभूतेषु मनोवाक्कायसंयमः ॥३५॥

34-35. Cleanliness; the sipping of water preparatory to certain functions;[1] performance of the

THE LAST MESSAGE OF SHRI KRISHNA 177

services due in the morning, noon, and evening; straightforwardness;[2] the visiting of holy places; repetition of the Mantra; avoidance of things[3] not to be touched or eaten, and of persons not to be accosted; looking upon all beings as Myself; and control of mind, speech, and body—these, O Uddhava, are the observances meant for all the orders of life.

[1] *Functions*—such as eating, or going through religious exercises.

[2] *Straightforwardness*—There is also a different reading: *Mamârchanam*—"Worship of Me".

[3] *Things etc.*—i.e. probable sources of disturbance to the chaste life.

एवं बृहद्व्रतधरो ब्राह्मणोऽग्निरिव ज्वलन् ।
मद्भक्तस्तीव्रतपसा दग्धकर्माशयोऽमलः ॥३६॥

36. The Brâhmana who thus practises Brahma-charya becomes as a blazing fire, and if he is unselfish, by this intense asceticism his desires are burnt out, and he attains[1] devotion to Me.

[1] *Attains etc.*—One practising lifelong celibacy, without any selfish motive, will be rewarded with liberation—this is the idea.

अथानन्तरमावेक्ष्यन्यथाजिज्ञासितागमः ।
गुरवे दक्षिणां दत्त्वा स्नायाद्गुर्वनुमोदितः ॥३७॥

37. Then, after having properly studied the Vedas, if the student wishes to enter the householder's

12

UDDHAVA GITA

178

life, he should make the teacher some reverential present, and with his permission perform the usual ablution.[1]

[1] *Ablution*—This marked the termination of the student life.

गृहं वनं वोपविशेत् प्रव्रजेद्वा द्विजोत्तमः ।
आश्रमादाश्रमं गच्छेन्नान्यथा मत्परश्चरेत् ॥३८॥

38. The qualified Dvija may enter[1] the house-holder's life, the hermit's life in the woods, or the monastic life; or, with his mind intent on Me, he may proceed from one order of life to the next; but never otherwise.[2]

[1] *Enter etc.*—He may marry if he has desires; may at once be a hermit if he wishes to purify his mind; or a monk even, if he is already pure.

[2] *Never otherwise*—i.e. must not go back to the previous order, or be without any order.

गृहार्थी सदृशीं भार्यामुद्वहेदजुगुप्सिताम् ।
यवीयसीं तु वयसा यां सवर्णामनुक्रमात् ॥३९॥

39. A person wishing to lead a householder's life should marry an unblemished girl of the same caste, who must be younger[1] in age; and if he wishes to marry any other, he should do so after the above marriage, and even then, in the succeeding order.[2]

[1] *Younger*—The object probably was to maintain a sufficient number of male issues.

[2] *Succeeding order*—i.e. a Brâhmana was allowed to marry in the three lower castes also; a Kshatriya in the

THE LAST MESSAGE OF SHRI KRISHNA
179

two lower; and a Vaishya in the Shudra caste also, the last being confined to his own caste. But not in the inverse order.

इज्याध्ययनदानानि सर्वेषां च द्विजन्मनाम् ।
प्रतिग्रहोऽध्यापनं च ब्राह्मणस्यैव याजनम् ॥४०॥

40. The performance of sacrifices, study, and the making of gifts are the duties of the twice-born. The acceptance of gifts, teaching, and the helping of others to perform sacrifices are the occupations of the Brâhmana.

प्रतिग्रहं मन्यमानस्तपस्तेजोयशोनुदम् ।
अन्याभ्यामेव जीवेत शिलैर्वा दोषदृक् तयोः ॥४१॥

41. A Brâhmana who regards the acceptance of gifts as destructive of austerity, spirit of independence, and fame, should live by either of the other two means, or if he considers them harmful, live upon the grains left ungathered[1] in the fields.

[1] *Ungathered*—by the owner as useless.

ब्राह्मणस्य हि देहोऽयं क्षुद्रकामाय नेष्यते ।
कृच्छ्राय तपसे चेह प्रेत्यानन्तसुखाय च ॥४२॥

42. The body of a Brâhmana is certainly not meant for the satisfaction of petty ends. It is for rigorous austerity here, and endless happiness hereafter.

180 UDDHAVA GITA

शिलोच्छवृत्त्या परितुष्टचित्तो
धर्मं महान्तं विरजं जुषाणः ।
मय्यर्पितात्मा गृह एव तिष्ठ-
न्नातिप्रसक्तः समुपैति शान्तिम् ॥४३॥

43. A Brâhmana content to live upon grains left
in the fields and in front of shops, and observing the
great taintless duty,[1] while he lives at home, with
his mind given up to Me and not over-attached, attains
Peace.

[1] *Duty*—consisting of hospitality etc.

समुद्धरन्ति ये विप्रं सीदन्तं मत्परायणम् ।
तानुद्धरिष्ये न चिरादापद्धृद्धो नौरिवार्णवात् ॥४४॥

44. Those that rescue a Brâhmana[1] devoted to
Me from his misfortune, I will quickly deliver from
dangers, as a boat picks up a drowning man from the
sea.

[1] *Brâhmana*—This should be taken as a type. Any
devotee is meant.

सर्वाः समुद्धरेद्राजा पितेव व्यसनात्प्रजाः ।
आत्मानमात्मना धीरो यथा गजपतिर्गजान् ॥४५॥

45. A king (specially) should deliver all his
subjects from misfortunes like a father, and as the
leader of elephants rescues the elephants in his herd,
he should, preserving his balance, deliver himself by
his own efforts.

THE LAST MESSAGE OF SHRI KRISHNA 181

एवंविधो नरपतिर्विमानेनार्कवर्चसा ।
विधूयेहाशुभं कृत्स्नमिन्द्रेण सह मोदते ॥४६॥

46. Such a king shakes off all his sins on earth, and ascending the heaven in an aerial car resplendent like the sun, enjoys in the company of Indra, the king of the gods.

सीदन्विप्रो वणिग्वृत्त्या पण्यैरेवापदं तरेत् ।
खड्गेन वाऽऽपदाक्रान्तो न श्ववृत्त्या कथंचन ॥४७॥

47. A helpless Brâhmana should get over his trouble by setting up as a merchant,[1] selling only things allowable.[2] If he is still overtaken by misfortune, he should have recourse to the sword, but never resort to dog-like servility.

The means of livelihood for all the castes in extremity are mentioned in verses 47-49.

[1] *Merchant*—This is in contravention of Gautama's injunction that the occupation of a next lower caste should be adopted in times of danger. The Lord prefers this course to the life of a Kshatriya, because it is free from injury to others.

[2] *Allowable*—not wine etc.

वैश्यवृत्त्या तु राजन्यो जीवेन्मृगययाऽऽपदि ।
चरेद्वा विप्ररूपेण न श्ववृत्त्या कथंचन ॥४८॥

48. A king in adversity should take up the occupation of a Vaishya, or live by hunting, or even as a Brâhmana; but never take to dog-like servility.

182   UDDHAVA GITA

शूद्रवृत्तिं भजेद्वैश्यः शूद्रः कारुकटक्रियाम् ।
कृच्छ्रान्मुक्तो न गर्ह्येण वृत्तिं लिप्सेत कर्मणा ॥४९॥

49. A Vaishya in trouble should lead the life of a
Shudra, and a Shudra adopt the weaving of mats etc.,
which is the occupation of the Kârus.[1] Once free from
the adversity, none should desire to maintain himself
by a despicable profession.

[1] *Kârus*—considered a very low class.

वेदाध्याय स्वधा स्वाहा बल्यन्नाद्यैर्यथोदयम् ।
देवर्षिपितृभूतानि मद्रूपाण्यन्वहं यजेत् ॥५०॥

50. By means of study of the Vedas, the utterance of Svadhâ,[1] and Svâhâ, little food-offerings and
distribution of food etc., a householder should,
according to his means, daily worship[2] the Rishis, the
manes, the gods, the lower animals, and men respectively, considering them as forms of Mine.

[1] *Svadhâ, and Svâhâ*—words used as Mantras in the
invocation of the Pitris and Devas respectively.

[2] *Worship etc.*—This is the fivefold Yajna or sacrifice
obligatory for every householder.

यदृच्छयोपपन्नेन शुक्लेनोपार्जितेन वा ।
धनेनापीडयन्भृत्यान् न्यायेनैवाहरेत्क्रतून् ॥५१॥

51. By means of wealth that comes of itself,
or is acquired legitimately, he should judiciously
perform the above sacrifices, without[1] taxing his
dependants.

THE LAST MESSAGE OF SHRI KRISHNA 183

[1]*Without etc.*—He should not starve his family to perform his Yajnas.

कुटुम्बेषु न सज्जेत न प्रमाद्येत्कुटुम्ब्यपि ।
विपश्चिन्नश्वरं पश्येददृष्टमपि दृष्टवत् ॥५२॥

52. He should not get attached to his family, and, even though he is a householder, should not forget God. The wise man should consider the unseen enjoyments of future life just as perishable as the visible enjoyments of this life.

पुत्रदारापबन्धूनां संगमः पान्थसंगमः ।
अनुदेहं वियन्त्येते स्वप्नो निद्रानुगो यथा ॥५३॥

53. The association with one's sons, wife, relatives, and friends is like the chance meeting of travellers. They depart with the end of each body, as dreams are inextricably bound to sleep.

इत्थं परिमृशन्मुक्तो गृहेष्वतिथिवद्वसन् ।
न गृहैरनुबध्येत निर्ममो निरहंकृतः ॥५४॥

54. One who reflecting thus lives at home without attachment and egoism, like[1] a guest, is not fettered by the home, and is free.

[1]*Like etc.*—i.e. indifferently.

कर्मभिर्गृहमेधीयैरिष्ट्वा मामेव भक्तिमान् ।
तिष्ठेद्वनं बोपविशेत्प्रजावान्वा परिव्रजेत् ॥५५॥

55. A devotee, worshipping Me through his household duties, may lead a householder's life, may

184   UDDHAVA GITA

retire into the forest, or, if he has progeny, may
embrace monasticism.

यस्त्वासक्तमतिर्गेहे पुत्रवित्तैषणातुरः ।
स्त्रैणः कृपणधीर्मूढो ममाहमिति बध्यते ॥५६॥

56. But he who is attached to his house, is
afflicted by the desire for sons and wealth, and is
henpecked—is foolish, and being beguiled, he comes
under the bondage of "I and mine".

The last three verses condemn attachment to the family-
life.

अहो मे पितरौ वृद्धौ भार्या बालात्मजाऽऽत्मजाः ।
अनाथा मामृते दीनाः कथं जीवन्ति दुःखिताः ॥५७॥

57. "Alas, my parents are old; my wife has got
young children; and how can she in her helpless state
live, with these poor children, without me?"

एवं गृहाशयाक्षिप्तहृदयो मूढधीरयम् ।
अतृप्तस्ताननुध्यायन्मृतोऽन्धं विशते तमः ॥५८॥

58. Thus does this foolish man, with his heart
distracted by thoughts of home, continue to think of
them without satisfaction. Then he dies and enters
into abysmal darkness.[1]

[1] *Darkness*—birth in a very undesirable body.

CHAPTER XIII

श्रीभगवानुवाच ।

वनं विविक्षुः पुत्रेषु भार्यां न्यस्य सहैव वा ।
वन एव वसेच्छान्तस्तृतीयं भागमायुषः ॥१॥

The Lord said:

1. When[1] a man wishes to retire into the woods, he should put his wife in the care of his sons, or go with her, and live peacefully in the woods the third quarter[2] of his span of life.

[1] *When etc.*.—The duties of the forest life are being enumerated.

[2] *Third quarter*—i.e. from 51 to 75. After this one may embrace the monastic life, even though he may not have attained to a perfect dispassion.

कन्दमूलफलैर्वन्यैर्मध्यैर्वृत्तिं प्रकल्पयेत् ।
वसीत वल्कलं वासस्तृणपर्णाजिनानि च ॥२॥

2. He should live on purifying wild tubers, roots, and fruits, and wear a bark, or a cloth, or a garment of straw, or leaves, or a deer-skin.

केशरोमनखश्मश्रुमलानि बिभृयादतः ।
न धावेदप्सु मज्जेत त्रिकालं स्थण्डिलेशयः ॥३॥

3. He should allow[1] the hair on his head and body as well as his beard to grow, and not remove

UDDHAVA GITA

the dirt on his person; he should not wash his teeth, should plunge in water thrice a day, and lie on the ground.

[1] *Allow etc.*—All this is for minimising the attention to the body.

प्रीष्मे तप्येत पञ्चाग्नीन्वर्षास्वासारषाड् जले ।
आकण्ठमग्नः शिशिर एवंवृत्तस्तपश्चरेत् ॥४॥

4. In the summer he should subject himself to the five fires,[1] in the rainy season expose himself to showers, and in the winter remain immersed up to his neck in water. Thus should he practise austerity.

Here is a series of austerities prescribed with a view to kindling the powers of the mind, by overlooking the demands of the body.

[1] *Five fires*—four fires lighted on four sides and the scorching sun overhead. All these austerities have got technical names.

अग्निपक्कं समश्रीयात्कालपक्कमथापि वा ।
उलूखलाश्मकुट्टो वा दन्तोलूखल एव वा ॥५॥

5. He should eat food cooked over a fire, or ripening naturally in the process of time, powdering it with a pestle or stone, or even making his teeth serve the purpose.

स्वयं संचिनुयात्सर्वमात्मनो वृत्तिकारणम् ।
देशकालबलाभिज्ञो नाददीतान्यदाऽऽहृतम् ॥६॥

THE LAST MESSAGE OF SHRI KRISHNA

187

6. Aware of the efficacy of place and time, he should himself collect[1] all his means of subsistence, and not eat things procured at some past time.

[1] *Collect*—from within the forest itself. This is suggested by the "efficacy of place".

वन्यैश्चरुपुरोडाशैर्निर्वपेत्कालचोदितान् ।
न तु श्रौतेन पशुना मां यजेत वनाश्रमी ॥७॥

7. The hermit living in the woods should perform his observances[1] of the season with oblations prepared from grains that grow in the woods and not with animal sacrifice as prescribed in the Vedas.

[1] *Observances etc.*—such as the *âgrayana*, a Vedic ceremony performed when the first harvest of the year is collected. Such harmless Vedic rites are to be preferred to those that entail injury to beings. This is the idea.

अग्निहोत्रं च दर्शश्च पूर्णमासश्च पूर्ववत् ।
चातुर्मास्यानि च मुनेराम्नातानि च नैगमैः ॥८॥

8. On the recluse the expounders of the Vedas also enjoin the daily tending of the sacrificial fires (Agnihotra), the observances in connection with the new moon and the full moon (Darsha and Purnamâsa), as well as that of Châturmâsya[1]—as in the household life.

[1] *Châturmâsya*—an observance extending over four months beginning with the rainy season.

एवं चीर्णेन तपसा मुनिर्धमनिसंततः ।
मां तपोमयमाराध्य ऋषिलोकादुपैति माम् ॥९॥

188 UDDHAVA GITA

9. The recluse, with arteries and veins prominent all over his body on account of this practice of austerity, worships Me, the embodiment of austerity, and attains to Me from the sphere[1] of the Rishis.

[1] *Sphere etc.*—i.e. Maharloka, which is the fourth among the seven spheres. A gradual attainment of liberation by passing through the successive spheres is meant.

यस्त्वेतत्कृच्छ्रतश्चीर्णं तपो निःश्रेयसं महत् ।
कामायाल्पीयसे युञ्ज्याद्वालिशः कोऽपरस्ततः ॥१०॥

10. Who is a greater fool than he who applies this great austerity practised with such hardship and calculated to confer liberation, to the fulfilment of petty desires?[1]

[1] *Petty desires*—including that of enjoying the pleasures of Brahmaloka even.

यदासौ नियमेऽकल्पो जरया जातवेपथुः ।
आत्मन्यग्नीन्समारोप्य मच्चित्तोऽग्निं समाविशेत् ॥११॥

11. When[1] the hermit is unable to observe those rules, being overtaken by a shaking of the limbs consequent on old age, he should mentally put the sacrificial fires within him, and with his mind intent on Me, enter[2] into fire.

[1] *When*—i.e. before his attaining the 75th year.
[2] *Enter etc.*—i.e. burn himself to death.

यदा कर्मविपाकेषु लोकेषु निर्यातमसु ।
विरागो जायते सम्यङ्न्यस्ताग्निः प्रव्रजेत्ततः ॥१२॥

THE LAST MESSAGE OF SHRI KRISHNA 189

12. When he is perfectly sick of the spheres that are the outcome of work, seeing that they are attended[1] with misery, he should discard the fires, and from that stage embrace the monastic life.

[1] *Attended etc.*—Because they are not eternal.

इष्ट्वा यथोपदेशं मां दत्त्वा सर्वस्वमृत्विजे ।
अग्नीन्स्वप्राण आवेश्य निरपेक्षः परिव्रजेत् ॥१३॥

13. Sacrificing unto Me according to scriptural injunctions and giving his all to the officiating priests, he should mentally put the sacrificial fires in his own self, and renounce without caring for anything.

This shows the method of becoming a Sannyâsin.

विप्रस्य वै संन्यसतो देवा दारादिरूपिणः ।
विघ्नान्कुर्वन्त्ययं ह्यस्मानाक्रम्य समियात्परम् ॥१४॥

14. To a Brâhmana who is about to renounce, the gods, thinking that he may verily transcend them and attain to Brahman, offer[1] obstructions in the form of the wife and other relations.

[1] *Offer etc.*—Therefore he must be on his guard against yielding to their entreaties.

बिभृयाच्चेन्मुनिर्वासः कौपीनाच्छादनं परम् ।
त्यक्तं न दण्डपात्राभ्यामन्यत्किंचिदनापदि ॥१५॥

15. If the monk retains a second piece of cloth, it should be only as much as covers the loin-cloth. And except in times of danger, he

190   UDDHAVA GITA

should not have anything that he has already[1] discarded, other than his staff[2] and his begging bowl.

[1] *Already*—i.e. at the time of Sannyâsa.
[2] *Staff etc.*—The barest necessities are meant.

दृष्टिपूतं न्यसेत्पादं वस्त्रपूतं पिबेज्जलम् ।
सत्यपूतां वदेद्वाचं मनःपूतं समाचरेत् ॥१६॥

16. He should[1] place his foot on the ground after looking well, should drink water filtered through a cloth, should speak words that have the stamp of truth on them, and act as his reason dictates.

[1] *He should etc.*—The general idea being non-injury and purity.

मौनानीहाऽनिलायामा दण्डा वाग्देहचेतसाम् ।
नह्येते यस्य सन्त्यङ्ग वेणुभिर्न भवेद्यतिः ॥१७॥

17. Silence, inaction,[1] and control[2] of the Prânas are the restraints of speech, body, and mind respectively. One who has not these, My friend, never becomes a Sannyâsin by simply carrying some staves.

[1] *Inaction.*—Giving up of works done with selfish motives is meant.
[2] *Control etc.*—i.e. Prâ nâyâma.

भिक्षां चतुषु वर्णेषु विगर्ह्यान्वर्जयंश्चरेत् ।
सप्तागारानसंक्लृप्तांस्तुष्येल्लब्धेन तावता ॥१८॥

18. A Sannyâsin should beg his food from the four castes,[1] excepting the culpable.[2] He should

THE LAST MESSAGE OF SHRI KRISHNA   191

visit not more than seven houses, must not think of
the food[3] beforehand, and must be satisfied with as
much as is obtained.

[1] *Four castes*—Each succeeding caste being resorted to
in the absence of the preceding one.

[2] *Culpable*—e.g. those under a curse or degraded.

[3] *Food etc.*—i.e. Such and such food is to be had from
such and such a house.

बहिर्जलाशयं गत्वा तत्रोपस्पृश्य वाग्यतः ।
विभज्य पावितं शेषं भुञ्जीताशेषमाहृतम् ॥१९॥

19. Going to a tank outside the village, and
bathing there, he should purify[1] the food he has
collected, and offering portions to the deities[2] and
all creatures silently eat the remnant, without saving[3]
anything.

[1] *Purify*—by sprinkling with water, and so on.

[2] *Deities*—Vishnu, Brahmâ, and the Sun.

[3] *Saving etc.*—So he must not beg in excess of one
meal.

एकश्चरेन्महीमेतां निःसङ्गः संयतेन्द्रियः ।
आत्मक्रीड आत्मरत आत्मवान्समदर्शनः ॥२०॥

20. He should roam over this earth alone,
without attachment, and with his senses under
control. All his pastimes should be in the Self, as
well as all his pleasures; he should be of a steady mind
and look evenly upon everything.

विविक्तक्षेमशरणो मद्भावविमलाशयः ।
आत्मानं चिन्तयेदेकमभेदेन मया मुनिः ॥२१॥

21. Taking shelter in a secluded and congenial spot, and with his mind purified by rapt devotion to Me, the sage should meditate on the One Self as identified with Me.

अन्वीक्षेतात्मनो बन्धं मोक्षं च ज्ञाननिष्ठया ।
बन्ध इन्द्रियविक्षेपो मोक्ष एषां च संयमः ॥२२॥

22. He should reflect on the bondage and liberation of the Self, through the pursuit of knowledge. Bondage consists in the outgoing of the senses, and liberation in their control.

तस्मान्नियम्य षड्वर्गं मद्भावेन चरेन्मुनिः ।
विरक्तः क्षुल्लकामेभ्यो लब्ध्वाऽऽत्मनि सुखं महत् ॥२३॥

23. Therefore the sage, controlling the senses, should roam, looking upon everything as Myself. Deriving great bliss from the Self, he should turn away from petty desires.

पुरग्रामव्रजान्सार्थान्भिक्षार्थं प्रविशंश्चरेत् ।
पुण्यदेशसरिच्छैलवनाश्रमवतीं महीम् ॥२४॥

24. Going to towns, villages, cowherd settlements, and assemblies of pilgrims for the purpose of begging his food, he should wander over the earth abounding in holy countries, rivers, mountains, forests, and hermitages.

वानप्रस्थाश्रमपदेष्वभीक्ष्णं भैक्ष्यमाचरेत् ।
संसिध्यत्याश्वसंमोहः शुद्धसत्त्वः शिलान्धसा ॥२५॥

THE LAST MESSAGE OF SHRI KRISHNA 193

25. He should beg his food mostly from the hermitages of people who have retired into the forest, for by partaking of their food consisting of grains picked up from the fields, he soon becomes purified in mind, and freed from delusion, attains perfection.

नैतद्वस्तुतया पश्येद्दृश्यमानं विनश्यति ।
असक्तचित्तो विरमेदिहामुत्र चिकीर्षितात् ॥२६॥

26. The visible world he should not[1] consider as a reality, for it perishes. With his mind unattached to this world and the next, he should desist from activities tending to enjoyments in them.

[1] *Should not etc.*—This is how he is to overcome temptations for nice food etc.

यदेतदात्मनि जगन्मनोवाक्प्राणसंहतम् ।
सर्वं मायेति तर्केण स्वस्थस्त्यक्ता न तत्स्मरेत् ॥२७॥

27. This world,[1] and this body[2] with the mind, speech, and Prânas, are all a delusive superimposition on the Self—reasoning thus he should take his stand on the Self, and giving the former up, should no more think of them.

[1] *World*—which we consider as "ours".
[2] *Body etc.*—which we consider as "ourselves".

ज्ञाननिष्ठो विरक्तो वा मद्भक्तो वाऽनपेक्षकः ।
सलिङ्गानाश्रमांस्त्यक्ता चरेद्विधिगोचरः ॥२८॥

28. He who, averse to the objective world, is devoted to knowledge,[1] or not caring even for liberation, is devoted to Me, should move about,

13

regardless[2] of the orders of life with their respective insignia; he should be above the ties of formality.

In the foregoing verses are set forth the duties of lower orders of Sannyâsins, e.g. the Bahudakas etc. Verses 28-37 describe those of the highest class, viz. the Paramahamsas.

[1] *Knowledge*—as a means to liberation.
[2] *Regardless etc.*—i.e. he should observe only the spirit of the rules guiding them, without being bound by their letter.

बुधो बालकवत्क्रीडेत्कुशलो जडवच्चरेत् ।
वदेदुन्मत्तवद्विद्वान्गोचर्यां नैगमश्चरेत् ॥२९॥

29. Though wise, he should play[1] as a child; though expert, he should move[2] about like an idiot; though erudite, he should talk[3] like a lunatic; and though well versed in the scriptures, he should live[4] as if he were a cow.

[1] *Play etc.*—without considerations of position.
[2] *Move etc.*—not having any definite plans.
[3] *Talk etc.*—not seeking applause from people.
[4] *Live etc.*—following no established code of conduct.

वेदवादरतो न स्यान्न पाखण्डी न हैतुकः ।
शुष्कवादविवादे न कंचित्पक्षं समाश्रयेत् ॥३०॥

30. He should not be fond of upholding the ritualistic portion of the Vedas, nor be a heretic,[1] nor be given to barren argument; in disputes arising out of empty discussions, he should take neither side.

[1] *Heretic*—acting contrary to the injunctions of the Shrutis and Smritis.

THE LAST MESSAGE OF SHRI KRISHNA

नोद्विजेत जनाद्धीरो जनं चोद्वेजयेन्न तु ।
अतिवादांस्तितिक्षेत नावमन्येत कंचन ।
देहमुद्दिश्य पशुवद्वैरं कुर्यान्न केनचित् ॥३१॥

31. The sage should not be vexed by people
nor vex them himself. He should put up with
vilifications and never insult anybody. For the sake
of the body he should bear enmity to none, as beasts
do.

एक एव परो ह्यात्मा भूतेष्वात्मन्यवस्थितः ।
यथेन्दुरूदपात्रेषु भूतान्येकात्मकानि च ॥३२॥

32. The One Supreme Self alone dwells in the
bodies of all beings and in one's own body, as the
moon is reflected in so many vessels of water. And
all bodies are of the same nature.

A twofold reason for practising non-injury is furnished:
First, as Ātman, all creatures are one; and secondly, there
is no essential difference between one body and another, all
being composed of matter.

अलब्ध्वा न विषीदेत काले कालेऽशानं क्वचित् ।
लब्ध्वा न हृष्येद्धृतिमानुभयं दैवतन्त्रितम् ॥३३॥

33. Possessed of steadiness, he should not be
sorry when he gets no food, nor be delighted when he
gets it, for both these are controlled by destiny.

आहारार्थं समीहेत युक्तं तत्प्राणधारणम् ।
तत्त्वं विमृश्यते तेन तद्विज्ञाय विमुच्यते ॥३४॥

UDDHAVA GĪTA

34. He should strive[1] to procure his food,[2] for continuity of life is desirable. Through it one can reflect on Truth, knowing which one becomes free.

[1] *Strive etc.*—He should not leave this also to destiny.
[2] *Food*—not delicacies.

यदृच्छयोपपन्नान्नमद्याच्छ्रेष्ठमुतापरम् ।
तथा वासस्तथा शय्यां प्राप्तं प्राप्तं भजेन्मुनिः ॥३५॥

35. The sage should eat food, good or bad, which comes of itself, and use clothes and bedding just as he obtains them.

This verse suggests that a Paramahamsa should not be anxious to avoid comforts when they chance to come.

शौचमाचमनं स्नानं न तु चोदनया चरेत् ।
अन्यांश्च नियमान् ज्ञानी यथाहं लीलयेश्वरः ॥३६॥

36. The man of realisation should observe cleanliness, wash his mouth, and bathe, and go through all other observances, but not[1] because of scriptural injunctions, as I, the Lord, do everything of My free will.

[1] *But not etc.*—He should do them with perfect non-attachment.

नहि तस्य विकल्पाख्या या च मद्वीक्षया हता ।
आदेहान्तात्कचित्ख्यातिस्ततः संपद्यते मया ॥३७॥

37. He has no perception of differences, and if he ever had any, it has been removed by his realisation of Me. Till the dissolution of his body he

THE LAST MESSAGE OF SHRI KRISHNA   197

sometimes has a semblance of it, and after that he is one with Me.

This verse gives the reason why he is not a slave to scriptural injunctions.

दुःखोदर्केषु कामेषु जातनिर्वेद आत्मवान् ।
अजिज्ञासितमद्धर्मो गुरुं मुनिमुपात्रजेत् ॥३८॥

38. A man[1] who has got sick of works that produce only pain, and is possessed of self-control, but has not inquired into the religion that leads to Me, should go to a sage as to a Master.

[1] *A man etc.*—Verses 38 and 39 deal with an aspirant after realisation.

तावत्परिचरेद्भक्तः श्रद्धावाननसूयकः ।
यावद्ब्रह्म विजानीयान्मामेव गुरुमाद्रतः ॥३९॥

39. Until[1] he has realised Brahman, he should serve the Teacher like Me, with care and devotion, having faith in him and never carping at him.

[1] *Until etc.*—After that he should behave like a Paramahamsa, as described in verses 28-37.

यस्त्वसंयतषड्वर्गः प्रचण्डेन्द्रियसारथिः ।
ज्ञानवैराग्यरहितस्त्रिदण्डमुपजीवति ॥४०॥

सुरानात्मानमात्मस्थं निह्नुते मां च धर्महा ।
अविपक्वकषायोऽस्मादमुष्माच्च विहीयते ॥४१॥

40-41. But one[1] who has not mastered his passions, whose intellect—the guide to his sense-organs—is wild, and who is devoid of discrimination and renunciation—such a man taking up the monk's triple staff for the sake of subsistence, is a destroyer of religion, and cheats the Gods,[2] cheats himself, and Me who reside in his self. With his impurities unconsumed, he is deprived of both this life and the life to come.

[1] *But one etc.*—Unqualified intruders into monasticism are condemned.

[2] *Gods*—to whom sacrifices are made.

भिक्षोर्धर्मः शमोऽहिंसा तप ईक्षा वनौकसः ।
गृहिणो भूतरक्षेज्या द्विजस्याचार्यसेवनम् ॥४२॥

42. The duties[1] of a monk are control of the mind and non-injury, those of a forest-dwelling hermit are austerity and discrimination; those of a householder are preservation of the lives of animals and performance of sacrifices; while the duty of a Brahmachârin is service unto the Teacher.

[1] *Duties*—i.e. principal ones.

ब्रह्मचर्यं तपः शौचं संतोषो भूतसौहृदम् ।
गृहस्थस्याप्यृतौ गन्तुः सर्वेषां मदुपासनम् ॥४३॥

43. Continence, with the option of deviating from it at prescribed times, the performance of his duties, purity, contentment, and kindness to animals are also duties for a householder. Worship of Me is a duty for all.

इति मां यः स्वधर्मेण भजन्नित्यमनन्यभाक् ।
सर्वभूतेषु मद्भावो मद्भक्तिं विन्दतेऽचिरात् ॥४४॥

THE LAST MESSAGE OF SHRI KRISHNA

199

44. He who[1] thus worships Me constantly and exclusively, through the performance of his duties, knowing My presence in all beings, soon attains to a steadfast devotion to Me.

[1] *He who etc.*—This and the next two verses set forth the result of the performance of one's prescribed duties.

भक्त्योद्धवानपायिन्या सर्वलोकमहेश्वरम् ।
सर्वोत्पत्त्यप्ययं ब्रह्म कारणं मोपयाति सः ॥४५॥

45. O Uddhava, through his undying devotion he comes to Me, the great Lord of all beings, the originator and destroyer of all, their cause, the Brahman.

इति स्वधर्मनिर्णिक्तसत्त्वो निर्ज्ञातमद्गतिः ।
ज्ञानविज्ञानसंपन्नो न चिरात्समुपैति माम् ॥४६॥

46. Having his mind thus purified by the performance of his duties, and knowing My Divinity, he becomes endowed with knowledge and realisation and soon attains to Me.

वर्णाश्रमवतां धर्म एष आचारलक्षणः ।
स एव मद्भक्तियुतो निःश्रेयसकरः परः ॥४७॥

47. All this duty, consisting of specific rites, of those belonging to the castes and orders of life, if[1] attended with devotion to Me, becomes supreme and conducive to liberation.

[1] *If etc.*—Without the devotion it would merely lead to the Pitriloka, the sphere of the manes. *Devotion* implies surrender of the fruits of work to God.

UDDHAVA GITA

एतत्तेऽभिहितं साधो भवान्पृन्छति यञ्च माम् ।
यथा स्वधर्मसंयुक्तो भक्तो मां समियात्परम् ॥४८॥

48. So I have told you, My friend, what you asked Me about, viz. how a person attending to his duties becomes a devotee and attains to Me the Supreme Being.

CHAPTER XIV

श्रीभगवानुवाच ।

यो विद्याश्रुतसंपन्न आत्मवान्नानुमानिकः ।
मायामात्रमिदं ज्ञात्वा ज्ञानं च मयि संन्यसेत् ॥१॥

The Lord said:

1. One who is endowed with scriptural erudition culminating in realisation, who has attained to the Self, and has not mere theoretical knowledge, should surrender[1] knowledge (with its means) to Me —knowing the universe to be but an illusion.

[1] *Surrender etc.*—After realisation he attains to a stage known as Vidvat-Sannyâsa. He remains with unconditional devotion to the Lord.

ज्ञानिनस्त्वहमेवेष्टः स्वार्थो हेतुश्च संमतः ।
स्वर्गश्चैवापवर्गश्च नान्योऽर्थो मद्वते प्रियः ॥२॥

2. For I am the desired goal of the Jnâni and its efficient means; I am his worldly prosperity as well as liberation. There is nothing else but Me which is dear to him.

ज्ञानविज्ञानसंसिद्धाः पदं श्रेष्ठं विदुर्मम ।
ज्ञानी प्रियतमोऽतो मे ज्ञानेनासौ बिभर्ति माम् ॥३॥

3. Those who have perfected themselves in knowledge and realisation attain to My Supreme

UDDHAVA GITA

abode. Since the Jnâni cherishes Me through his knowledge, therefore he is the most beloved of Me.

तपस्तीर्थं जपो दानं पवित्राणीतराणि च ।
नालं कुर्वन्ति तां सिद्धिं या ज्ञानकलया कृता ॥४॥

4. Austerity, pilgrimage, repetition of the Mantra, charity, and whatever else is sacred, cannot improve that perfection which springs from even a modicum of realisation.

तस्माज्ज्ञानेन सहितं ज्ञात्वा स्वात्मानमुद्धव ।
ज्ञानविज्ञानसंपन्नो भज मां भक्तिभावतः ॥५॥

5. Therefore, O Uddhava, dwelling on your own Self till the attainment of realisation, be endowed with knowledge and realisation, and worship Me with devotion.

ज्ञानविज्ञानयज्ञेन मामिष्टाऽऽत्मानमात्मनि ।
सर्वयज्ञपतिं मां वै संसिद्धिं मुनयोऽगमन् ॥६॥

6. Sacrificing unto Me, the Self and Lord of all sacrifices, in their own selves, through the sacrifice of knowledge and realisation, sages[1] have attained to perfection in that they have realised Me.

[1] *Sages*—in ancient times.

त्वय्युद्धवाश्रयति यस्त्रिविधो विकारो
मायान्तराऽऽपतति नाद्यपवर्गयोर्यत् ।
जन्मादयोऽस्य यदमी तव तस्य किं स्यु-
राद्यन्तयोर्यदसतोऽस्ति तदेव मध्ये ॥७॥

THE LAST MESSAGE OF SHRI KRISHNA 203

7. The threefold[1] modification, O Uddhava, which has come upon you is an illusion, for it only comes in the middle,[2] and is not at the beginning and end. When birth and such other things befall it,[3] what is that to you? For that[4] which exists at the beginning and end of an unreality, alone persists in the middle.

[1] *Threefold etc.*—Gross, subtle, and causal bodies are meant.

[2] *Middle*—like a snake or garland in the rope.

[3] *It*—refers to "modification" in line 1.

[4] *That etc.*—e.g. the rope in a false perception of snake or garland.

उद्धव उवाच ।
ज्ञानं विशुद्धं विपुलं यथैत-
द्वैराग्यविज्ञानयुतं पुराणम् ।
आख्याहि विश्वेश्वर विश्वमूर्ते
त्वद्भक्तियोगं च महद्विमृग्यम् ॥८॥

Uddhava said:

8. O Lord of the universe, O Thou whose form is the universe, please tell me how this pure and ancient knowledge, which is coupled with dispassion and realisation, becomes steady. Please also tell me about the systematic practice of that devotion to Thee which the great[1] seek.

[1] *Great*—great sages, and even Brahmâ.

UDDHAVA GITA

तापत्रयेणाभिहतस्य घोरे
संतप्यमानस्य भवाध्वनीश ।
पश्यामि नान्यच्छरणं तवांघ्रि-
द्वन्द्वातपत्रादमृताभिवर्षात् ॥६॥

9. O Lord, for a man smitten by the threefold[1] affliction and suffering torment in the dire
pathway[2] of the world, I see no other refuge than
Thy feet, which[3] act not only like an umbrella but
also rain nectar.

[1] *Threefold etc.*—troubles due to physical disorders, to
denizens of the earth, and to natural phenomena.
[2] *Pathway etc.*—labyrinth of births and deaths.
[3] *Which etc.*—which not only remove temporal evils, but
also confer immortality.

दष्टं जनं संपतितं बिलेऽस्मि-
न्कालाहिना क्षुद्रसुखोरुतर्षम् ।
समुद्धरैनं कृपयापवर्ग्यै-
र्वचोभिरासिञ्च महानुभाव ॥१०॥

10. O Thou of wonderful powers, deign to save
this man fallen into this worldly pit and bitten by
the snake of Time, and withal thirsting violently
after trivial pleasures, and sprinkle him over with
words that conduce to liberation.

The metaphor is changed in this verse.

THE LAST MESSAGE OF SHRI KRISHNA 205

श्रीभगवानुवाच ।

इत्थमेतत्पुरा राजा भीष्मं धर्मभृतां वरम् ।

अजातशत्रुः पप्रच्छ सर्वेषां नोऽनुश्रृण्वताम् ॥११॥

The Lord said:

11. In days gone by King Yudhishthira asked the very same thing of Bhishma, the best of pious men, in exactly this way, to which We all listened.

निवृत्ते भारते युद्धे सुहृन्निधनविह्वलः ।

श्रुत्वा धर्मान्बहून्पश्चान्मोक्षधर्मानपृच्छत ॥१२॥

12. When the Mahâbhârata War was finished, he, overwhelmed at the death of his relatives, after listening to various other religions, inquired about the religion of liberation.

तानहं तेऽभिधास्यामि देवव्रतमुखाच्छ्रुतान् ।

ज्ञानवैराग्यविज्ञानश्रद्धाभक्त्युपबृं हितान् ॥१३॥

13. That religion—enriched with knowledge, dispassion, realisation, faith, and devotion—I am relating to thee, as heard from the lips of Bhishma.

नवैकादशपञ्चत्रीन्भावान्भूतेषु येन वै ।

ईक्षेतायैकमप्येषु तज्ज्ञानं मम निश्चितम् ॥१४॥

14. I consider that as knowledge by means of which one sees the nine,[1] the eleven,[2] the five[3] and the three[4] things in beings, and also sees the One in all these beings.

206   UDDHAVA GITA

[1] *Nine*—Prakriti, Purusha, Mahat (Cosmic Intelligence), Ahamkâra (ego), and the five Tanmâtras (fine matter).

[2] *Eleven*—five organs of action, five organs of knowledge, and Manas (mind).

[3] *Five*—the elements: earth, water, fire, air, and ether.

[4] *Three*—the Gunas: Sattva, Rajas, and Tamas.

By means of knowledge one sees the multiple universe as not essentially distinct from Brahman, the Supreme Cause. This is the idea.

एतदेव हि विज्ञानं न तथैकेन येन यत् ।
स्थित्युत्पत्त्यप्ययान्पश्येद्भावानां त्रिगुणात्मनाम् ॥१५॥

15. This very knowledge becomes realisation when[1] one no more sees things pervaded by the One as before. One should see that things composed of the three Gunas are subject to origin, continuity, and dissolution.

[1] *When etc.*—When he sees only the Brahman, and not the multiplicity. The line is too elliptical.

आदावन्ते च मध्ये च सृज्यात्सृज्यं यदन्वियात् ।
पुनस्तत्प्रतिसंक्रामे यच्छिष्येत तदेव सत् ॥१६॥

16. That which, when one object[1] is transformed into another, abides at its beginning, middle, and end, and remains when those objects return to their cause, is verily the Real.[2]

[1] *Object*.—lit. effect. Every object is an effect, Brahman being the cause.

[2] *Real*—One should see that Brahman alone is eternal in an ever-changing world.

THE LAST MESSAGE OF SHRI KRISHNA

श्रुतिः प्रत्यक्षमैतिह्यमनुमानं चतुष्टयम् ।
प्रमाणेष्वनवस्थानाद्विकल्पात्स विरज्यते ॥१७॥

17. Vedic texts, direct perception, tradition and inference—these are the four proofs of knowledge. Since this ever-changing phenomenal world does not stand[1] the test of these, the wise man turns away from it.

[1] *Does not stand etc.—Vedic texts* : such as, "Multiplicity is a fiction." *Direct perception* : e.g. a cloth never exists apart from the threads that go to make it; similarly the world does not exist apart from the Âtman. *Tradition* : Big authorities have declared the unreality of the world. *Inference* : e.g. the universe must be unreal, for it is a mere phenomenon like silver in a mother-of-pearl.

कर्मणां परिणामित्वादाविरिञ्चादमङ्गलम् ।
विपश्चिन्नश्वरं पश्येददृष्टमपि दृष्टवत् ॥१८॥

18. Since all work[1] is subject to change, the wise man should look upon unseen happiness[2] also, even in the sphere of Brahmâ, as misery and transient, just like the happiness we experience here below.

[1] *Work etc.*—It can never produce eternal results.
[2] *Unseen happiness*—which one gets in heaven acquired through work.

भक्तियोगः पुरैवोक्तः प्रीयमाणाय तेऽनघ ।
पुनश्च कथयिष्यामि मद्भक्तेः कारणं परम् ॥१६॥

19. O sinless one, I have already expounded the philosophy of devotion to thee, but since thou

UDDHAVA GITA

hast taken a fancy to it, I shall again describe the chief means to the attainment of devotion to Me.

श्रद्धाऽमृतकथायां मे शश्वन्मदनुकीर्तनम् ।
परिनिष्ठा च पूजायां स्तुतिभिः स्तवनं मम ॥२०॥

20. A constant[1] regard for the wonderfully sweet tales of My deeds, expounding them to others after hearing, attachment to the worship of Me, and praising Me with hymns.

[1] *Constant*—This epithet is to be repeated in all the succeeding phrases.

आदरः परिचर्यायां सर्वाङ्गैरभिवन्दनम् ।
मद्भक्तपूजाभ्यधिका सर्वभूतेषु मन्मतिः ॥२१॥

21. Delight in service unto Me, making prostrations before Me, worshipping My devotees—which is even greater than the worship of Me—and looking upon all beings as Myself.

मदर्थेष्वङ्गचेष्टा च वचसा मद्गुणेरणम् ।
मय्यर्पणं च मनसः सर्वकामविवर्जनम् ॥२२॥

22. Moving the limbs so as to serve Me, recapitulating My attributes through speech, surrendering the mind unto Me, and banishing all desires from it.

मदर्थेऽर्थपरित्यागो भोगस्य च सुखस्य च ।
इष्टं दत्तं हुतं जप्तं मदर्थं यद्व्रतं तपः ॥२३॥

THE LAST MESSAGE OF SHRI KRISHNA
209

23. Giving up riches, enjoyment and happiness for My sake; making sacrifices, gifts and Homa,[1] repeating My name, undertaking vows and austerities—all for My sake.[2]

[1] *Homa*—offering of oblations in the sacred fire.

[2] *For My sake*—Every act may be conducive to devotion if only it is performed for the sake of the Lord.

एवं धर्मैर्मनुष्याणामुद्धवात्मनिवेदिनाम् ।
मयि संजायते भक्तिः कोऽन्योऽर्थोऽस्यावशिष्यते ॥२४॥

24. O Uddhava, by such pious acts men who have surrendered themselves unto Me acquire devotion to Me. What other[1] objects remain to be achieved by such devotees?

[1] *What other etc.*—Devotion perfectly satisfies the aspirant.

यदाऽऽत्मन्यर्पितं चित्तं शान्तं सत्त्वोपबृंहितम् ।
धर्मं ज्ञानं सवैराग्यमैश्वर्यं चाभिपद्यते ॥२५॥

25. When the mind, pacified and enriched with Sattva,[1] is surrendered unto Me who am the Atman, the devotee attains to religion, knowledge, dispassion, and extraordinary powers.

[1] *Sattva*—balance of mind, with which are associated such qualities as purity, a capacity to illuminate a subject, etc.

यदर्पितं तद्विकल्पे इन्द्रियैः परिधावति ।
रजस्खलं चासन्निष्ठं चित्तं विद्धि विपर्ययम् ॥२६॥

14

UDDHAVA GITA

26. But when that mind, placed on sense-objects, pursues them by means of the organs, it becomes Râjasika,[1] and attached to unreal things, whence, you must know, proceed the very reverse[2] of the above four qualities.

[1] *Râjasika*—engrossed in activity.
[2] *Reverse etc.*—i.e. irreligion, ignorance, attachment, and impotence.

धर्मो मद्भक्तिकृत्प्रोक्तो ज्ञानं चैकात्म्यदर्शनम् ।
गुणेष्वसङ्गो वैराग्यमैश्वर्यं चाणिमादयः ॥२७॥

27. That religion is called[1] the best which makes for devotion to Me; knowledge is the realisation of the unity of Self; dispassion is non-attachment to sense-objects; and extraordinary powers comprise extreme minuteness and so forth.

In this verse the Lord explains in His own way the four virtues mentioned in verse 25.

[1] *Called*—in the Vaishnava scriptures.

उद्धव उवाच ।
यमः कतिविधः प्रोक्तो नियमो वाऽऽरिकर्शन ।
कः शमः को दमः कृष्ण का तितिक्षा धृतिः प्रभो ॥२८॥

Uddhava said:

28. Of how many kinds is Yama,[1] O Chastiser of foes, and Niyama[2] also? What is calmness, and what is self-control, O Krishna? What is fortitude and what is patience, O Lord?

[1] *Yama*—universal moral observances.
[2] *Niyama*—particular moral observances.

THE LAST MESSAGE OF SHRI KRISHNA 211

किं दानं किं तपः शौर्यं किं सत्यमृतमुच्यते ।
कस्त्यागः किं धनं चेष्टं को यज्ञः का च दक्षिणा ॥२९॥

29. What is charity? What is penance? What
is valour? What is honesty, and what is truthfulness? What is renunciation? What is wealth worth
coveting? What is sacrifice, and what is religious
remuneration?

पुंसः किंस्विद्बलं श्रीमन्भगो ळाभश्च केशव ।
का विद्या ह्रीः परा का श्रीः किं सुखं दुःखमेव च ॥३०॥

30. What is the strength of a man, O Sire?
What is fortune, and what is profit, O Keshava?
What is learning? What is shyness? What is the
highest beauty? What is happiness, and what is
misery?

कः पण्डितः कश्च मूर्खः कः पन्था उत्पथश्च कः ।
कः स्वर्गो नरकः कः स्विक्को बन्धुरुत किं गृहम् ॥३१॥

31. Who is a scholar, and who is a fool? What
is the way, and what is its reverse? What is heaven,
and what is hell? Who is a friend, and what is a
house?

क आढ्यः को दरिद्रो वा कृपणः क ईश्वरः ।
एतान्प्रश्नान्मम ब्रूहि विपरीतांश्च सत्पते ॥३२॥

32. Who is rich, and who is poor? Who is
mean, and who is lordly? O Lord of the virtuous,
answer these questions of mine, together with their
opposites.

UDDHAVA GITA

श्रीभगवानुवाच ।

अहिंसा सत्यमस्तेयमसङ्गो ह्रीरसंचयः ।

आस्तिक्यं ब्रह्मचर्यं च मौनं स्थैर्यं क्षमाऽभयम् ॥३३॥

The Lord said:

33. Non-injury, truthfulness, non-stealing, non-attachment, shame, non-accumulation of wealth, faith in God, chastity, silence, patience, forgiveness, fearlessness,

This enumeration differs from that of Patanjali, who in his Yoga Aphorism II. 30 mentions only five virtues under this head (Yama). The same is the case with Niyama also in the next verse.

शौचं जपस्तपो होमः श्रद्धातिथ्यं मदर्चनम् ।

तीर्थाटनं परार्थेहा तुष्टिराचार्यसेवनम् ॥३४॥

34. Purity[1] of mind and of body, repetition of the Lord's name, austerity, offering of oblations in the sacred fire, faith in one's self, hospitality, worship of Me, visiting of holy places, working for the good of others, contentment, and service unto the teacher:

[1] *Purity*—This should be counted as two.

एते यमाः सनियमा उभयोर्द्वादश स्मृताः ।

पुंसामुपासितास्तात यथाकामं दुहन्ति हि ॥३५॥

35. These groups of twelve virtues enumerated in the above two verses constitute the Yamas and the Niyamas. These, my friend, if rightly practised by men, surely produce results[1] according to their desires.

THE LAST MESSAGE OF SHRI KRISHNA

[1] *Results etc.*—i.e. liberation or material prosperity according as the person practising them is free from desires or possessed of desires.

शमो मन्निष्ठता बुद्धे र्देम इन्द्रियसंयमः ।
तितिक्षा दुःखसंमर्षो जिह्वोपस्थजयो धृतिः ॥३६॥

36. Calmness is a steady attachment of the mind to Me. Self-control is control of the sense-organs. Fortitude is the bearing of grief. Patience is a perfect control over the palate and sex-impulse.

It will be seen that the Lord in most cases gives novel interpretations of His own, which, differing as they do from the popular notions of the terms, lend a peculiar piquancy to them. For instance, calmness is not mere control of the mind, but its being fixed on the Lord. Similarly in the other cases.

दण्डन्यासः परं दानं कामत्यागस्तपः स्मृतम् ।
स्वभावविजयः शौर्यं सत्यं च समदर्शनम् ॥३७॥

37. The highest charity is the relinquishing of the idea of violence towards beings. Penance is the giving up[1] of desires. Valour is the conquest of one's nature. Honesty is looking upon everything with an equal eye.

[1] *Giving up etc.*—not undergoing austerities merely.

ऋतं च सूनृता वाणी कविभिः परिकीर्तिता ।
कर्मस्वसंगमः शौचं त्यागः संन्यास उच्यते ॥३८॥

38. Truthfulness is true and agreeable speech which the sages praise. Purity[1] is non-attachment to work, and renunciation is the giving up of work.

[1] *Purity*—This is introduced to distinguish renunciation from it.

धर्मं इष्टं धनं नृणां यज्ञोऽहं भगवत्तमः ।
दक्षिणा ज्ञानसंदेशः प्राणायामः परं बलम् ॥३९॥

39. Religion is that wealth which men may covet. I, the Supreme Lord, am the sacrifice. The imparting of knowledge is religious remuneration. The highest strength is the control of Prâna.

भगो मे ऐश्वरो भावो लाभो मद्भक्तिरुत्तमः ।
विद्याऽऽत्मनि भिदाबाधो जुगुप्सा ह्रीरकर्मसु ॥४०॥

40. Fortune is my Divine State. The best profit is devotion to Me. Learning is the destruction of the idea of multiplicity in the Self. Shyness is abhorrence of evil deeds.

श्रीर्गुणां नैरपेक्ष्याद्याः सुखं दुःखसुखात्ययः ।
दुःखं कामसुखापेक्षा पण्डितो बन्धमोक्षवित् ॥४१॥

41. Beauty consists in virtues such as a spirit of independence. Happiness is the transcending of pleasure and pain. Misery is the hankering after sense-pleasures. A scholar is one who can distinguish between bondage and liberation.

मूर्खो देहाद्यहंबुद्धिः पन्था मन्निगमः स्मृतः ।
उत्पथश्चित्तविक्षेपः स्वर्गः सत्त्वगुणोदयः ॥४२॥

42. A fool is one who identifies oneself with the body etc. The right way is that which leads to

THE LAST MESSAGE OF SHRI KRISHNA 215

Me. The wrong way is that[1] which causes disturbance of the mind. Heaven is the rise of Sattva[2] in the mind.

[1] *That etc.*—i.e. seeking material prosperity.
[2] *Sattva*—blessed qualities.

नरकस्तम उन्नाहो बन्धुर्गुरुरहं सखे ।
गृहं शरीरं मानुष्यं गुणाढ्यो ह्याढ्य उच्यते ॥४३॥

43. Hell is the rise of Tamas in the mind. The teacher, who is no other than Myself, is the friend, O Uddhava. The human body is the home. He indeed is called rich who is rich in virtues.

दरिद्रो यस्त्वसंतुष्टः कृपणो योऽजितेन्द्रियः ।
गुणेष्वसक्तधीरीशो गुणसङ्गो विपर्ययः ॥४४॥

44. One who is discontented is poor. He who is not a master of his senses is mean. One who is not attached to sense-objects is lordly. One who is attached to sense-objects is the reverse[1] of him.

[1] *Reverse*—The Lord mentions only one opposite quality, as an illustration. The others are to be inferred.

एत उद्धव ते प्रश्नाः सर्वे साधु निरूपिताः ।
किं वर्णितेन बहुना लक्षणं गुणदोषयोः ।
गुणदोषदृशिर्दोषो गुणस्तूभयवर्जितः ॥४५॥

45. Here, O Uddhava, I have fully answered all your questions. Well, what is the use of dilating on the characteristics of merit and defect? Defect is distinguishing between merit and defect, and to be free from both is merit.

CHAPTER XV

उद्धव उवाच ।

विधिश्च प्रतिषेधश्च निगमो हीश्वरस्य ते ।
अवेक्षतेऽरविन्दाक्ष गुणं दोषं च कर्मणाम् ॥१॥

वर्णाश्रमविकल्पं च प्रतिलोमानुलोमजम् ।
द्रव्यदेशवयःकालान्स्वर्गं नरकमेव च ॥२॥

Uddhava said:

1-2. O Lotus-eyed Lord, injunctions and prohibitions constitute Thy commandment, the Vedas, which adjudged the merits[1] and defects of work, of the various castes and orders of life, of the issues of Anuloma[2] and Pratiloma marriages, of substance, place, age, and time, and of heaven and hell.

The first five verses attempt a *prima facie* refutation of what has been said in the last verse of the preceding chapter, viz that one should make no distinction between the merits and defects of work.

[1] *Merits etc.*—Certain kinds of work are higher and are to be preferred to other kinds which are lower. Similarly with the other terms that follow. The phrase "merits and defects" is to be repeated with each.

[2] *Anuloma etc.*—An Anuloma marriage is one in which the husband belongs to a higher caste and the wife to a lower caste. *Pratiloma* is the reverse of it.

गुणदोषभिदादृष्टिमन्तरेण वचस्तव ।
निःश्रेयसं कथं नॄणां निषेधविधिलक्षणम् ॥३॥

THE LAST MESSAGE OF SHRI KRISHNA

3. How can Thy utterances[1] consisting of injunctions and prohibitions conduce to the liberation of men without[2] observing the distinction between merits and defects?

[1] *Utterances*—the Vedas.

[2] *Without etc.*—For it is by shunning the lower and adhering to the higher courses of action that progress is possible.

पितृदेवमनुष्याणां वेदश्चक्षुस्तवेश्वर ।
श्रेयस्त्वनुपलब्धेऽर्थे साध्यसाधनयोरपि ॥४॥

4. O Lord, the Vedas uttered by Thee are the highest source of illumination for the manes, the gods, and men, regarding things unseen[1] as well as means[2] and ends.

[1] *Unseen*—such as liberation and heaven, etc.
[2] *Means etc.*—which is which.

गुणदोषभिदादृष्टिर्निगमात्ते न हि स्वतः ।
निगमेनापवादश्च भिदाया इति हि भ्रमः ॥५॥

5. The distinction between merits and defects is to be observed through Thy commandment, the Vedas, and not according to the promptings of nature. Here is again Thy commandment[1] which refutes the idea of distinction. This is exceedingly puzzling.[2]

[1] *Commandment*—uttered at the end of the preceding chapter.

[2] *Puzzling*—So kindly enlighten me on the point.

श्रीभगवानुवाच ।

योगास्त्रयो मया प्रोक्ता नॄणां श्रेयोविधित्सया ।

ज्ञानं कर्म च भक्तिश्च नोपायोऽन्योऽस्ति कुत्रचित् ॥६॥

The Lord said:

6. With a view to effecting the liberation of men I have inculcated[1] three Yogas or methods, viz. those of knowledge, work, and devotion. There is no other[2] means anywhere.

He first deals with the three Yogas in order to show that the apparent contradiction is to be solved by a reference to the qualification of the aspirant. During the period of striving, there is all that distinction; but after realisation there is none.

[1] *Inculcated*—in the sections dealing with Brahman, ritual, and the gods respectively.

[2] *No other etc.*—such as work done with a selfish motive.

निर्विण्णानां ज्ञानयोगो न्यासिनामिह कर्मसु ।

तेष्वनिर्विण्णचित्तानां कर्मयोगस्तु कामिनाम् ॥७॥

यदृच्छया मत्कथादौ जातश्रद्धस्तु यः पुमान् ।

न निर्विण्णो नातिसक्तो भक्तियोगोऽस्य सिद्धिदः ॥८॥

7-8. Of these the path of knowledge is for those who have got disgusted with work[1] and have renounced it; for those who have not been disgusted with it and desire its fruits, there is the path of work; but for the man who somehow[2] has got a veneration for tales about Me and such other things, and who is

THE LAST MESSAGE OF SHRI KRISHNA

neither disgusted with nor grossly attached to work, the path of devotion[3] is successful.

[1] *Work*—knowing it is fraught with evil.

[2] *Somehow*—by a rare stroke of good fortune.

[3] *Devotion*—So this is intermediate between the other two.

तावत्कर्माणि कुर्वीत न निर्विद्येत यावता ।
मत्कथाश्रवणादौ वा श्रद्धा यावन्न जायते ॥६॥

9. One should perform work[1] until one has got disgusted[2] with it, or until one has developed a veneration[3] for listening to tales about Me and that kind of thing.

Verses 9-17 treat of Karma-Yoga as being the first step.

[1] *Work*—obligatory and occasional.

[2] *Disgusted etc.*—Then he is qualified for Jnâna-Yoga.

[3] *Veneration etc.*—Then he can take up Bhakti-Yoga.

स्वधर्मस्थो यजन्यज्ञैरनाशीःकाम उद्धव ।
न याति स्वर्गनरकौ यद्यन्यन्न समाचरेत् ॥१०॥

10. O Uddhava, a man discharging his own duties and performing sacrifices without any desire for results, goes neither to heaven[1] nor to hell,[2] unless he practises evil.

Verses 10 and 11 show how the Karma-Yogi can rise to the level of a Jnâna-Yogi or Bhakti-Yogi.

[1] *Heaven*—Because he does not want it.

[2] *Hell*—Because he has been doing his duties and avoiding evil.

UDDHAVA GITA

अस्मिँल्लोके वर्तमानः स्वधर्मस्थोऽनघः शुचिः ।
ज्ञानं विशुद्धमाप्नोति मद्भक्तिं वा यदृच्छया ॥११॥

11. Such a man, becoming sinless and pure, attains to pure knowledge, or perchance devotion to Me, while remaining in this very world.

स्वर्गिणोऽप्येतमिच्छन्ति लोकं निरयिणस्तथा ।
साधकं ज्ञानभक्तिभ्यामुभयं तदसाधकम् ॥१२॥

12. Even the dwellers of heaven as well as of hell desire this world, which is conducive to knowledge[1] and devotion. But the other two[2] do not serve this purpose.

The human body is praised in verses 12-17.

[1] *Knowledge etc.*—The fifth case in the text stands for the sixth case.

[2] *Other two*—heaven and hell. The former having too much of pleasure and the latter too much of pain, seldom incline the mind to higher things.

न नरः स्वर्गतिं कांक्षेन्नारकीं वा विचक्षणः ।
नेमं लोकं च कांक्षेत देहावेशात्प्रमाद्यति ॥१३॥

13. The wise man should seek neither[1] heaven nor hell, nor desire to return to this world, for he comes under delusion through attachment to the body.

[1] *Neither etc.*—Because both are lower.

एतद्विद्वान्पुरा मृत्योरभवाय घटेत सः ।
अप्रमत्त इदं ज्ञात्वा मर्त्यमप्यर्थसिद्धिदम् ॥१४॥

THE LAST MESSAGE OF SHRI KRISHNA

14. Conscious of this fact, he should be alert and struggle for liberation before death comes on, knowing that the body, even though mortal, can help him to attain his goal.

छिद्यमानं यमैरेतैः कृतनीडं वनस्पतिम् ।
खगः स्वकेतमुत्सृज्य क्षेमं याति ह्यलम्पटः ॥१५॥

15. Seeing that the tree on which it built its nest is being felled by cruel hands, the bird giving up attachment leaves its home and attains[1] to well-being.

[1] *Attains etc.*—is saved.

अहोरात्रैश्छिद्यमानं बुद्ध्वायुर्भयवेपथुः ।
मुक्तसङ्गः परं बुद्ध्वा निरीह उपशाम्यति ॥१६॥

16. Similarly, knowing that his span of life is being cut short by the rotation of days and nights, the wise man trembles in fear, and giving up all attachment realises the Supreme Being. Then he is free from activity[1] and is at peace.

[1] *Activity*—for his own sake.

नृदेहमाद्यं सुलभं सुदुर्लभं
प्लवं सुकल्पं गुरुकर्णधारम् ।
मयानुकूलेन नभस्वतेरितं
पुमान्भवाब्धिं न तरेत्स आत्महा ॥१७॥

17. Getting the first and foremost requisite, viz a human body which is like a strong boat—so

UDDHAVA GITA

difficult to secure, yet within[1] easy reach—with the teacher[2] as its helmsman, and propelled by Me[3] as by a favourable wind—with such means as these, the man who does not strive to cross the ocean of Samsâra,[4] is verily a suicide.

[1] *Within etc.*—by a rare piece of good luck.
[2] *Teacher*—whom one has but to approach.
[3] *Me*—as soon as I am prayed to.
[4] *Samsâra*—rotation of birth and death.

यदारम्भेषु निर्विण्णो विरक्तः संयतेन्द्रियः ।
अभ्यासेनात्मनो योगी धारयेदचलं मनः ॥१८॥

18. When he has got disgusted with under-takings and is averse to their results, the Yogi, with his senses under control, should hold the mind steady by the practice of meditation on the Âtman.

Verse 18-26 deal with Jnâna-Yoga and its preliminary steps.

धार्यमाणं मनो यर्हि भ्राम्यदाश्वनवस्थितम् ।
अतन्द्रितोऽनुरोधेन मार्गेणात्मवशं नयेत् ॥१९॥

19. When the mind, in the act of being concen-trated, begins immediately to wander and is unsteady, then being alert he should bring it within his control by following[1] a conciliatory way.

[1] *Following etc.*—allowing some concessions to its weak-nesses.

मनोगतिं न विसृजेज्जितप्राणो जितेन्द्रियः ।
सत्त्वसंपन्नया बुद्ध्या मन आत्मवशं नयेत् ॥२०॥

THE LAST MESSAGE OF SHRI KRISHNA

20. He should not lose[1] sight of the course of his mind, but holding his Prâna and sense-organs in subjugation, he should bring the mind under his control by means of an intellect charged with Sattva.

[1] *Not lose etc.*—not allow it to drift altogether.

एष वै परमो योगो मनसः संग्रहः स्मृतः ।
हृदयज्ञत्वमन्विच्छन् दम्यस्येवार्बतो मुहुः ॥२१॥

21. This sort of control of the mind is, spoken of[1] as the highest Yoga—like[2] the control of an unruly horse with a view to making him conform to his rider's wishes at every step.

[1] *Spoken of etc.*—i.e. by way of compliment, since it leads to that.

[2] *Like etc.*—As the breaker of a horse has to run some distance with the animal, holding however the reins tight in his hands, so the Yogi in certain cases should allow the mind to wander a little, keeping a strict watch on its movements, and then little by little gain mastery over it.

सांख्येन सर्वभावानां प्रतिलोमानुलोमतः ।
भवाप्ययावनुध्यायेन्मनो यावत्प्रसीदति ॥२२॥

22. One should reflect through discrimination on the origin and dissolution of all things[1] in their backward[2] and forward order, till the mind is at rest.

Verses 22-25 set forth the method of bringing under complete control the partially controlled mind.

[1] *All things*—from the subtlest to the grossest manifestations.

[2] *Backward etc.*—tracing them successively to their ultimate cause, Prakriti, and again reversing the process.

224

UDDHAVA GITA

निर्विण्णस्य विरक्तस्य पुरुषस्योक्तवेदिनः ।
मनस्त्यजति दौरात्म्यं चिन्तितस्यानुचिन्तया ॥२३॥

23. The mind of a man who is disgusted with the world, is possessed of dispassion, and has understood the teachings of his Guru, gives up its wickedness[1] by repeatedly reflecting on them.

[1] *Wickedness*—A literal interpretation would yield the meaning, "identification with things other than the Self, such as the body etc."

यमादिभिर्योगपथैरान्वीक्षिक्या च विद्यया ।
ममार्चोपासनाभिर्वा नान्यैर्योग्यं स्मरेन्मनः ॥२४॥

24. The mind should think of the Paramâtman with whom union is sought through the path of Yoga comprising Yama etc., or through logical analysis,[1] or through the worship and meditation etc., of Me; but by no other means.

[1] *Logical analysis*—Reflecting on the true meaning of *Tat-tvam-asi* or "Thou art That", by eliminating respectively the ideas of Ishvara and Jiva from the first two words, and arriving at the identity of both in Brahman which is their substratum.

यदि कुर्यात्प्रमादेन योगी कर्म विगर्हितम् ।
योगेनैव दहेद्दंहो नान्यत्तत्र कदाचन ॥२५॥

25. If through inadvertence the Yogi does some culpable deed, he should burn the sin thereof through Yoga[1] alone. There is no other[2] way.

THE LAST MESSAGE OF SHRI KRISHNA   225

[1] *Yoga*—the practice of Jnâna. This implies also the taking of the Lord's name and such other means in the case of the Bhakti-Yogi.

[2] *No other way*—such as expiation.

स्वे स्वेऽधिकारे या निष्ठा स गुणः परिकीर्तितः ।
कर्मणां जात्यशुद्धानामनेन नियमः कृतः ।
गुणदोषविधानेन सङ्गानां त्याजनेच्छया ॥२६॥

26. The steadfastness[1] to the duties of one's own sphere is considered as merit. By the declaration[2] of their merits and defects, a restriction[3] is made with regard to actions, which are impure in their very nature, in order to remove people's attachment to them.

[1] *Steadfastness etc.*—This explains why his sins would be burnt without the help of expiation, which is meant for those who work for selfish ends.

[2] *Declaration etc.*—enjoining some and prohibiting others. See verse I.

[3] *Restriction etc.*—So that man's natural tendency for work—which is the root of all mischief—may be gradually controlled and finally overcome.

जातश्रद्धो मत्कथासु निर्विण्णः सर्वकर्मसु ।
वेद दुःखात्मकान्कामान्परित्यागेऽप्यनीश्वरः ॥२७॥
ततो भजेत मां प्रीतः श्रद्धालुर्दृढनिश्चयः ।
जुषमाणश्च तान्कामान्दुःखोदर्कांश्च गर्हयन् ॥२८॥

27-28. Should a man who has got faith in tales about Me and is disgusted with all kinds of work,[1] know desires to be full of misery and yet fail to give them up, then this man of faith, with firm

15

226 UDDHAVA GITA

conviction,[2] should cheerfully worship Me, as he goes on satisfying those desires fraught with painful consequences, condemning[3] them all the while.

Bhakti-Yoga is described in verses 27-35.

[1] *Work*—but not with their fruits.

[2] *Conviction*—that devotion alone will achieve everything.

[3] *Condemning etc.*—This discrimination gradually weans the mind from such desires, when devotion does its full work.

प्रोक्तेन भक्तियोगेन भजतो माऽसकृन्मुनेः ।
कामा हृदय्या नश्यन्ति सर्वे मयि हृदि स्थिते ॥२६॥

29. If a meditative man constantly worships Me through the path of devotion mentioned above,[1] all the desires of his heart are destroyed, for I[2] reside in his heart.

The method of worship and its effect are set forth in this and the next verse.

[1] *Above*—e.g. in verses 20-23 of the preceding chapter.

[2] *For I etc.*—And the two cannot live together, like light and darkness.

भिद्यते हृदयग्रन्थिश्छिद्यन्ते सर्वसंशयाः ।
क्षीयन्ते चास्य कर्माणि मयि दृष्टेऽखिलात्मनि ॥३०॥

30. When he sees Me, the Self of all, the knot[1] of his heart breaks to pieces, all his doubts are dispelled, and his Karma[2] is destroyed.

A close reproduction of Mundaka II. ii. 8.

[1] *Knot etc.*—i.e. egoism.

[2] *Karma*—the resultant of past works stored as tendencies in the mind. Of these tendencies some are

THE LAST MESSAGE OF SHRI KRISHNA   227

very strong and work themselves out in this birth. They are called *prârabdha* (the commenced). Others, forming by far the greater portion, are comparatively feeble in strength. These are destroyed on the dawning of realisation. But not the former, which persist till the fall of the body. A special name, viz *âgâmi* or the forthcoming, is given to those works which a man does after the attainment of realisation. But these cannot bind him any more. For a discussion on the subject *vide* the Brahma-Sutras IV. i. 13-15.

तस्मान्मड्रक्तियुक्तस्य योगिनो वै मदात्मनः ।
न ज्ञानं न च वैराग्यं प्रायः श्रेयो भवेदिह ॥३१॥

31. Hence the practice of knowledge or dispassion is scarcely of any use to the Yogi who is devoted to Me and has his mind centred in me.

Devotion is extolled in verses 31-33.

यत्कर्मभिर्यत्तपसा ज्ञानवैराग्यतश्च यत् ।
योगेन दानधर्मेण श्रेयोभिरितररैरपि ॥३२॥
सर्वं मड्रक्तियोगेन मड्रक्तो लभतेऽञ्जसा ।
स्वर्गापवर्गं मद्धाम कथंचिद्यदि वाञ्छति ॥३३॥

32-33. Whatever is acquired through works, austerities, knowledge, dispassion, Yoga, or charity, or through any other means of well-being, My devotee easily attains to it all through devotion to me—aye, even heaven, or liberation, or My abode, should he care to have it.

UDDHAVA GITA

न किंचित्साधवो धीरा भक्ता ह्येकान्तिनो मम ।
वाञ्छन्त्यपि मया दत्तं कैवल्यमपुनर्भवम् ॥३४॥

34. Those saintly persons who are of a steady mind and are devoted exclusively to Me, never desire absolute[1] independence, even if I offer it to them.

[1] *Absolute*—literally, free from birth.

नैरपेक्ष्यं परं प्राहुर्निःश्रेयसमनल्पकम् ।
तस्मान्निराशिषो भक्तिर्निरपेक्षस्य मे भवेत् ॥३५॥

35. Caring for nothing has been called the highest and the fullest well-being. Therefore the man who has no desires, and cares for naught, attains devotion to Me.

न मय्येकान्तभक्तानां गुणदोषोद्भवा गुणाः ।
साधूनां समचित्तानां बुद्धेः परमुपेयुषाम् ॥३६॥

36. Merits[1] and defects, arising from the performance of acts enjoined and prohibited, do not affect those saints who are exclusively devoted to Me, who are of an even mind, and who have realised the Being[2] who is beyond the intellect.

[1] *Merits etc.*—For the idea compare Taittiriya Upanishad II. ix. I, and Brihadâranyaka Upanishad IV. iv. 23.
[2] *Being etc.*—viz the Paramâtman.

THE LAST MESSAGE OF SHRI KRISHNA 229

एवमेतन्मयाऽऽदिष्टाननुतिष्ठन्ति मे पथः ।
क्षेमं विन्दन्ति मत्स्थानं यद्ब्रह्म परमं विदुः ।।३७।।

37. Those who thus practise these means[1] to My attainment, which I have just taught, attain to My abode, which is all bliss, and also realise the Supreme Brahman.

[1] *Means etc.*—viz the three Yogas.

CHAPTER XVI

श्रीभगवानुवाच ।
य एतान्मत्पथो हित्वा भक्तिज्ञानक्रियात्मकान् ।
क्षुद्रान्कामांश्चलैः प्राणैर्जुषन्तः संसरन्ति ते ॥१॥

The Lord said:

1. Those[1] who discarding these three ways of devotion, knowledge, and work taught by Me, feed through their restless organs their petty desires, pass on from birth to death.

[1] *Those etc.*—This is a class of utterly selfish people who are distinct from both men of realisation and the seekers after truth described in the preceding chapter.

स्वे स्वेऽधिकारे या निष्ठा स गुणः परिकीर्तितः ।
विपर्ययस्तु दोषः स्यादुभयोरेष निश्चयः ॥२॥

2. The steadfastness[1] to the duties of one's particular sphere is described as merit, and the reverse is defect. This is the criterion about them.

[1] *Steadfastness etc.*—i.e. no action is by itself right or wrong.

शुद्धयशुद्धी विधीयेते समानेष्वपि वस्तुषु ।
द्रव्यस्य विचिकित्सार्थं गुणदोषौ शुभाशुभौ ॥३॥

3. With a view to test[1] the fitness of things, purity and impurity, merit and defect, as well as

THE LAST MESSAGE OF SHRI KRISHNA 231

conduciveness to well-being and its opposite are enjoined even with regard to things[2] of the same group, for the sake of piety,[3] of practice,[4] and of the maintenance[5] of life respectively.

[1] *Test etc.*—so as to put a check on man's natural proneness to them.

[2] *Things etc.*—viz place, time, things, agent, Mantra, and action, dealt with later.

[3] *Piety etc.*—e.g. pure things conduce to piety (by which formal religion is meant), and impure things to its opposite.

[4] *Practice etc.*—In the absence of specific declarations, what great personages do is also right, and the reverse is wrong.

[5] *Maintenance etc.*—One may have just as much of even a questionable thing as will save one's life, but no more.

धर्मार्थं व्यवहारार्थं यात्रार्थमिति चानघ ।
दर्शितोऽयं मयाऽऽचारो धर्ममुद्वहतां धुरम् ।।४।।

4. O sinless one, for those[1] to whom piety is but a burden, I[2] have laid down the above rule of conduct.

[1] *Those etc.*—i.e. grossly selfish people.
[2] *I etc.*—as Manu and other law-givers.

भूम्यम्ब्वग्न्यनिलाकाशा भूतानां पञ्च धातवः ।
आब्रह्मस्थावरादीनां शरीरा आत्मसंयुताः ।।५।।

5. Earth, water, fire, air, and ether are the five common factors of the bodies of all beings from

232 UDDHAVA GITA

Brahmâ down to a tree etc., and they are equally connected with a soul.[1]

[1] *Soul*—So from both standpoints they are alike.

वेदेन नामरूपाणि विषमाणि समेष्वपि ।
धातुपूर्वव कल्प्यन्त एतेषां स्वार्थसिद्धये ॥६॥

6. O Uddhava, though their bodies are thus similar, yet for their[1] own good the Vedas have fashioned diverse names and forms for them.

[1] *Their etc.*—in order that they may attain the end of their life by regulating their propensities.

देशकालादिभावानां वस्तूनां मम सत्तम ।
गुणदोषौ विधीयेते नियमार्थं हि कर्मणाम् ॥७॥

7. O best of men, with a view to circumscribing work I enjoin merits and defects regarding things in accordance with the exigencies of place,[1] time, etc.

[1] *Place etc.*—See note 2 on verse 3.

अकृष्णसारो देशानामब्रह्मण्योऽशुचिर्भवेत् ।
कृष्णसारोऽप्यसौवीरकीकटासंस्कृतेरिणम् ॥८॥

8. Of lands those that are devoid of spotted antelopes and where, in particular, devotion to Brâhmanas is absent, should be considered impure. And even if they are rich in antelopes tracts designated as Kikata[1] and those that are not swept, or are

THE LAST MESSAGE OF SHRI KRISHNA   233

barren, should be regarded as impure, unless[2] there be worthy people in them.

The purity or impurity of the six items is set forth in verses 8-15, as helping piety.

[1] *Kikata*—Probably Bihar, the lower part of East Bengal and the northern portion of the Madras Presidency.

[2] *Unless etc.*—This in any case is the chief determining factor.

कर्मण्यो गुणवान्कालो द्रव्यतः स्वत एव वा ।
यतो निवर्तते कर्म स दोषोऽकर्मकः स्मृतः ॥६॥

9. That time is efficacious which owing to the abundance of requisite materials, or through inherent properties of its own, is conducive to any particular work; while that in which work stops[1] or is prohibited[2] is considered unfit.

[1] *Stops*—owing to the scarcity of materials, or for political unrest etc.

[2] *Prohibited*—by the scriptures. For example, those attending a birth or death in the family.

द्रव्यस्य शुद्धशुद्धी च द्रव्येण वचनेन च ।
संस्कारेणाथ कालेन महत्त्वाल्पतयाऽथवा ॥१०॥
शक्त्याशक्त्याऽथवा बुद्धया समृद्धया च यदात्मने ।
अर्घं कुर्वन्ति हि यथा देशावस्थानुसारतः ॥११॥

10-11. The purity or impurity of a thing is determined by other things,[1] by the verdict of competent persons, by specific acts, by durations of time,[2] by its greatness[3] or smallness, by strength[4] or infirmity,

234   UDDHAVA GITA

by knowledge,[5] and by affluence[6] or otherwise. They bring demerit on a person according[7] to place and circumstances.

The purity or impurity of "things" (the third item) is described in verses 10-13.

[1] *Things*—coming in contact with it.

[2] *Time*—e.g. rain-water collected in a tank is considered pure after the lapse of ten days. Food, on the contrary, loses its value on being stale.

[3] *Greatness etc.*—e.g. a jar of water is easily defiled, but not a tank.

[4] *Strength etc.*—Infirm people are generally made certain allowances over the able-bodied ones.

[5] *Knowledge*—e.g. if a man comes to know of the birth of his son within ten days, he comes under the usual ban of uncleanliness, but not after that period.

[6] *Affluence etc.*—e.g. wearing tattered clothes will be wrong for a rich man, but not for a poor man.

[7] *According etc.*—e.g. under normal conditions. In exceptional circumstances the strictures should be relaxed.

धान्यदार्वस्थितन्तूनां रसतैजसचर्मणाम् ।
कालवाय्वग्निमृत्तोयैः पार्थिवानां युतायुतैः ॥१२॥

12. The purity of corn, wood, bone,[1] textiles, liquids, metallic wares, skins, and earthen things[2] is effected, as the case may be, by time, air, fire, earth, and water, either singly or in combination.

[1] *Bone*—such as ivory.

[2] *Earthen things*—including unmetalled roads, mud, etc.

अमेध्यलिप्तं यद्येन गन्धं लेपं व्यपोहति ।
भजते प्रकृतिं तस्य तच्छौचं तावदिष्यते ॥१३॥

THE LAST MESSAGE OF SHRI KRISHNA

13. That through which a thing coated with some impure stuff gives up its foreign smell and coating and returns to its natural state, is considered a purifying agency for that[1] thing, and should be made use of till the desired result is produced.

[1] *That etc.*—Different means should be adopted according as it is made of wood, or metal, or cloth, etc.

स्नानदानतपोऽवस्थावीर्यसंस्कारकर्मभिः ।
मत्स्मृत्या चात्मनः शौचं शुद्धः कर्माचरेद् द्विजः ॥१४॥

14. Ablution, charity, austerities, ceremonies,[1] and observances[2] performed according to stages of life and strength, and remembrance of Me, serve to purify a person. Thus purified, a twice-born[3] should perform religious acts.

The means of purification for the agent are being described.

[1] *Ceremonies*—such as the investiture with the holy thread.

[2] *Observances*— such as evening prayers and meditation.

[3] *Twice-born*—here including the Shudra also.

मन्त्रस्य च परिज्ञानं कर्मशुद्धिर्मदर्पणम् ।
धर्मः संपद्यते षड्भिरधर्मस्तु विपर्ययः ॥१५॥

15. The purity of a Mantra consists in its being duly understood[1]; that of work in being offered unto Me. The purity of the above six factors leads to piety, and the reverse of it to impiety.

[1] *Understood*—from a qualified teacher.

UDDHAVA GITA

कचिद्गुणोऽपि दोषः स्याद्दोषोऽपि विधिना गुणः ।
गुणदोषार्थनियमस्तद्विदामेव बाधते ॥१६॥

16. Sometimes a merit even turns into demerit, and a demerit into merit by virtue of an injunction. Thus the regulation with regard to merit and demerit merely annuls their distinction.

समानकर्माचरणं पतितानां न पातकम् ।
औत्पत्तिको गुणः सङ्गो न शयानः पतत्यधः ॥१७॥

17. The doing of the identical deed[1] is no sin in the case of those already much too degraded; while association with the opposite sex is allowable to those[2] to whom it is in order. A man already lying low on the ground can no more fall.

[1] *Deed*—i.e. evil deed.
[2] *Those etc.*—i.e. householders only.

यतो यतो निवर्तेत विमुच्येत ततस्ततः ।
एष धर्मो नॄणां क्षेमः शोकमोहभयापहः ॥१८॥

18. From whatever[1] one abstains, one gets rid of that. This is the righteous conduct that leads to the well-being of men and removes their grief, infatuation and fear.

[1] *Whatever etc.*—Hence the scriptures only advise the restricted exercise of our lower tendencies with a view to getting rid of them finally.

THE LAST MESSAGE OF SHRI KRISHNA 237

विषयेषु गुणाध्यासात्पुंसः सङ्गस्ततो भवेत् ।
सङ्गात्तत्र भवेत्कामः कामादेव कलिर्नृणाम् ॥१६॥

19. By ascribing[1] worth to sense-objects a man
comes to be attached to them; from attachment arises
the desire for them; and desire leads to dispute among
men.

The path of enjoyment is condemned in verses 19-22.
Compare Gita II. 62-63.

[1] *Ascribing etc.*—fancying it where there is none. The
real source of Bliss is the Ātman.

कलेर्दुर्विषहः क्रोधस्तमस्तमनुवर्तते ।
तमसा ग्रस्यते पुंसश्चेतना व्यापिनी द्रुतम् ॥२०॥

20. Dispute engenders vehement anger, which
is followed by infatuation. Infatuation quickly over-
powers his hitherto abiding consciousness of right and
wrong.

तया विरहितः साधो जन्तुः शून्याय कल्पते ।
ततोऽस्य स्वार्थविभ्रंशो मूर्च्छितस्य मृतस्य च ॥२१॥

21. O noble soul, when a man is deprived of this
consciousness, he becomes almost a zero. Like a man
in stupor or half-dead, he then misses the end of his
life.

विषयाभिनिवेशेन नात्मानं वेद नापरम् ।
वृक्षजीविकया जीवन्व्यर्थं भस्त्रेव यः श्वसन् ॥२२॥

238 UDDHAVA GITA

22. Engrossed in sense-objects, he knows neither himself nor the Supreme Self, but vainly lives a vegetative life and breathes but like a pair of bellows.

फलश्रुतिरियं नॄणां न श्रेयो रोचनं परम् ।
श्रेयोविवक्षया प्रोक्तं यथा भैषज्यरोचनम् ॥२३॥

23. The Vedic passages treating of fruits of work[1] do not set forth the highest well-being of men, but are mere inducements[2]—like those for taking a medicine—spoken with a view to leading people to their highest good.

[1] *Work*—i.e. work done with selfish motives.

[2] *Inducements etc.*—As a child is induced to take a bitter medicine by promises of candy, and obtains as a result much more than the candy, viz recovery from his illness, so people are led by means of these tempting prospects to Self-realisation which confers liberation.

उत्पत्त्यैव हि कामेषु प्राणेषु स्वजनेषु च ।
आसक्तमनसो मर्त्या आत्मनोऽनर्थहेतुषु ॥२४॥

24. Men are from their very birth attached to sense-objects, to things affecting their physical welfare, and to their relatives—all of which are but sources of danger to them.

न तानविदुषः स्वार्थं भ्राम्यतो वृजिनाध्वनि ।
कथं युञ्ज्यात्पुनस्तेषु तांस्तमो विशतो बुधः ॥२५॥

25. How can the all-knowing Vedas again recommend sense-enjoyments to people who, ignorant

THE LAST MESSAGE OF SHRI KRISHNA 239

of their true well-being, wander in the paths of enjoyment, only to enter into deeper gloom,[1] and who submit[2] to the guidance of the Vedas themselves?

[1] *Deeper gloom*—as they more and more lose sight of the ideal.

[2] *Submit etc.*—who believe in the portion of the Vedas dealing with work and cite it as the basis of their conduct.

एवं व्यवसितं केचिदविज्ञाय कुबुद्धयः ।
फलश्रुतिं कुसुमितां न वेदज्ञा वदन्ति हि ॥२६॥

26. Certain fools,[1] not knowing this trend of the Vedas, speak of the flowery descriptions in them of the fruits of work as all in all. But the real knowers[2] of the Vedas do not say like that.

[1] *Fools etc.*—A fling at the Mimâmsaka school who advocate work.

[2] *Real knowers*—like Vyâsa and others.

कामिनः कृपणा लुब्धाः पुष्पेषु फलबुद्धयः ।
अग्निमुग्धा धूमतान्ताः स्वं लोकं न विदन्ति ते ॥२७॥

27. People hankering after desires, mean-spirited and avaricious, who mistake flowers[1] for fruits, are deluded[2] by work performed with the help of fire, which but leads to the path of Smoke,[3]—and never know the truth of their Self.

[1] *Flowers etc.*—passing states for the abiding Reality.

[2] *Deluded etc.*—A reproduction of the Shruti passage: "Some departing from this world realise their identity with the Self, while others do not know the truth of their Self, being deluded by work", etc.

240 UDDHAVA GITA

[3] *Path of Smoke*—the Pitriyâna, leading to the lunar sphere, whence at the completion of their term of enjoyment they are reborn on earth.

न ते मामङ्ग जानन्ति हृदिस्थं य इदं यतः ।
उक्थशस्त्रा ह्यसुतृपो यथा नीहारचक्षुषः ॥२८॥

28. My friend, though I am in their heart and am the cause of the universe, yet they do not know Me, because[1] they only talk of work and seek to satisfy their senses, as is the case with those who have been blinded[2] by a fog.

[1] *Because etc.*—An echo of a well-known verse from the Samhitâ.

[2] *Blinded*—i.e. for the time being.

ते मे मतमविज्ञाय परोक्षं विषयात्मकाः ।
हिंसायां यदि रागः स्याद्यज्ञ एव न चोदना ॥२९॥
हिंसाविहारा ह्यालब्धैः पशुभिः स्वसुखेच्छया ।
यजन्ते देवता यज्ञैः पितृभूतपतीन्खलाः ॥३०॥

29-30. These cruel people addicted to the senses, not knowing My covert import—that if[1] one has a natural craving for killing animals, then one may satisfy it only in sacrifices, and that it is never an injunction—revel in such killing and for their own pleasure worship the gods, the manes, and the leaders of ghosts by means of animals slaughtered in sacrifices.

[1] *That if etc.*—that these are merely *permissive* measures and are not to be confounded with *obligatory* duties.

THE LAST MESSAGE OF SHRI KRISHNA 241

स्वप्नोपममममुं लोकमसन्तं श्रवणप्रियम् ।
आशिषो हृदि सङ्कल्प्य त्यजन्त्यर्थान्यथा वणिक् ॥३१॥

31. Imagining in their heart a future world,[1]
which is dream-like, unreal, and agreeable to the ear
only, they spend their money (in sacrifices) like[2] a
trader.

[1] *World*—as a place of intense enjoyment. See verse
33.

[2] *Like etc.*—As a trader stakes his capital on a perilous
venture and loses it.

रजःसत्त्वतमोनिष्ठा रजःसत्त्वतमोजुषः ।
उपासत इन्द्रमुख्यान्देवादीन् न तथैव माम् ॥३२॥

32. Attached to Rajas, Sattva, and Tamas,
they worship not Me,[1] but the gods etc., who have
Indra for their chief and are concerned with Rajas,
Sattva, and Tamas—and even that not[2] in the right
way.

[1] *Me*—who am beyond the three Gunas.

[2] *Not etc.*—The right way of worshipping the gods
would be to think of them as manifestations of the Lord.

इष्ट्रेह देवता यज्ञैर्गत्वा रंस्यामहे दिवि ।
तस्यान्त इह भूयास्म महाशाला महाकुलाः ॥३३॥

33. (They think:) Worshipping the gods here
through sacrifices we shall go to heaven and enjoy
there, at the end of which[1] we shall (again) be born
in noble families with large mansions.

[1] *Which*—period of enjoyment.

16

UDDHAVA GITA

एवं पुष्पितया वाचा व्याक्षिप्तमनसां नृणाम् ।
मानिनाश्चातिस्तब्धानां मद्वार्तापि न रोचते ॥३४॥

34. These men, who with their minds thus upset by the flowery statements in the scriptures, are vain and exceedingly greedy, never like[1] even a reference to Me.

[1] *Never like etc.*—and are therefore degraded.

वेदा ब्रह्मात्मविषयास्त्रिकाण्डविषया इमे ।
परोक्षवादा ऋषयः परोक्षं मम च प्रियम् ॥३५॥

35. The Vedas comprising three sections[1] (really) deal with the identity of Jiva and Brahman. But the Mantras are indirect in their import, and this indirectness I like.[2]

[1] *Three sections*—dealing respectively with ceremonials, Brahman, and the gods.

[2] *I like*—Because thus only pure souls who understand the true import give up ceremonials. If, instead, these had been openly denounced, all people who should rather pass through these lower stages would have been misled into renouncing work prematurely.

शब्दब्रह्म सुदुर्बोधं प्राणेन्द्रियमनोमयम् ।
अनन्तपारं गम्भीरं दुर्विगाह्यं समुद्रवत् ॥३६॥

36. The manifestation[1] of Brahman as the Word, which is conditioned[2] by the Prânas, the mind, and the organs, is most subtle,[3] limitless, profound, and unfathomable like the ocean.

THE LAST MESSAGE OF SHRI KRISHNA 243

The elaborate theory of the origin of speech is introduced in verses 36-43 to indicate the abstruseness of the Vedas. No wonder, therefore, that even sages like Jaimini have got so confounded as to build their ritualistic philosophy out of the Vedas.

[1] *Manifestation etc.*—The word Shabda-Brahma means the Vedas also as the most authoritative body of words.

[2] *Conditioned etc.*—Speech has a subtle and a gross form. The former again is subdivided into three stages of varying fineness, known as Parâ, Pashyanti, and Madhyamâ. The first two are those manifested in the Prânas and the mind respectively, and the third is that stage which is about to issue through the vocal organs as articulate speech, which is the gross form of speech known as Vaikhari.

[3] *Subtle*—both as to nature, as described in the previous note, and as to import.

मयोपबृं'हितं भूम्ना ब्रह्मणानन्तशक्तिना ।
भूतेषु घोषरूपेण बिसेषूर्णेव लक्ष्यते ॥३७॥

37. Strengthened by Me, the infinite Brahman, of limitless powers, it is noticed[1] as the *subtle* Om in beings, like the slender fibres in a lotus stalk.

[1] *Noticed*—by the penetrative insight of the Yogis only.

यथोर्णनाभिर्हृ'दयादूर्णामुद्ग्रमते मुखात् ।
आकाशाद्घोषवान् प्राणो मनसा स्पर्शरूपिणा ॥३८॥
छन्दोमयोऽमृतमयः सहस्रपदवीं प्रभुः ।
ओङ्कारादृयञ्जितस्पर्शस्वरोष्मान्तस्थभूषिताम् ॥३९॥
विचित्रभाषाविततां छन्दोभिश्चतुरुत्तरैः ।
अनन्तपारां बृहतीं सृजत्याक्षिपते स्वयम् ॥४०॥

244   UDDHAVA GITA

38-40. As the spider projects its web from its heart through its mouth, so the immortal Lord Hiranyagarbha, the Cosmic Prâna, whose form is the Vedas, projects out of[1] the subtle Om from the space of his heart, through his mind which scans the entire alphabet, the infinite mass of words known as the Vedas. These issue in a thousand channels, are enriched with the consonants (classified[2] into the Sparsha, the Antastha, and the Ushma group) and the vowels—all fashioned[3] by the subtle Om. They are expressed in diverse forms of language, by means of metres with four additional letters in each succeeding variety. And Hiranyagarbha again winds[4] all up.

[1] *Out of etc.*—first as Parâ (which is the same as the subtle Om), then as Pashyanti, and so on.

[2] *Classified etc.*—The twenty-five letters to comprise the Sparsha group, the next four the Antastha, and the last four the Ushma. The vowels are sixteen in number.

[3] *Fashioned etc.*—in conjunction with the different parts of the vocal system.

[4] *Winds etc.*—at the end of a cycle, as the spider also is believed to swallow its web.

गायत्र्युष्णिगनुष्टुप् च बृहती पंक्तिरेव च ।
त्रिष्टुब्जगत्यतिच्छन्दो ह्यत्यष्ट्यतिजगद्विराट् ॥४१॥

41. (These are some of the metres:) Gâyatri,[1] Ushnik, Anushtup, Brihati, Pankti, Trishtup, Jagati, Atijagati (which belongs to a class known as Atichchhandas), Atyashti, and Ativirât.

[1] *Gâyatri*—has 24 letters. Each of the succeeding varieties has 4 additional letters, up to Atijagati, which thus has 52 letters. Then the order breaks.

THE LAST MESSAGE OF SHRI KRISHNA 245

किं विधत्ते किमाचष्टे किमनूद्य विकल्पयेत् ।
इत्यस्या हृदयं लोके नान्यो मद्वेद कश्चन ॥४२॥

42. What the Vedas enjoin, what they express,[1] and what they tentatively state merely to refute —the secret of this none in the world knows except Myself.

[1] *Enjoin*—in the ritualistic section; *express*—through the Mantras of the section dealing with the gods; and *state etc.*—in the section treating of the highest knowledge.

मां विधत्तेऽभिधत्ते मां विकल्प्यापोह्यते त्वहम् ।
एतावान्सर्ववेदार्थः शब्द आस्थाय मां भिदाम् ।
मायामात्रमनूद्यान्ते प्रतिषिध्य प्रसीदति ॥४३॥

43. Me[1] they enjoin, and Me[2] express, and what is stated therein only to be refuted is also I. This is the import of the entire Vedas. With Me as their substratum[3] the Vedas tentatively state duality as an illusion, and refuting it at the end are satisfied.[4]

[1] *Me etc.*—as Yajna or sacrifice.

[2] *And Me etc.*—as the Antaryâmi or Internal Ruler manifested through the gods.

[3] *Substratum etc.*—Just as the sap that is in a tiny seedling runs through the whole developed tree, so the import of the Om (viz the Supreme Lord) is also that of the entire Vedas.

[4] *Are satisfied*—finish their task.

CHAPTER XVII

उद्धव उवाच ।

कति तत्त्वानि विश्वेश संख्यातान्यृषिभिः प्रभो ।
नवैकादशपञ्चत्रीण्यात्थ त्वमिह शुश्रुम ॥१॥

Uddhava said:

1. How many[1] are the categories enumerated by the sages, O Lord of the Universe? O Lord, regarding this I hear that Thou speakest of twenty-eight, divided into nine, eleven, five, and three.

[1] *How many etc.*—He means, which enumeration is correct?

केचित्षड्विंशतिं प्राहुरपरे पञ्चविंशतिम् ।
सप्तैके नव षट् केचिच्चत्वार्येकादशापरे ।
केचित्सप्तदश प्राहुः षोडशैके त्रयोदश ॥२॥

2. Some[1] speak of twenty-six, and others twenty-five; some speak of seven, some nine, or six, or four, and others eleven; some speak of seventeen, or sixteen, and some again thirteen.

[1] *Some etc.*—These will be touched on later.

एतावत्त्वं हि संख्यानामृषयो यद्विवक्षया ।
गायन्ति पृथगायुष्मन्निदं नो वक्तुमर्हसि ॥३॥

THE LAST MESSAGE OF SHRI KRISHNA

247

3. Thou shouldst tell me, O Immortal One, the purpose which the sages have in view in thus differently enumerating them.

श्रीभगवानुवाच ।

युक्तं च सन्ति सर्वत्र भाषन्ते ब्राह्मणा यथा ।
मायां मदीयामुद्गृह्य वदतां किं नु दुर्घटम ॥४॥

The Lord said:

4. Howsoever the sages may speak, it is quite in order, for all the categories are included[1] in every enumeration. And what is impossible[2] for those who speak accepting My wonder-working Mâyâ?

[1] *Included*—tacitly or otherwise. The construction is highly elliptical.

[2] *Impossible etc.*—When plurality itself is an illusion, one may easily indulge in any sort of speculation about it.

नैतदेवं यथाऽऽत्थ त्वं यदहं वच्मि तत्तथा ।
एवं विवदतां हेतुं शक्तयो मे दुरत्ययाः ॥५॥

5. "It is not as you put it, but it is as I put it"—this sort of fighting over the issue is due to My powers, Sattva,[1] Rajas, and Tamas, which are so difficult to get rid of.

[1] *Sattva etc.*—transformed as particular mental states.

यासां व्यतिकरादासीद्विकल्पो वदतां पदम् ।
प्राप्ते शमदमेऽप्येति वादस्तमनु शाम्यति ॥६॥

UDDHAVA GITA

248

6. It is the disturbance among these[1] that caused[2] the doubt which is the ground of contention among the disputants. This doubt vanishes when one attains calmness of mind and self-control, and after that dispute, too, is at an end.

[1] *These*—held in equilibrium in the Prakriti.

[2] *Caused etc.*—evolved the entire universe of mind and matter, including, of course, doubt.

परस्परानुप्रवेशात्तत्त्वानां पुरुषर्षभ ।
पौर्वापर्यप्रसंख्यानं यथा वक्तुर्विवक्षितम् ॥७॥

7. O best of men, it is owing to their mutual interpenetration[1] that the categories are enumerated in a relation of cause and effect, according to the view of the particular exponent.

[1] *Interpenetration*—to be explained in the next verse.

एकस्मिन्नपि दृश्यन्ते प्रविष्टानीतराणि च ।
पूर्वस्मिन्वा परस्मिन्वा तत्त्वे तत्त्वानि सर्वशः ॥८॥

8. In the same category, be it cause or effect, all the other categories are seen to be included.[1]

[1] *Included*—The effects (the jar etc.) are inherent in a subtle form in the cause (the clay), which, again, runs through the effects.

पौर्वापर्यमतोऽमीषां प्रसंख्यानमभीप्सताम् ।
यथा विविक्तं यद्वक्तृं गृह्लीमो युक्तिसंभवात् ॥९॥

THE LAST MESSAGE OF SHRI KRISHNA   249

9.   Therefore we accept as true the causal order and enumeration of the categories upheld by the different exponents, just as[1] their mouth utters them; for there is reason behind them all.

[1] *Just as etc.*—The construction is again elliptical.

अनाद्यविद्यायुक्तस्य पुरुषस्यात्मवेदनम् ।
स्वतो न संभवादन्यस्तत्त्वज्ञो ज्ञानदो भवेत् ॥१०॥

10.   Some[1] hold: Since a man, under the grip of beginningless nescience, cannot realise his Self unaided, the Omniscient Giver of knowledge must be a different Being from him.

Verses 10 and 11 show how, apart from the categories among which a causal relation subsists, and which, therefore, can be grouped variously, the question of identity or difference between God and the soul leads to two schools.

[1] *Some*—the upholders of twenty-six categories.

पुरुषेश्वरयोरत्र न वैलक्षण्यमण्वपि ।
तदन्यकल्पनापार्था ज्ञानं च प्रकृतेर्गुणः ॥११॥

11.   On this point others[1] hold: There is not[2] the least difference between the soul and God. Therefore it is futile to make a distinction between them. And knowledge[3] is but an attribute[4] of the Prakriti.

[1] *Others*—those who are twenty-five categories.
[2] *Not etc.*—Since both are Knowledge Absolute.

250   **UDDHAVA GITA**

[3] *Knowledge etc.*—It cannot form a separate category to vitiate both the above enumerations.

[4] *Attribute etc.*—being the function of Sattva.

प्रकृतिर्गुणसाम्यं वै प्रकृतेर्नात्मनो गुणाः ।
सत्त्वं रजस्तम इति स्थित्युत्पत्त्यन्तहेतवः ॥१२॥

12. The Prakriti is but the equilibrium of the Gunas, which are Sattva, Rajas, and Tamas. These, leading respectively to the maintenance, origin, and destruction of the world, belong to the Prakriti and not to the Âtman.

सत्त्वं ज्ञानं रजः कर्म तमोऽज्ञानमिहोच्यते ।
गुणव्यतिकरः कालः स्वभावः सूत्रमेव च ॥१३॥

13. Now, knowledge[1] is said to be the outcome of Sattva, activity, of Rajas, and ignorance, of Tamas. Time[2] is no other than God who causes the disturbance among the Gunas, and tendency is identical with the Cosmic Prâna.[3]

[1] *Knowledge etc.*—So all these must, according to this school, come under the Prakriti.

[2] *Time etc.*—So neither it nor "tendency" (the resultant impressions of work) can form separate categories.

[3] *Cosmic Prâna*—the same as Cosmic Intelligence or Mahat.

पुरुषः प्रकृतिर्व्यक्तमहंकारो नभोऽनिलः ।
ज्योतिरापः क्षितिरिति तत्त्वान्युक्तानि मे नव ॥१४॥

14. Purusha, Prakriti, Mahat, Egoism, ether, air, fire, water, and earth—these are the nine categories enumerated by Me.

THE LAST MESSAGE OF SHRI KRISHNA 251

The Lord enumerates the three Gunas apart from the Prakriti, because they come and go. He now proceeds to enumerate in verses 14-16 the other twenty-five categories which are common to both the schools referred to in verses 10 and 11.

श्रोत्रं त्वग्दर्शनं घ्राणो जिह्वेति ज्ञानशक्तयः ।
वाक्पाण्युपस्थपाय्वंघ्रिः कर्माण्यङ्गोभयं मनः ॥१५॥

15. My friend, the ear, skin, eye, nose, and palate are the five organs of knowledge; the tongue, hand, leg, etc., are the organs of action; and the mind is both.[1]

[1] *Both*—organ of knowledge and action. These are the eleven categories referred to in verse 1.

शब्दः स्पर्शो रसो गन्धो रूपं चेत्यर्थजातयः ।
गत्युक्त्युत्सर्गशिल्पानि कर्मायतनसिद्धयः ॥१६॥

16. Sound, touch, taste, smell, and colour are the five sense-objects. Motion, speech, excretion, and manual art are but the effects[1] of the organs of action.

[1] *Effects etc.*—hence not to be enumerated separately.

सर्गादौ प्रकृतिर्ह्यस्य कार्यकारणरूपिणी ।
सत्त्वादिभिर्गुणैर्धत्ते पुरुषोऽव्यक्त ईक्षते ॥१७॥

17. In the projection[1] etc., of this universe, the Prakriti, transformed into causes and effects,[2] assumes, through the Gunas such as the Sattva etc.,

252 UDDHAVA GITA

the conditions for such modification. But the Purusha, unmodified,[3] merely looks on.

[1] *Projection etc.*—i.e. projection, continuity, and dissolution.

[2] *Causes and effects*—The causes are: Mahat, egoism, and the five subtle elements. The effects are: the five gross elements, the ten organs, and the Manas or mind.

[3] *Unmodified etc.*—Hence it is distinct from the Prakriti.

व्यक्तादयो विकुर्वाणा धातवः पुरुषेक्षया ।
लब्धवीर्याः सृजन्त्यण्डं संहताः प्रकृतेर्बलात् ॥१८॥

18. The component elements such as the Mahat etc., while being transformed, are charged with power under the glance of the Purusha, and, supported by the Prakriti, combine[1] and form the universe.

[1] *Combine etc.*—Hence the universe can be grouped under those several categories.

सप्तैव धातव इति तत्रार्थाः पञ्च खादयः ।
ज्ञानमात्मोभयाधारस्ततो देहेन्द्रियासवः ॥१९॥

19. The view that the components are only seven in number, comprises the five elements such as ether[1] etc., together with the Jiva, and the Supreme Self, which is the substratum of both subject and object. From these seven proceed[2] the body, the organs and the Prânas.

[1] *Ether etc.*—The five gross elements. The causes from Prakriti down to the subtle elements inhere in these.

[2] *Proceed etc.*—Hence the remaining sixteen categories are accounted for.

THE LAST MESSAGE OF SHRI KRISHNA   253

षडित्यत्रापि भूतानि पञ्च षष्ठः परः पुमान् ।
तैर्युक्त आत्मसम्भूतैः सृष्ट्वेदं समुपाविशत् ॥२०॥

20. The view that there are six categories, comprises the five elements and the Supreme Self,[1] which makes up the sixth. The Supreme Self, being provided with the five elements, which have emanated out of It, has made all this[2] and entered into it.

[1] *Supreme Self*—which includes the Jiva of the previous enumeration.

[2] *All this*—the body and everything else.

चत्वार्येवेति तत्रापि तेज आपोऽन्नमात्मनः ।
जातानि तैरिदं जातं जन्मावयविनः खलु ॥२१॥

21. In the view limiting the categories to four only, fire, water, and earth, together with the Âtman from which they have sprung, are meant. It is from these[1] that the origin of all effects has taken place.

[1] *From these etc.*—So they are all included in these four.

संख्याने सप्तदशके भूतमात्रेन्द्रियाणि च ।
पञ्चपञ्चैकमनसा आत्मा सप्तदशः स्मृतः ॥२२॥

22. In the enumeration of seventeen categories the gross elements, the subtle elements, and the organs —five of each—together with the mind and the Âtman constitute the seventeen.

UDDHAVA GITA

तद्वत्षोडशसंख्याने आत्मैव मन उच्यते ।
भूतेन्द्रियाणि पञ्चैव मन आत्मा त्रयोदश ॥२३॥

23. Similarly, in the enumeration of sixteen categories the Âtman[1] itself is taken as the mind. The five elements, the five organs, the mind, and the twofold[2] Âtman—these make up the thirteen categories.

[1] *Âtman etc.*—as cogitating.
[2] *Twofold etc.*—as Jiva and Paramâtman.

एकादशत्व आत्मासौ महाभूतेन्द्रियाणि च ।
अष्टौ प्रकृतयश्चैव पुरुषश्च नवेत्यथ ॥२४॥

24. In the enumeration of eleven categories this Âtman, the five elements, and the five organs are taken into consideration. While the eight causes[1] and the Purusha make up the nine categories.

[1] *Eight causes*—i.e. Prakriti, Mahat, egoism, and the five subtle elements.

इति नानाप्रसंख्यानं तत्त्वानामृषिभिः कृतम् ।
सर्वं न्याय्यं युक्तिमत्त्वाद्विदुषां किमशोभनम् ॥२५॥

25. Thus the sages have made various enumerations of the categories. All of these, being reasonable, are apposite. What indeed is inappropriate for the learned?

THE LAST MESSAGE OF SHRI KRISHNA 255

उद्धव उवाच ।

प्रकृतिः पुरुषश्चोभौ यद्यप्यात्मविलक्षणौ ।
अन्योन्यापाश्रयात्कृष्ण दृश्यते न भिदा तयोः ।
प्रकृतौ लक्ष्यते ह्यात्मा प्रकृतिश्च तथाऽऽत्मनि ॥२६॥

Uddhava said:

26. O Krishna, though the Prakriti and the Purusha are mutually distinct[1] by their very nature, yet their distinction is not perceived as they are never found apart. The Âtman, verily, is seen in the Prakriti,[2] and likewise the Prakriti in the Atman.

[1] *Distinct*—one being sentient and the other insentient.

[2] *Prakriti*—i.e. its effect, the body. They are mixed up and perceived as the "I".

एवं मे पुण्डरीकाक्ष महान्तं संशयं हृदि ।
छेत्तुमर्हसि सर्वज्ञ वचोभिर्नयनैपुणैः ॥२७॥

27. O Lotus-eyed, Omniscient Lord, Thou shouldst dispel this great doubt in my heart with words skilled in reasoning.

त्वत्तो ज्ञानं हि जीवानां प्रमोषस्तेऽत्र शक्तितः ।
त्वमेव ह्यात्ममायाया गतिं वेत्थ न चापरः ॥२८॥

28. For it is from Thee that people get illumination, and through Thy power[1] it is that they are robbed of it. Thou alone knowest the course of Thy inscrutable Power and none else.

[1] *Power*—Mâyâ.

UDDHAVA GITA

श्रीभगवानुवाच ।

प्रकृतिः पुरुषश्च ति विकल्पः पुरुषर्षभ ।
एष वैकारिकः सर्गो गुणव्यतिकरात्मकः ॥२६॥

The Lord said:

29. O best of men, the Prakriti and the Purusha are entirely distinct[1] entities. This projected universe is subject to modifications, for it has sprung from a disturbance among the Gunas.

[1] *Distinct*—This distinction is brought out first by describing the ever-changing nature of the Parkriti in this and the next two verses.

ममाङ्ग माया गुणमय्यनेकधा
विकल्पबुद्धीश्च गुणैर्विधत्ते ।
वैकारिकस्त्रिविधोऽध्यात्ममेक-
मथाधिदैवमधिभूतमन्यत् ॥३०॥

30. My friend, My inscrutable Power, consisting of the Gunas, creates through these Gunas innumerable modifications and ideas relating thereto. Even though subject to all sorts of modifications, yet the universe is, broadly speaking, threefold[1]—one pertaining to the body, another to the gods, and a third to the creatures.

[1] *Threefold*—This will be expanded in the next verse.

THE LAST MESSAGE OF SHRI KRISHNA

द्रूपमार्कं वपुरत्र रन्ध्रे
परस्परं सिध्यति यः स्वतः खे ।
आत्मा यदेषामपरो य आद्यः
स्वयानुभूत्याखिलसिद्धिसिद्धिः ।
एवं त्वगादि श्रवणादि चक्षु-
जिह्वादि नासादि च चित्तयुक्तम् ॥३१॥

31. The eye,[1] the form, and the solar rays
penetrating the eye-ball—these depend[2] upon one
another for their manifestation; but the sun which is
in the sky exists independently.[3] Because the Âtman[4]
is the primeval cause of these,[5] It is distinct from
them. By Its self-effulgence It is the Illuminer of all
those that help to manifest one another. Similarly[6]
with reference to the skin, the ear, the eye, the tongue,
the nose, the mind, etc.

[1] *The eye etc.*—exemplifying respectively the three
aspects spoken of in verse 30.

[2] *Depend etc.*—We see the form and infer the other
two factors in its perception.

[3] *Independently*—It does not require any support and
is not affected by the defects of the latter.

[4] *Âtman etc.*—The distinctive character of the Purusha
is being pointed out: It is the only unchanging self-effulgent
Principle.

[5] *These*—three divisions of the universe.

[6] *Similarly etc.*—Each of these has its triangular relation with two other things. For example, the skin has got
touch and air; the ear, sound and the quarters; the
tongue, taste and Varuna; the nose, smell and the Ashvins;
Chitta, object of recognition and Vâsudeva; Manas, object

17

258 UDDHAVA GITA

of cogitation and the Moon; Buddhi, object of determination and Brahmâ; and egoism, object of identification and Rudra.

योऽसौ गुणक्षोभकृतो विकार:
प्रधानमूलान्महतः प्रसूतः ।
अहं त्रिवृन्मोहविकल्पहेतु-
वैंकारिकस्तामस ऐन्द्रियश्च ॥३२॥

32. This modification, due to God[1] who upsets the equilibrium of the Gunas, produced from the Mahat which, again, has for its cause the Prakriti, is known as egoism. It is threefold—Vaikârika,[2] Tâmasa, and Aindriya—and is the cause of doubt characterised by ignorance.

[1] *God*—as the operative cause.

[2] *Vaikârika etc.*—The same as Sâttvika, Tâmasa and Râjasa, representing the divisions of Adhidaiva, Adhibhuta, and Adhyâtma respectively.

One must realise the Âtman by rooting out egoism—this is the suggestion of this and the next verse.

आत्मापरिज्ञानमयो विवादो
ह्यस्तीति नास्तीति भिदार्थनिष्ठः ।
व्यर्थोऽपि नैवोपरमेत पुंसां
मत्तः परावृत्तधियां स्वलोकात् ॥३३॥

33. The dispute as to whether the Âtman is or is not, hinges on a difference of views merely, and is due to the non-perception of the Âtman. Even though

THE LAST MESSAGE OF SHRI KRISHNA   259

it is baseless, it never ceases[1] for men who are averse
to Me, their own Self.

[1] *Never ceases*—and creates an endless round of births
and deaths.

उद्धव उवाच ।

त्वत्तः परावृत्तधियः स्वकृतैः कर्मभिः प्रभो ।
उच्चावचानन्यथा देहान्गृह्णन्ति विसृजन्ति च ॥३४॥

तन्ममाख्याहि गोविन्द दुर्विभाव्यमनात्मभिः ।
न ह्येतत्प्रायशो लोके विद्वांसः सन्ति वञ्चिताः ॥३५॥

Uddhava said:

34-35. Tell me, O Lord, O Govinda, how[1] men
averse to Thee obtain and give up, through their own
actions, bodies high and low. It is inscrutable for
those who are addicted to the senses. Few are the
men who know it in the world; the majority are
deluded.

[1] *How etc.*—He asks about transmigration.

श्रीभगवानुवाच ।

मनः कर्ममयं नृणामिन्द्रियैः पञ्चभिर्युतम् ।
लोकाल्लोकं प्रयात्यन्य आत्मा तदनुवर्तते ॥३६॥

The Lord said:

36. The mind[1] of man, swayed by past work,
goes from one sphere to another, accompanied by the

260 UDDHAVA GITA

five[2] organs. The Âtman, which is distinct from it, follows[3] it.

[1] *Mind etc.*—The whole thing, says the Lord, is due to the "subtle body".

[2] *Five*—implies all the ten.

[3] *Follows*—through identification.

ध्यायन्मनोऽनुविषयान् दृष्टान् वानुश्रुतानथ ।
उद्यत्सीदत्कर्मतन्त्रं स्मृतिस्तदनुशाम्यति ॥३७॥

37. The mind swayed by past work, as it dwells on sense-objects experienced or heard of, flashes[1] up with regard to those and sleeps over the past. After this memory is lost.

[1] *Flashes etc.*—It is all a question of memory. The new body is remembered and the old forgotten. The centre of identification is thus changed.

विषयाभिनिवेशेन नात्मानं यत्स्मरेत्पुनः ।
जन्तोर्वैं कस्यचिद्धेतोर्मृत्युरत्यन्तविस्मृतिः ॥३८॥

38. Being engrossed in a particular sense-object,[1] man no more recollects himself. This utter self-forgetfulness of man, from any cause,[2] is verily his death.

[1] *Sense-object*—the new body produced by past work. So also in the next verse.

[2] *Any cause*—either the intense enjoyment of an angelic body or the extreme pain of a low body undergoing tortures.

THE LAST MESSAGE OF SHRI KRISHNA

261

जन्म त्वात्मतया पुंसः सर्वभावेन भूरिद ।
विषयस्वीकृतिं प्राहुर्यथा स्वप्नमनोरथः ॥३६॥

39. O generous one, the complete acceptance[1]
by a man of a particular sense-object as himself is
called his birth—as in the case of dream and
imagination.

> [1] *Acceptance etc.*—It is all due to identification.

स्वप्नं मनोरथं चेत्थं प्राक्तनं न स्मरत्यसौ ।
तत्र पूर्वमिवात्मानमपूर्वं चानुपश्यति ॥४०॥

40. In a similar way, he no more remembers the
old dream[1] and imagination. In the new experience
he considers his old self as just come into being.

> [1] *Dream etc.*—of the body.

इन्द्रियायनसृष्ट्यर्थं दं त्रैविध्यं भाति वस्तुनि ।
बहिरन्तर्भिदाहेतुर्जनोऽसज्जनकृद्यथा ॥४१॥

41. As a man creates phantom bodies in a dream,
so this threefold division[1] which is the creation of
mind *appears* in the Âtman, which becomes[2] the
cause of the division of interior and exterior.

> [1] *Division*—into Adhidaiva etc.
> [2] *Becomes etc.*—in this instance, through identification,
> i.e. the man has subjective and objective experiences.

UDDHAVA GITA

नित्यदा ह्यङ्ग भूतानि भवन्ति न भवन्ति च ।
कालेनालक्ष्यवेगेन सूक्ष्मत्वात्तन्न दृश्यते ॥४२॥

42. My friend, through the imperceptible march of Time creatures are being continually born and dying. But this is not observed because of its subtlety.

The Lord refers unasked to the constant molecular change in the body to stimulate a spirit of dispassion.

यथार्चिषां स्रोतसां च फलानां वा वनस्पतेः ।
तथैव सर्वभूतानां वयोऽवस्थादयः कृताः ॥४३॥

43. As in the case of flames, or streams, or the fruits of a tree, even so are the conditions of age[1] etc., brought about (by Time).

[1] *Age etc.*—The change in the body can be easily inferred from its effects, as in the examples given.

सोऽयं दीपोऽर्चिषां यद्वत्स्रोतसां तदिदं जलम् ।
सोऽयं पुमानिति नृणां मृषा गीर्धीर्मृषायुषाम् ॥४४॥

44. As in the case of flames the idea and the statement that this is that very lamp, or in the case of streams, that this is that very water, are false,[1] so also are the idea and the statement that this is that very man, with reference to men whose lives are vain.[2]

[1] *False*—the recognition being merely based on a semblance.

[2] *Vain*—because enveloped in ignorance.

THE LAST MESSAGE OF SHRI KRISHNA 263

मा स्वस्य कर्मबीजेन जायते सोऽप्ययं पुमान् ।
म्रियते वामरो भ्रान्त्या यथाग्निर्दारुसंयुतः ॥४५॥

45. Neither[1] is this man born nor does he die
through the instrumentality of his own works. It
is all a mistake. He is immortal. The case is ana-
logous to that of fire which is manifested[2] through
the wood.

[1] *Neither etc.*—Even in the case of an ignorant man
it is the body that dies and not the Self.
[2] *Manifested etc.*—even though surviving indefinitely as
subtle fire.

निषेकगर्भजन्मानि बाल्यकौमारयौवनम् ।
वयोमध्यं जरा मृत्युरित्यवस्थास्तनोर्नव ॥४६॥

46. Conception, embryo state, birth, childhood,
boyhood, youth, middle age, decay, and death—these
are the nine states of the body.

एता मनोरथमयीर्हान्यस्योच्चावचास्तनूः ।
गुणसङ्गादुपादत्ते क्वचित्कश्चिज्जहाति च ॥४७॥

47. Owing to his attachment to the Gunas, the
Jiva assumes these imaginary states, high and low,
belonging clearly to something else,[1] and some,[2]
under[3] exceptional circumstances, give them up.

[1] *Something else*—viz. the body.
[2] *Some*—who are fortunate enough to obtain the grace
of God.
[3] *Under etc.*—by the practice of discrimination.

264   UDDHAVA GITA

आत्मनः पितृपुत्राभ्यामनुमेयौ भवाप्ययौ ।
न भवाप्ययवस्तूनामभिज्ञो द्वयलक्षणः ॥४८॥

48. One's own birth and death may be inferred from those of one's son and father. The Witness[1] of things possessed of birth and death is not affected by either of them.

[1] *Witness*—the Âtman. So in the next verse.

तरोर्बीजविपाकाभ्यां यो विद्धाञ्जन्मसंयमौ ।
तरोर्विलक्षणो द्रष्टा एवं द्रष्टा तनोः पृथक् ॥४९॥

49. He who sees the origin and death of a plant from its seed and final transformation—this observer is distinct from the plant. Similarly is the Witness of the body distinct from it.

प्रकृतेरेवमात्मानमविविच्याबुधः पुमान् ।
तत्त्वेन स्पर्शसंमूढः संसारं प्रतिपद्यते ॥५०॥

50. The ignorant man, failing to rightly discriminate thus the Âtman from the Prakriti, is deluded by the sense-objects and goes from birth to death.

The transmigratory existence of the ignorant man is set forth in verses 50-54.

सत्त्वसङ्गादृपीन्देवान् रजसाऽसुरमानुषान् ।
तमसा भूततिर्यक्त्वं भ्रामितो याति कर्मभिः ॥५१॥

THE LAST MESSAGE OF SHRI KRISHNA 265

51. Swayed by his past works, a man[1] through his attachment to Sattva becomes a sage or a god, under the influence of Rajas an Asura or a man, and under the influence of Tamas a ghost or a beast.

[1] *Man etc.*—Because Sattva is characterised by purity or balance, Rajas by activity, and Tamas by dullness or inertia.

नृत्यतो गायतः पश्यन् यथैवानुकरोति तान् ।
एवं बुद्धिगुणान्पश्यन्ननीहोऽप्यनुकार्यते ॥५२॥

52. Just as a man watching a band of dancers or singers imitates[1] them, so the Âtman, even though without activity, is moved to imitate the attributes of the Buddhi (intellect).

[1] *Imitates*—spontaneously in his mind.

यथाम्भसा प्रचलता तरवोऽपि चला इव ।
चक्षुषा भ्राम्यमाणेन दृश्यते भ्रमतीव भूः ॥५३॥

53. As[1] trees reflected in moving water seem to be moving also, and as, when the eyes whirl, the land also seems to be whirling:

[1] *As etc.*—So the movements of the Prakriti are superimposed on the Âtman.

यथा मनोरथधियो विषयानुभवो मृषा ।
स्वप्नदृष्टाश्च दाशार्ह तथा संसार आत्मनः ॥५४॥

54. As imaginations and dream-perceptions are unreal, so also, O Uddhava, is the relative existence of sense-experience of the Âtman.

UDDHAVA GITA

अर्थे ह्यविद्यमानेऽपि संसृतिर्न निवर्तते ।
ध्यायतो विषयानस्य स्वप्नेऽनर्थागमो यथा ॥५५॥

55. Even though the sense-world is unreal, the relative existence of a man who dwells on sense-objects is never at an end, as troubles come in dreams.[1]

[1] *Dreams*—which, as everybody knows, are the effects of the impressions of the waking state.

तस्मादुद्धव मा भुङ्क्ष्व विषयानसदिन्द्रियैः ।
आत्माग्रहणनिर्भातं पश्य वैकल्पिकं भ्रमम् ॥५६॥

56. Therefore, O Uddhava, cease to experience the sense-objects through the outgoing organs. Look upon the delusion of plurality as caused by the non-perception of the Âtman.

क्षिप्तोऽवमानितोऽसद्भिः प्रलब्धोऽसूयितोऽथवा ।
ताडितः संनिबद्धो वा वृत्त्या वा परिहापितः ॥५७॥
निष्ठितो मूत्रितो वाज्ञैर्बहुधैवं प्रकम्पितः ।
श्रेयस्कामः कृच्छ्रगत आत्मनाऽऽत्मानमुद्धरेत् ॥५८॥

57-58. Even though scolded by the wicked, or insulted, ridiculed, calumniated, beaten, bound, robbed of his living, or spat upon, or otherwise abominably treated by the ignorant—being thus variously shaken[1] and placed in dire extremities, the man

THE LAST MESSAGE OF SHRI KRISHNA

who desires his well-being should deliver himself by
his own effort.[2]

[1] *Shaken*—from his faith in God.
[2] *Own effort*—through patience and discrimination.

उद्धव उवाच ।

यथैवमनुबुध्येयं वद नो वदतां वर ।
सुदुःसहमिमं मन्य आत्मन्यसदतिक्रमम् ॥५९॥
विदुषामपि विश्वात्मन् प्रकृतिर्हि बलीयसी ।
ऋते त्वद्धर्मनिरतान् शान्तांस्ते चरणालयान् ॥६०॥

Uddhava said:

59-60. O Best of Teachers, kindly instruct me
about this so that I may understand it. O Self of
the Universe, this insult to oneself by the wicked I
consider as most difficult to put up with even by the
learned, excepting those who practise the religion
taught by Thee, are equanimous, and have taken refuge at Thy feet, for nature[1] is too strong for men.

[1] *Nature*—the instinct to retaliate.

CHAPTER XVIII

बादरायणिरुवाच ।

स एवमाशंसित उद्धवेन
　　भागवतमुख्येन दाशार्हमुख्यः ।
सभाजयन्भृत्यवचो मुकुन्द-
　　स्तमाबभाषे श्रवणीयवीर्यः ॥१॥

Shuka said:

1. Being thus asked by the great devotee
Uddhava, Shri Krishna, the chief of the Dâshârhas—
whose mighty deeds are worth hearing—praised his
servant's question and spoke to him.

श्रीभगवानुवाच ।

बार्हस्पत्य स वै नात्र साधुर्वै दुर्जनेरितैः ।
दुरुक्तैर्भिन्नमात्मानं यः समाधातुमीश्वरः ॥२॥

The Lord said:

2. O disciple of Brihaspati, there is not in the
world a sage who can control his mind when it has
been pierced by harsh words hurled by the wicked.

न तथा तप्यते विद्धः पुमान्बाणैः सुमर्मगैः ।
यथा तुदन्ति मर्मस्था ह्यसतां परुषेषवः ॥३॥

THE LAST MESSAGE OF SHRI KRISHNA

3. Arrows penetrating the most vital parts of a man do not so wound him as do the harsh words of the wicked which rankle in the bosom for ever.

कथयन्ति महत्पुण्यमितिहासमिहोद्भव ।
तमहं वर्णयिष्यामि निबोध सुसमाहितः ॥४॥
केनचिद्भिक्षुणा गीतं परिभूतेन दुर्जनैः ।
स्मरता धृतियुक्तन विपाकं निजकर्मणाम् ॥५॥

4-5. O Uddhava, there is a fine story on this subject which is full of spiritual significance. I am narrating it to you. Listen to it with all attention. It was recited by a mendicant who was maltreated by the wicked, but who bore it with patience, considering it as but the effect of his own past deeds.

अवन्तिषु द्विजः कश्चिदासीदाढ्यतमः श्रिया ।
वार्तावृत्तिः कदर्यस्तु कामी लुब्धोऽतिकोपनः ॥६॥

6. There lived in Avanti a Brâhmana who was immensely rich, but who led a miserable life, doing business, and was greedy, avaricious, and exceedingly irritable.

ज्ञातयोऽतिथयस्तस्य वाङ्मात्रेणापि नार्चिताः ।
शून्यावसथ आत्मापि काले कामैरनर्चितः ॥७॥

7. He never greeted his relatives or guests with kind words even, and living in that God-forsaken

house, he never gave even his own body occasional comforts.

दुःशीलस्य कदर्यस्य द्रुह्यन्ते पुत्रबान्धवाः ।
दारा दुहितरो भृत्या विषण्णा नाचरन्प्रियम् ॥८॥

8. As he led such an impious and despicable life, his sons and relatives did not like him; and his wife, daughters, and servants were sad and did not act up to his wishes.

तस्यैवं यक्षवित्तस्य च्युतस्योभयलोकतः ।
धर्मकामविहीनस्य चुक्रुधुः पञ्चभागिनः ॥९॥

9. As he took pleasure only in hoarding money, and never cared for the acquisition of virtue or the legitimate satisfaction of desires, he lost both this life and the next, and the five sharers[1] of his wealth were wroth.

[1] *Five sharers etc.*—viz. the gods, the seers, the manes, men, and animals, who are entitled to daily offerings from a householder.

तदवध्यानविस्रस्तपुण्यस्कन्धस्य भूरिद ।
अर्थोऽप्यगच्छन्निधनं बह्वायासपरिश्रमः ॥१०॥

10. O generous one, through his disregard of them, his stock of merits[1] was exhausted; and that wealth, too, which he was at such pains to accumulate, vanished.

[1] *Merits*—that portion which had contributed to wealth.

THE LAST MESSAGE OF SHRI KRISHNA 271

ज्ञातयो जगृहुः किंचित्किंचिद्दस्यव उद्धव ।
दैवतः कालतः किंचिद् ब्रह्मबन्धोर्नृपार्थिवात् ॥११॥

11. O Uddhava, some of that wretched Brâhmana's wealth was taken by his relatives and some by robbers; some part was destroyed by accident or worn out through the lapse of time; and some of it was taken by men or kings.

स एवं द्रविणे नष्टे धर्मकामविवर्जितः ।
उपेक्षितश्च स्वजनैश्चिन्तामाप दुरत्ययाम् ॥१२॥

12. When his wealth was thus gone and he was ignored by his own people, he was exceedingly anxious about his future, for he had neglected the acquisition of virtue or the legitimate satisfaction of desires.

तस्यैवं ध्यायतो दीर्घं नष्टरायस्तपस्विनः ।
खिद्यतो बाष्पकण्ठस्य निर्वेदः सुमहानभूत् ॥१३॥

13. He was a penniless man now, in dire extremities; and as he was thus reflecting long on his condition, his voice choked with repentence, and he was seized with a tremendous disgust for the world.

स चाहेदमहो कष्टं वृथाऽऽत्मा मेऽनुतापितः ।
न धर्माय न कामाय यस्यार्थायास ईदृशः ॥१४॥

14. And he said to himself: Woe, alas, unto me! I have for nothing tormented the body in this

UDDHAVA GITA

mad quest for riches, neglecting the acquisition of
virtue and the legitimate satisfaction of desires.

प्रायेणार्थाः कदर्याणां न सुखाय कदाचन ।
इह चात्मोपतापाय मृतस्य नरकाय च ॥१५॥

15. Riches seldom bring happiness to the despicable man. They only cause the mortification of
his body while he is alive, and pave the way for hell[1]
after he is dead.

[1] *Hell*—because of the misuse of wealth.

यशो यशस्विनां शुद्धं श्लाघ्या ये गुणिनां गुणाः ।
लोभः स्वल्पोऽपि तान्हन्ति श्वित्रो रूपमिवेप्सितम् ॥१६॥

16. Even a modicum of greed is enough to destroy the untarnished reputation of a renowned man,
and the most praiseworthy attributes of a virtuous
man, as leucoderma spoils the most graceful
features.

अर्थस्य साधने सिद्धे उत्कर्षे रक्षणे व्यये ।
नाशोपभोग आयासस्त्रासश्चिन्ता भ्रमो नृणाम् ॥१७॥

17. Whether in the acquisition of wealth, or,
after it has been acquired, in the increase, maintenance, expenditure, enjoyment, or loss of it, men
undergo exertion,[1] fear, anxiety, and delusion.

[1] *Exertion etc.*—as the case may be.

THE LAST MESSAGE OF SHRI KRISHNA 273

स्तेयं हिंसाऽनृतं दम्भः कामः क्रोधः स्मयो मदः ।
भेदो वैरमविश्वासः संस्पर्धा व्यसनानि च ॥१८॥
एते पञ्चदशानर्था ह्यर्थमूला मता नृणाम् ।
तस्मादनर्थमर्थाख्यं श्रेयोऽर्थी दूरतस्त्यजेत् ॥१९॥

18-19. Theft, injury to others, falsehood, ostentation, lust, anger, pride, haughtiness, dissension, enmity, distrust, competition, and the three kinds[1] of indulgence—these fifteen evils pertaining to men are considered to be the outcome of wealth. Therefore one desirous of well-being should shun from a distance the evil known as wealth.

The evil effects of riches are set forth in verses 18-21.
[1] *Three kinds etc.*—viz. those relating to sex, wine, and gambling.

भिद्यन्ते भ्रातरो दाराः पितरः सुहृदस्तथा ।
एकाक्ष्णिग्धाः काकिणिना सद्यः सर्वेऽरय कृताः ॥२०॥

20. Brothers, wives, fathers, and friends, who were very near and dear to the heart, are all instantly alienated and turned into foes by even an insignificant sum of money.

अर्थेनाल्पीयसा ह्येते संरब्धा दीप्तमन्यवः ।
त्यजन्त्याशु स्पृधो घ्नन्ति सहसोत्सृज्य सौहृदम् ॥२१॥

21. Even the least amount of money upsets them and inflames their anger, so that they immediately

18

part company, and all at once abandoning cordiality they rival and even kill one another.

लब्ध्वा जन्मामरप्रार्थ्यं मानुष्यं तद्द्विजाग्रयताम् ।
तदनाद्रत्य ये स्वार्थं घ्नन्ति यान्त्यशुभां गतिम् ॥२२॥

22. Attaining a human birth which even the gods covet, and being good Brâhmanas at that, those who disregard this and mar their own interests,[1] meet with an evil end.

[1] *Interests*—viz. Self-realisation.

स्वर्गापवर्गयोर्द्वारं प्राप्य लोकमिमं पुमान् ।
द्रविणे कोऽनूषज्जेत मर्त्योंऽनर्थस्य धामनि ॥२३॥

23. What mortal man would, after attaining this body which is the gateway to heaven and liberation, get attached to money which is the abode of evil?

देवर्षिपितृभूतानि ज्ञातीन्बन्धूंश्च भागिनः ।
असंविभज्य चात्मानं यक्षवित्तः पतत्यधः ॥२४॥

24. The miser who hoards money like the proverbial Yaksha,[1] without sharing it with the gods,[2] the Rishis, the manes, lower animals, relatives,[3] friends, and other legitimate sharers in it as well as himself, goes to degradation.

[1] *Yaksha*—a species of superhuman beings possessing immense wealth which they simply keep hidden without using it for themselves or others.

THE LAST MESSAGE OF SHRI KRISHNA   275

[2] *Gods etc.*—The reference is to the Panchayajna or the fivefold sacrifice which every householder is required to perform. See note on verse 9.

[3] *Relatives etc.*—coming under the head of 'man' in the list.

व्यर्थयाऽर्थेहया वित्तं प्रमत्तस्य वयो बलम् ।
कुशला येन सिध्यन्ति जरठः किं नु साधये ॥२५॥

25. Oh, I was deluded by a fruitless search for wealth, which has now gone, along with my age and strength. Well, what could a decrepit man like me achieve through that which helps men of discrimination alone to attain the goal?

कस्मात्संक्लिश्यते विद्वान् व्यर्थयाऽर्थेहयाऽसकृत् ।
कस्यचिन्मायया नूनं लोकोऽयं सुविमोहितः ॥२६॥

26. Why are even learned men tormented time and again by the vain quest for wealth? Surely this world is utterly deluded by Somebody's inscrutable Power.

किं धनैर्धनदैर्वा किं कामैर्वा कामदैरुत ।
मृत्युना ग्रस्यमानस्य कर्मभिर्वोत जन्मदैः ॥२७॥

27. What can a man in the jaws of death want with wealth or the bestower of wealth, with desires or those who fulfil those desires, or with works[1] which but lead to rebirth?

[1] *Works*—such as the Agnihotra which being done with selfish motives never confer liberation.

UDDHAVA GITA

नूनं मे भगवांस्तुष्टः सर्वदेवमयो हरिः ।
येन नीतो दशामेतां निर्वेदश्चात्मनः प्रुवः ॥२८॥

28. Surely the Lord Hari, who is the embodiment of all the gods, is pleased with me, for He has brought me to such a crisis, in which I have got that world-weariness which is a raft[1] for the struggling soul.

[1] *Raft*—to cross the ocean of transmigration.

सोऽहं कालावशेषेण शोषयिष्येऽङ्गमात्मनः ।
अप्रमत्तोऽखिलस्वार्थे यदि स्यात्सिद्ध आत्मनि ॥२९॥

29. So during the remainder of my life—if at all there is any left—I shall mortify the body, satisfied with the Self alone and attending to all that conduces to well-being.

तत्र मामनुमोदेरन् देवास्त्रिभुवनेश्वराः ।
मुहूर्तेन ब्रह्मलोकं खट्वाङ्गः समसाधयत् ॥३०॥

30. May the gods who rule the three worlds bless me in this! Well, Khatvānga[1] attained to the sphere of the Lord in about forty-eight minutes.[2]

[1] *Khatvânga*—was a king, who, coming to know through the kindness of the gods that only about 48 minutes of his life were left, devoted himself whole-heartedly to the meditation of God and in that short time attained realisation.

[2] A Muhurta, being one-fifteenth of a day or night, varies in length daily.

THE LAST MESSAGE OF SHRI KRISHNA 277

श्रीभगवानुवाच ।

इत्यभिप्रेत्य मनसा ह्यावन्त्यो द्विजसत्तमः ।
उन्मुच्य हृदयग्रन्थीन् शान्तो भिक्षुरभून्मुनिः ॥३१॥

The Lord said:

31. Thus resolved in his mind, the good Brâhmana of Avanti succeeded in removing the knots[1] of his heart and become a Sannyâsin, calm and silent.

[1] *Knots etc.*—viz. egoism which superimposes the universe on the Âtman. The ego has been aptly called the "knot between Pure Intelligence and matter".

स चचार महीमेतां संयतात्मेन्द्रियानिलः ।
भिक्षार्थं नगरग्रामानसङ्गोऽलक्षितोऽविशत् ॥३२॥

32. With his mind, organs, and Prânas under control, he wandered over the earth alone, entering towns and villages only to beg his food, and none knew who he was.

तं वै प्रवयसं भिक्षुमवधूतमसज्जनाः ।
दृष्ट्वा पर्यभवन्भद्र बह्वीभिः परिभूतिभिः ॥३३॥

33. Seeing that aged shabby-looking monk, the wicked people, My friend, insulted him with various indignities.

केचित्त्रिवेणुं जगृहुरेके पात्रं कमण्डलुम् ।
पीठं चैकेऽक्षसूत्रं च कन्थां चीराणि केचन ॥३४॥

34. Some took his triple staff and some his begging-bowl and water-pot; some took his seat and rosary of Rudrâksha beads and some his tattered clothes and wrapper.

प्रदाय च पुनस्तानि दर्शितान्यादददुर्मुनेः ।
अन्नं च भैक्ष्यसंपन्नं भुंजानस्य सरित्तटे ॥३५॥
मूत्रयन्ति च पापिष्ठाः ष्ठीवन्त्यस्य च मूर्धनि ।
यतवाचं वाचयन्ति ताडयन्ति न वक्ति चेत् ॥३६॥

35-36. Then, showing them to him they returned those things, but again snatched them from the silent monk. When he was eating on a river-side the food he had collected by begging, the rascals defiled it abominably and spat on his head. He was observing silence, but they made him speak, and threatened him if he did not do so.

तर्जयन्त्यपरे वाग्भिः स्तेनोऽयमिति वादिनः ।
बध्नन्ति रज्ज्वा तं केचिद् बध्यतां बध्यतामिति ॥३७॥

37. Others rated him with harsh words, saying, "This man is a thief." Some bound him with a rope, and some said, "Bind him! Bind him!"

क्षिपन्त्येकेऽवजानन्त एष धर्मध्वजः शठः ।
क्षीणवित्त इमां वृत्तिमग्रहीत्स्वजनोज्झितः ॥३८॥

38. Some taunted him insultingly, saying, "He is a sharper who has put on a mask of religion.

THE LAST MESSAGE OF SHRI KRISHNA

Having lost his wealth and being discarded by his kinsmen, he has taken to this profession."

अहो एष महासारो धृतिमान्गिरिराडिव ।
मौनेन साधयत्यर्थं बकवद् ढनिश्चयः ॥३६॥

39. "Oh, he is exceptionally strong, and as steady as the Himalayas! He is firm in resolution like a heron[1] and seeks to gain his object by observing silence!"

[1] *Like a heron*—Just as a heron waits silently on the margin of a lake to catch the unwary fish.

इत्येके विहसन्त्येनमेके दुर्वातयन्ति च ।
तं बबन्धुर्निरुरुधुर्यथा क्रीडनकं द्विजम् ॥४०॥

40. Thus did some ridicule him. Others treated him shamefully, and some bound and confined him as they do a plaything such as a bird.

एवं स भौतिकं दुःखं दैविकं दैहिकं च यत् ।
भोक्तव्यमात्मनो दिष्टं प्राप्तं प्राप्तमबुध्यत ॥४१॥

41. Thus whatever troubles befell him—whether[1] they sprang from the animal kingdom, natural phenomena, or bodily ailments—he thought they were predestined and therefore must be silently borne.

[1] *Whether etc.*—These are the three usual divisions of human ills.

280 UDDHAVA GITA

परिभूत इमां गाथामगायत नराधमैः ।
पातयद्भिः स्वधर्मस्थो धृतिमास्थाय सात्त्विकीम् ॥४२॥

42. Even though insulted by rascals who sought
to lead him astray, he clung to his path of duty by
practising the pure form[1] of steadiness, and sang this
song:

[1] *Pure form etc.*—Vide Gîtâ XVIII. 33.

द्विज उवाच ।
नायं जनो मे सुखदुःखहेतु-
र्न देवतात्मा ग्रहकर्मकालाः ।
मनः परं कारणमामनन्ति
संसारचक्रं परिवर्तयेद्यत् ॥४३॥

The Brâhmana said:

43. Neither[1] is this body[2] the cause of my
pleasure or pain, nor the Âtman, nor the gods, nor
the planets, nor work, nor Time. The only cause of
pleasure and pain, the Shrutis[3] declare, is the mind,
which sets in motion[4] this cycle of transmigration.

[1] *Neither etc.*—All these items will be taken up one
by one in verses 51-56.

[2] *Body*—From the derivative meaning of the word,
"that which is produced". So also in verses 51 and 54.

[3] *Shrutis*—e.g. Brihadâranyaka III. ix. 20.—"Through the
mind alone one sees, through the mind one hears," etc.

[4] *Sets in motion etc.*—The next verses explains how.

THE LAST MESSAGE OF SHRI KRISHNA 281

मनो गुणान्वै सृजते बलीय-
　स्ततश्च कर्माणि विलक्षणानि ।
शुक्लानि कृष्णान्यथ लोहितानि
　तेभ्यः सवर्णाः सृतयो भवन्ति ॥४४॥

44. It is the formidable mind which creates desire[1] and the like; thence proceed varieties of work such as Sâttvika, Râjasika, and Tâmasika; and these lead to births of a type[2] which is in accordance with them.

　[1] *Desire etc.*—for sense-objects.
　[2] *Type etc.*—Good works producing angelic bodies, bad works animal (or still worse) bodies, and mixed works human bodies.

अनीह आत्मा मनसा समीहता
　हिरण्मयो मत्सख उद्विचष्टे ।
मनः स्वलिङ्गं परिगृह्य कामा-
　न्जुषन्निबद्धो गुणसङ्गतोऽसौ ॥४५॥

45. The inactive, resplendent[1] Self, the Friend[2] of the Jiva, looks on[3] from above while the mind works. The Jiva, however, identifying itself with the mind—which presents the world to it—is connected with works, which belong to the mind, and in the act of enjoying sense-objects comes to be bound.

　The idea is this: The real Self never transmigrates. It is Existence-Knowledge-Bliss Absolute. It is only the apparent self, the Jiva, which through nescience connects itself with the mind and goes from one body to another.

282 UDDHAVA GITA

[1] *Resplendent*—Because It is Knowledge Absolute.
[2] *Friend etc.*—Because the two are identical.
[3] *Looks on etc.*—as mere Witness, without being attached.

दानं स्वधर्मो नियमो यमश्च
श्रुतं च कर्माणि च सद्व्रतानि ।
सर्वे मनोनिग्रहलक्षणान्ताः
परो हि योगो मनसः समाधिः ॥४६॥

46. Charity, the performance of one's duty, the observance of vows, general and particular, the hearing of the scriptures, meritorious acts, and all other works—all these culminate in the control of the mind. The control of the mind is the highest Yoga.

So one must control the mind first—this is the purpose of verses 46 and 47.

समाहितं यस्य मनः प्रशान्तं
दानादिभिः किं वद तस्य कृत्यम् ।
असंयतं यस्य मनो विनश्य-
ज्ञानादिभिश्चेदपरं किमेभिः ॥४७॥

47. Say of what use are charity[1] and the rest to one whose mind is controlled and pacified? Of what use, again, are this charity and the rest to one whose mind is restless or lapsing into dullness?

[1] *Charity etc.*—referred to in the previous verse.

THE LAST MESSAGE OF SHRI KRISHNA 283

मनोवशेऽन्ये ह्यभवंसम देवा
मनश्च नान्यस्य वशं समेति ।
भीष्मो हि देवः सहसः सहीया-
न्युञ्ज्याद्दशे तं स हि देवदेवः ॥४८॥

48. The other gods[1] are under the sway of the mind, but the mind never comes under the sway of any one else. This is a terrible[2] god, stronger than the strongest, and he is the God of gods[3] who can control the mind.

[1] *Gods*—may also mean the organs (Indriyas). So also in verse 52.

[2] *Terrible*—even to the Yogis.

[3] *God of gods*—The phrase may also mean "the master of all the organs".

तं दुर्जेयं शत्रुमसह्यवेग-
मरुन्तुदं तन्न विजित्य केचित् ।
कुर्वन्त्यसद्विग्रहमत्र मर्त्यैं-
र्मिन्राण्युदासीनरिपून्विमूढाः ॥४९॥

49. There are some foolish people who, without conquering that invincible foe, whose onset is unbearable and who pierces the very vitals of a man, are for that very reason[1] engaged in vain quarrels with mortals here, and (in the course of it) convert others into friends, or neutrals, or enemies.

[1] *For that very reason*—Because they have not controlled the mind.

UDDHAVA GITA

देहं मनोमात्रमिमं गृहीत्वा
ममाहमित्यन्धधियो मनुष्याः ।
एषोऽहमन्योऽयमिति भ्रमेण
दुरन्तपारे तमसि भ्रमन्ति ॥५०॥

50. Foolish men, coming to look upon the body, which is but a phantasm of the mind, as "I am mine",[1] and thinking erroneously, "Here am I, but this other man is different", wander in a limitless wilderness of ignorance.

[1] *I and mine*—applied respectively to their own bodies and those of their near and dear ones.

जनस्तु हेतुः सुखःदुःखयोश्चे-
त्किमात्मनश्चात्र ह भौमयोस्तत् ।
जिह्वां कचित्संदशति स्वदद्भि-
स्तद्वेदनायां कतमाय कुप्येत् ॥५१॥

51. If the body be the cause of pleasure and pain, the Âtman has nothing[1] to do with it, for it all concerns the gross and subtle bodies, which are material in their nature. If one[2] chances to bite one's tongue with one's own teeth, whom should one be angry with for causing that pain?

Verses 51-56 elaborate the idea of verse 43.
[1] Has *nothing etc.*—Neither causes nor experiences pleasure and pain.
[2] *If one etc.*—The point of the illustration is this: Supposing that the pain caused by another did affect the

THE LAST MESSAGE OF SHRI KRISHNA

Âtman, still there is no ground for anger, for the same Âtman is present in all. The two bodies are virtually one body.

दुःखस्य हेतुर्यदि देवतास्तु
किमात्मनस्तत्र विकारयोस्तत् ।
यदङ्गमङ्गेन निहन्यते कचि-
त्कुध्येत कस्मै पुरुषः स्वदेहे ॥५२॥

52. If the gods be the cause of pain, the Âtman has nothing to do with it, for it concerns the two gods which alone are affected by it. If one[1] limb of a person be struck by another limb, with whom should he be angry in his own body?

[1] *If one etc.*—Suppose the hand strikes the mouth, or the mouth bites the hand, then it is the respective presiding deities, viz. Fire and Indra, who, being finite, are concerned in it. And if this happens between two bodies, instead of one, then also the situation is unaltered, for the presiding deity of each organ is the same in all bodies. The Âtman in any case is unaffected.

आत्मा यदि स्यात्सुखदुःखहेतुः
किमन्यतस्तत्र निजस्वभावः ।
न ह्यात्मनोऽन्यद्यदि तन्मृषा स्यात्-
कुध्येत कस्मान्न सुखं न दुःखम् ॥५३॥

53. If the Âtman[1] be the cause of pleasure and pain, nothing in that case happens through any extraneous agency; that pleasure and pain are of the essence of itself, for there is nothing[2] other than the Âtman; if there be, it must be a fiction.[3] So whom

286　UDDHAVA GITA

should one be angry with? There is neither[4] pleasure nor pain.

[1] *Âtman*—in its individual aspect as Jiva, that is.

[2] *Nothing etc.*—as is borne out by numerous Shruti texts.

[3] *Fiction*—being superimposed by nescience.

[4] *Neither etc.*—Only the Âtman exists.

ग्रहा निमित्तं सुखदुःखयोश्चे -
त्किमात्मनोऽजस्य जनस्य ते वै।
ग्रहैर्ग्रहस्यैव वदन्ति पीडां
क्रुध्येत कस्मै पुरुषस्ततोऽन्यः ॥५४॥

54. If the planets be the cause of pleasure and pain, the birthless Âtman has nothing to do with it, for the planets influence the body only. Besides, one planet is said to influence adversely another planet. And the Âtman[1] is different from either the planet or the body. So whom should one be angry with?

[1] *Âtman etc.*—It is only due to his mistaken identification with the body, born under a particular constellation, that a man comes under planetary influence. In reality he is the ever-free Âtman.

कर्मास्तु हेतुः सुखदुःखयोश्चे -
त्किमात्मनस्तद्धि जडाजडत्वे।
देहस्त्वचित्पुरुषोऽयं सुपर्णः
क्रुध्येत कस्मै नहि कर्ममूलम् ॥५५॥

THE LAST MESSAGE OF SHRI KRISHNA
287

55. If indeed work[1] be the cause of pleasure and pain, how does it affect the Âtman, for work is possible to an agency which is both sentient[2] and insentient?[3] But the body is insentient, and the Âtman is Pure Intelligence. So there is no such thing as work, the (alleged) root of pleasure and pain. Then whom should one be angry with?

[1] *Work etc.*—as the Mimâmsakas hold.

[2] *Sentient*—Because without intelligence purposive activity is impossible.

[3] *Insentient*—Because only matter, and not Spirit, is subject to change.

कालस्तु हेतुः सुखदुःखयोश्चे-
त्किमात्मनस्तत्र तदात्मकोऽसौ ।
नाग्नेर्हि तापो न हिमस्य तत्स्या-
त्क्व् ध्येत कस्मै न परस्य द्वन्द्वम् ॥५६॥

56. If Time be the cause of pleasure and pain, how does it affect the Âtman, for It is one[1] with Time? Surely[2] a flame is not adversely affected by fire, nor a hailstone by cold. The Supreme Self is never affected by the pairs of opposites.[3] So whom should one be angry with?

[1] *One etc.*—Because Time is identified with Brahman.

[2] *Surely etc.*—Things which are of the same essence never harm one another.

[3] *Pairs of opposites*—such as pleasure and pain, etc.

UDDHAVA GITA

288

न केनचित्कापि कथंचनास्य
द्वन्द्वोपरागः परतः परस्य ।
यथाहमः संसृतिरूपिणः स्या-
देवं प्रबुद्धो न बिभेति भूतैः ॥५७॥

57. This Âtman, which is beyond Prakriti,[1] is nowhere subjected in any way to the pairs of opposites by anything, as is the case with the ego,[2] which conjures up the relative existence. The illumined man is never afraid of the material world.

[1] *Prakriti*—which alone, as the primal state of the universe, is subject to modifications.

[2] *Ego etc.*—Vide verse 31.

एतां स आस्थाय परात्मनिष्ठा-
मध्यासिता पूर्वतमैर्महर्षिभिः ।
अहं तरिष्यामि दुरन्तपारं
तमो मुकुन्दांघ्रिनिषेवयैव ॥५८॥

58. So I shall practise this devotion to the Supreme Self which the great sages of old had recourse to, and only worshipping the feet of the Lord, I shall cross the limitless wilderness of ignorance.

श्रीभगवानुवाच ।
निर्विद्य नष्टद्रविणो गतक्लमः
प्रव्रज्य गां पर्यटमान इत्थम् ।
निराकृतोऽसद्भिरपि स्वधर्मा-
दकम्पितोऽमुं मुनिराह गाथाम् ॥५९॥

THE LAST MESSAGE OF SHRI KRISHNA 289

The Lord said:

59. This was the song sung by that sage who, having lost his wealth and getting disgusted with the world, wandered over the earth as a monk, free from anxiety, and who, though insulted thus by the wicked, remained unshaken in his path of duty.

सुखदुःखप्रदो नान्यः पुरुषस्यात्मविभ्रमः ।
मित्रोदासीनरिपवः संसारस्तमसः कृतः ॥६०॥

60. The world, consisting of friends, neutrals, and foes, which affects a man with pleasure and pain, is a phantasm of his mind owing to ignorance and nothing but that.

तस्मात्सर्वात्मना तात निगृहाण मनो धिया ।
मय्यावेशितया युक्त एतावान्योगसंग्रहः ॥६१॥

61. Therefore, My friend, possessed of an intellect wholly attached to Me, control the mind perfectly. This is the very gist of Yoga.

य एतां भिक्षुणा गीतां ब्रह्मनिष्ठां समाहितः ।
धारयन्श्रावयन्श्रृण्वन्द्वन्द्वैर्नैवाभिभूयते ॥६२॥

62. He who listens to, understands and recites before others this song of steadfastness in Brahman, as sung by the Sannyâsin, is no more overcome by the pairs of opposites.

CHAPTER XIX

श्रीभगवानुवाच ।

अथ ते संप्रवक्ष्यामि सांख्यं पूर्वं विनिश्चितम् ।
यद्विज्ञाय पुमान्सद्यो जह्याद्वैकल्पिकं भ्रमम् ॥१॥

The Lord said:

1. Now I shall tell you about the Sânkhya system propounded by the ancients,[1] knowing which a man can immediately give up the error caused by the seeing of multiplicity.

[1] *Ancients*—Kapila and others.

आसीज्ज्ञानमथो ह्यर्थ एकमेवाविकल्पितम् ।
यदा विवेकनिपुणा आदौ कृतयुगेऽयुगे ॥२॥

2. Before[1] the origin of the Yugas, the knower and the entire objective universe were verily one[2] and homogeneous. The same was the case in the Satya Yuga, at the beginning of the cycle, when people were skilled in discrimination.[3]

[1] *Before etc.*—i. e. at the state of Pralaya or cosmic involution.

[2] *One etc.*—There was no division of subject and object. Only Brahman was—the One without a second.

[3] *Discrimination*—which obliterates duality.

तन्मायाफलरूपेण केवलं निर्विकल्पितम् ।
वाङ्मनोऽगोचरं सत्यं द्विधा समभवद्बृहत् ॥३॥

THE LAST MESSAGE OF SHRI KRISHNA   291

3. That absolute and homogeneous Reality, the Brahman, which transcends mind and speech, became split into two—the objective world and the thinking subject.

तयोरेकतरो ह्यर्थः प्रकृतिः सोभयात्मिका ।
ज्ञानं त्वन्यतरो भावः पुरुषः सोऽभिधीयते ॥४॥

4. Of these two things one is Prakriti, which has a dual nature,[1] and the other Knowledge Absolute, which is called Purusha.

[1] *Dual nature*—as cause and effect—e.g. Mahat is a cause, and the ether etc., are effects.

तमो रजः सत्त्वमिति प्रकृतेरभवन्गुणाः ।
मया प्रक्षोभ्यमाणायाः पुरुषानुमतेन च ॥५॥

5. From the Prakriti as I agitated it, there emanated the Gunas,[1] Sattva, Rajas, and Tamas, with the approval[2] of the Purusha.

[1] *Gunas etc.*—tendencies to illumination, activity, and dullness, respectively.

[2] *Approval etc.*—Since creation takes place according to the past Karma of the Jivas.

तेभ्यः समभवत्सूत्रं महान्सूत्रेण संयुतः ।
ततो विकुर्वतो जातो योऽहंकारो विमोहनः ॥६॥

6. From them emanated the Sutra, with which the Mahat is united.[1] From the transformation of that was produced egoism, which deludes[2] all.

UDDHAVA GITA

[1] *With which etc.*—Though Sutra is characterised by activity and Mahat by intelligence, yet they are but aspects of one principle. This is what is meant.

[2] *Deludes etc.*—causing them to see difference.

वैकारिकस्तैजसश्च तामसश्चेत्यहं त्रिवृत् ।
तन्मात्रेन्द्रियमनसां कारणं चिदचिन्मयः ॥७॥

7. Egoism is threefold—Sâttvika, Râjasa, and Tâmasa, which are respectively the cause of the mind, the organs, and the fine particles of matter. It is both sentient[1] and insentient.

[1] *Sentient*—because of the reflection of the Âtman. It thus serves as a nexus between the Âtman, which is Pure Intelligence, and matter.

अर्थस्तन्मात्रिकाज्ज्ञे तामसादिन्द्रियाणि च ।
तैजसादे्वता आसन्नेकादश च वैकृतात् ॥८॥

8. From the Tâmasa aspect of egoism there emanated the five elements; from the Râjasa aspect the organs; and from the Sâttvika aspect the eleven gods[1] and the mind.[2]

[1] *Eleven gods*—viz the god representing the quarters, Vâyu (Wind), the sun, Varuna, the two Ashvins, Agni (Fire), Indra, Vishnu, Mitra, and the moon.

[2] *Mind*—This is suggested by the particle *cha* in the text.

मया संचोदिता भावाः सर्वे संहत्यकारिणः ।
अण्डमुत्पादयामासुर्ममायतनमुत्तमम् ॥६॥

THE LAST MESSAGE OF SHRI KRISHNA 293

9. Directed by me, all these things, acting together, made up an oval structure which was an excellent abode for Me.[1]

[1] *Me*—as the Indwelling Ruler of the Universe.

तस्मिन्नहं समभवमण्डे सलिलसंस्थितौ ।
मम नाभ्यामभूत्पद्मं विश्वाख्यं तत्र चात्मभूः ॥१०॥

10. In that oval structure floating in water I dwelt. From My navel grew a lotus epitomising the world, and there the self-born Brahmâ manifested himself.

सोऽसृजत्तपसा युक्तो रजसा मदनुग्रहात् ।
लोकान्सपालान्विश्वात्मा भूर्भुवःस्वरिति त्रिधा ॥११॥

11. With My grace he, the Universal Soul, endowed with activity, projected through hard reflection the three spheres, Bhur,[1] Bhuvar, and Svar,[2] together with their rulers.

[1] *Bhur*—including the seven nether spheres, Atala and so on.
[2] *Svar*—including the four higher spheres, Mahar and the rest.

देवानामोक आसीत्स्वर्भूतानां च भुवः पदम् ।
मर्त्यादीनां च भूर्लोकः सिद्धानां त्रितयात्परम् ॥१२॥

12. The Svar became the abode of the gods; the Bhuvar that of the spirits; the earth that of men; and the spheres beyond the Svar the abode of the Siddhas.[1]

[1] *Siddhas*—Highly advanced souls with extraordinary powers.

अधोऽसुराणां नागानां भूमेरोकोऽसृजत्प्रभुः ।
त्रिलोक्यां गतयः सर्वाः कर्मणां त्रिगुणात्मनाम् ॥१३॥

13. The Lord Brahmâ made the regions below the earth the abode of the Asuras and Nâgas. Works characterised by the three Gunas[1] lead to the three spheres.[2]

[1] *Gunas*—Sattva etc.
[2] *Three spheres*—viz Bhur, Bhuvar, Svar.

योगस्य तपसश्चैव न्यासस्य गतयोऽमलाः ।
महर्जनस्तपः सत्यं भक्तियोगस्य मद्गतिः ॥१४॥

14. Yoga, asceticism, and renunciation lead to the pure spheres of Mahar, Jana, Tapas, and Satya, but Bhakti-Yoga leads to My abode.[1]

[1] *My abode*—Vaikuntha.

मया कालात्मना धात्रा कर्मयुक्तमिदं जगत् ।
गुणप्रवाह एतस्मिन्नुन्मज्जति निमज्जति ॥१५॥

15. Owing to Me who am Time and the Ordainer of everything, this world with diverse Karma[1] rises[2] and sinks[3] in this stream[4] of the Gunas.

[1] *Karma*—the resultant of one's entire past work.
[2] *Rises*—up to the Brahmaloka.
[3] *Sinks*—down to vegetable existence.
[4] *Stream etc.*—i.e. relative existence.

THE LAST MESSAGE OF SHRI KRISHNA

295

अणुबृहत्कृशः स्थूलो यो यो भावः प्रसिध्यति ।
सर्वोऽप्युभयसंयुक्तः प्रकृत्या पुरुषेण च ॥१६॥

16. Whatever things come into being—minute
or vast, thin or stout—all partake of the two principles, Purusha and Prakriti.

यस्तु यस्यादिरन्तश्च स वै मध्यं च तस्य सन् ।
विकारो व्यवहारार्थो यथा तैजसपार्थिवाः ॥१७॥

17. That from which a thing originates and into
which it dissolves, abides also in the intermediate
stage. That[1] alone is real. The modifications have
a mere phenomenal existence, as in the case of metallic
and earthen wares.

[1] *That etc.*—The effect is but the cause in another
form. A gold ring is nothing but gold, an earthen jar nothing
but earth. The passage is an echo of the Chhândogya
Upanishad VI. i. 4-6.

यदुपादाय पूर्वस्तु भावो विकुरुतेऽपरम् ।
आदिरन्तो यदा यस्य तत्सत्यमभिधीयते ॥१८॥

18. That, using which as material[1] an antecedent
state[2] produces a consequent one,[3] is alone the reality.
A state from which another state originates and into
which it is dissolved, is also relatively called[4] real.[5]

[1] *That etc.*—e.g. earth.
[2] *Antecedent state*—e.g. that of an amorphous lump.
[3] *Consequent one*—e.g. that of a jar.
[4] *Called*—by the Shruti.

296 UDDHAVA GITA

[5] *Real*—with reference to the consequent state. So each of the intermediate links in a causal chain is only *relatively* real, the First Cause or Brahman being alone real in the absolute sense.

प्रकृतिर्ह्यस्योपादानमाधारः पुरुषः परः ।
सतोऽभिव्यञ्जकः कालो ब्रह्म तत्त्रितयं त्वहम् ॥१९॥

19. Prakriti which is the material cause of this manifested universe, Purusha which is its substratum,[1] and Time which is a factor in its manifestation—all these three[2] verily am I, the Brahman.

[1] *Substratum*—the efficient cause.
[2] *These three etc.*—The first is but Its energy, and the last two Its states.

सर्गः प्रवर्तते तावत्पौर्वापर्येण नित्यशः ।
महान्गुणविसर्गार्थः स्थित्यन्तो यावदीक्षणम् ॥२०॥

20. Projection[1] in its varied forms goes on for the experience of the soul, through an unbroken succession[2] of causes and effects, until the term of continuance of the world is over, according to the will of the Lord.

[1] *Projection*—the more correct word for "creation".
[2] *Succession etc.*—e.g. from father to son.

विराण्मयाऽऽसाद्यमानो लोककल्पविकल्पकः ।
पञ्चत्वाय विशेषाय कल्पते भुवनैः सह ॥२१॥

THE LAST MESSAGE OF SHRI KRISHNA

21. Then the universe which, pervaded by Me,[1] is the scene of the births and deaths of multifarious creatures, is, together with the spheres, ready for the state called dissolution.

[1] *Me*—as Time.

अन्ने प्रलीयते मर्त्यमन्नं धानासु लीयते ।
धाना भूमौ प्रलीयन्ते भूमिर्गन्धे प्रलीयते ॥२२॥

22. Thus the bodies[1] of animals are dissolved into food,[2] food[3] into seeds, seeds into earth, and earth into odour.

The order of evolution of the universe has been set forth in the Taittiriya Upanishad II. I. The dissolutoin naturally proceeds in the inverse order. Some intermediate stages have been added in the list here given.

[1] *Bodies etc.*—From this up to "sound particles" in verse 24 runs the series of effects of Tâmasa egoism. The series is resumed in the last part of verse 25.

[2] *Food*—Particles of earth constituting food are meant.

[3] *Food etc.*—i.e. seeds never sprout.

अप्सु प्रलीयते गन्ध आपश्च स्वगुणे रसे ।
लीयते ज्योतिषि रसो ज्योती रूपे प्रलीयते ॥२३॥

23. Odour dissolves into water, water into its own essence—sap, sap into fire, and fire into colour.

रूपं वायौ स च स्पर्शे लीयते सोऽपि चाम्बरे ।
अम्बरं शब्दतन्मात्र इन्द्रियाणि स्वयोनिषु ॥२४॥

UDDHAVA GITA

24. Colour dissolves into air, air into touch, touch into ether, and ether into sound particles. The organs are dissolved into their efficient causes, the gods.[1]

[1] *Gods*—The organs, being characterised by activity which is guided by the gods, are here said to be dissolved into the gods. Really they merge in Râjasa egoism, which is their material cause.

योनिर्वैकारिके सौम्य लीयते मनसीश्वरे ।
शब्दो भूतादिमप्येति भूतादिर्महति प्रभुः ॥२५॥

25. The gods, My friend, are dissolved into the mind[1] which rules over all, and the mind into Sâttvika egoism. Sound is dissolved into Tâmasa egoism, and the all-powerful egoism into the Cosmic Intelligence.

[1] *Mind etc.*—Strictly speaking, the mind together with the gods, which are swayed by it, merges in Sâttvika egoism.

स लीयते महान्स्वेषु गुणेषु गुणवत्तमः ।
तेऽव्यक्ते संप्रलीयन्ते तत्काले लीयतेऽव्यये ॥२६॥

26. That Cosmic Intelligence, endowed[1] with the noblest qualities, is dissolved into its own causes—the Gunas, the Gunas[2] into Prakriti, and that[3] again into eternal Time.

[1] *Endowed etc.*—Because it is both active and sentient.
[2] *Gunas etc.*—i.e. they regain their lost balance.
[3] *That etc.*—i.e. it remains identified with Time considered as an undivided whole.

THE LAST MESSAGE OF SHRI KRISHNA

कालो मायामये जीवे जीव आत्मनि मय्यजे ।
आत्मा केवल आत्मस्थो विकल्पापायलक्षणः ॥२७॥

27. Time is dissolved into the omniscient Being,[1] that Being[2] again into Me, the birthless Âtman. The Âtman, which is inferred[3] from the projection and dissolution of the universe, is absolute and rests on Itself.

[1] *Being*—the "Mahâpurusha" who projected the universe. He is that state of the Paramâtman in which It beholds the Prakriti.

[2] *That Being etc.*—Because all duality has then ceased, and there is no more subject-object relation.

[3] *Inferred etc.*—as their substratum, the reality behind them.

एवमन्वीक्षमाणस्य कथं वैकल्पिको भ्रमः ।
मनसो हृदि तिष्ठेत व्योम्नीवार्कोदये तमः ॥२८॥

28. How can delusions caused by the seeing of difference rise in the mind or stay in the heart of a man who reasons in this way—like darkness in the sky at sunrise?

एष सांख्यविधिः प्रोक्तः संशयग्रन्थिभेदनः ।
प्रतिलोमानुलोमाभ्यां परावरदृशा मया ॥२९॥

29. Here, in both[1] a direct and an inverse order, I have described the Sânkhya system, which breaks the knot of doubt. I am the Witness of the high[2] and the low.

[1] *In both*—by tracing the processes of involution as well as evolution.

[2] *High etc.*—cause and effect.

CHAPTER XX

श्रीभगवानुवाच ।
गुणानामसमिश्राणां पुमान्येन यथा भवेत् ।
तन्मे पुरुषवर्येदमुपधारय शंसतः ॥१॥

The Lord said:

1. O best of men, learn it of Me as I tell you,
how a man is affected by each of the Gunas unmixed
with the others.

शमो दमस्तितिक्षेक्षा तपः सत्यं दया स्मृतिः ।
तुष्टिस्त्यागोऽस्पृहा श्रद्धा ह्रीर्दयादिः स्वनिर्वृतिः ॥२॥

2. Control[1] of the mind and the senses, fortitude,
discrimination, devotion to duty, truthfulness, compassion, circumspection, contentment, generosity, dispassion, faith, shame, charity and the like,[2] and
taking pleasure in the Self.

[1] *Control etc.*—These are the modifications of Sattva.
[2] *And the like*—such as sincerity, modesty, etc.

काम ईहा मदस्तृष्णा स्तम्भ आशीर्भिदा सुखम् ।
मदोत्साहो यशः प्रीतिर्हास्यं वीर्यं बलोद्यमः ॥३॥

3. Desire,[1] activity, pride, covetousness, haughtiness, praying for comforts, seeing of difference,
sense-pleasure, a militant disposition due to pride, love

THE LAST MESSAGE OF SHRI KRISHNA   301

of fame, making fun, display of powers, and aggressive enterprise.

[1] *Desire etc.*—These are the effects of Rajas.

क्रोधो लोभोऽनृतं हिंसा याच्चा दम्भः क्षमः कलिः ।
शोकमोहौ विषादार्ती निद्राऽऽशा भीरनुद्यमः ॥४॥

4. Anger,[1] greed, falsehood, cruelty, begging, simulation of piety fatigue, quarrel, grief, infatuation, dejection, a miserable feeling, sleep, expectation, fear, and inertia.

[1] *Anger etc.*—These are the results of Tamas.

सत्त्वस्य रजसश्चैतास्तमसश्चानुपूर्वशः ।
वृत्तयो वर्णितप्रायाः संनिपातमथो शृणु ॥५॥

5. Thus have I almost exhaustively described the effects of Sattva, Rajas, and Tamas in order. Now listen to the effects of the mixed Gunas.

संनिपातस्त्वहमिति ममेत्युद्धव या मतिः ।
व्यवहारः संनिपातो मनोमात्रेन्द्रियासुभिः ॥६॥

6. The ideas[1] of "I" and "mine", O Uddhava, constitute the effects of the mixed Gunas, since all intercourse through the mind,[2] sense-objects, organs, and Prânas is the effect of a mixture of the Gunas.

The effects of the mixed Gunas are dealt with in verses 6-8.

[1] *Ideas etc.*—We sometimes identify ourselves with the

302 **UDDHAVA GITA**

body, organs, etc., as when we say we are stout or deaf, and more often we call external objects our own.

[2] *Mind etc.*—which are all the outcome of one or other of the three Gunas.

धर्मे चार्थे च कामे च यदाऽसौ परिनिष्ठितः ।
गुणानां संनिकर्षोऽयं श्रद्धारतिधनावहः ॥७॥

7.   When a man is devoted to the performance of his duty, to the acquisition of wealth and to the satisfaction of his desires, this is the result of a mixture of the Gunas. These contribute respectively to faith, to riches, and to attachment.

प्रवृत्तिलक्षणे निष्ठा पुमान्यर्हि गृहाश्रमे ।
स्वधर्मे चानुतिष्ठेत गुणानां समितिर्हि सा ॥८॥

8.   When a man is attached to a course leading to material prosperity, when he devotes himself to a householder's life and also to the performance of his duty, it is a case[1] of a mixture of the Gunas.

[1] *Case etc.*—Because these three are the outcome of Rajas, Tamas, and Sattva, respectively.

पुरुषं सत्त्वसंयुक्तमनुमीयाच्छमादिभिः ।
कामादिभी रजोयुक्तं क्रोधाद्यैस्तमसा युतम् ॥९॥

9.   By control of the mind and the like, a man should be inferred as possessed of Sattva; by desire and so forth, as possessed of Rajas; and by anger etc., as possessed of Tamas.

THE LAST MESSAGE OF SHRI KRISHNA

The different effects of the Gunas on character are described in verses 9-11.

यदा भजति मां भक्त्या निरपेक्षः स्वकर्मभिः ।
तं सत्त्वप्रकृतिं विद्यात्पुरुषं स्त्रियमेव वा ॥१०॥

10. When a man or a woman worships Me with devotion through works, without any selfish motive, they should be known as possessed of a Sâttvika temperament.

यदा आशिष आशास्य मां भजेत स्वकर्मभिः ।
तं रजःप्रकृतिं विद्याद्विसामाशास्य तामसम् ॥११॥

11. When they worship Me through works for some definite purpose, they should be known as possessed of the Râjasika temperament; and if thereby they meditate injury to others, they should be considered to have a Tâmasika temperament.

सत्त्वं रजस्तम इति गुणा जीवस्य नैव मे ।
चित्तजा यैस्तु भूतानां सज्जमानो निबध्यते ॥१२॥

12. The Gunas Sattva, Rajas, and Tamas affect not Me, but the Jiva. They manifest themselves in his mind and serve to bind him by attaching him to material objects.

यदेतरौ जयेत्सत्त्वं भास्वरं विशदं शिवम् ।
तदा सुखेन युज्येत धर्मज्ञानादिभिः पुमान् ॥१३॥

13. When Sattva, which is bright, pure, and placid, overcomes the other two Gunas, then a man

304   UDDHAVA GITA

is endowed with happiness, virtue, knowledge and the
like.[1]

The effects of the prevalence of each of the Gunas
are set forth in verses 13-29.

[1] *And the like*—such as control of the mind, the senses,
etc.

यदा जयेत्तमः सत्त्वं रजः सङ्गं भिदा चलम् ।
तदा दुःखेन युज्येत कर्मणा यशसा श्रिया ॥१४॥

14. When Rajas, which is characterised by
attachment, differentiation, and activity, overcomes
Tamas and Sattva, then he gets work, fame, opulence,
and pain.

यदा जयेद्रजः सत्त्वं तमो मूढं लयं जडम् ।
युज्येत शोकमोहाभ्यां निद्रया हिंसयाऽऽशया ॥१५॥

15. When Tamas, which is characterised by infatuation, ignorance, and dullness, overcomes Rajas
and Sattva, then he is stricken with grief, infatuation,
sleep, cruelty, and expectation.[1]

[1] *Expectation*—Since he lacks the energy of obtaining
things through self-exertion.

यदा चित्तं प्रसीदेत इन्द्रियाणां च निर्वृतिः ।
देहेऽभयं मनोऽसङ्गं तत्सत्त्वं विद्धि मत्पदम् ॥१६॥

16. When the mind-stuff is cheerful, the senses
subdued, the body intrepid, and the mind unattached,
know that to be Sattva, through which I am realised.

THE LAST MESSAGE OF SHRI KRISHNA

विकुर्वन्क्रियया चाधीरनिर्वृत्तिश्च चेतसाम् ।
गात्रास्वास्थ्यं मनो भ्रान्तं रज एतैर्निशामय ॥१७॥

17. When a man under the influence of work
has his intellect going hither and thither, the sensory
organs restless, the organs of action in a frenzy, and
the mind wandering—know by these signs that Rajas
is up.

सीदच्चित्तं विलीयेत चेतसो ग्रहणेऽक्षमम् ।
मनो नष्टं तमो ग्लानिस्तमस्तदुपधारय ॥१८॥

18. When the mind-stuff being fatigued, is unable to reflect the Self and droops, when the mind is
vacant, and there are ignorance and dejection—know
these to be signs of Tamas.

एधमाने गुणे सत्त्वे देवानां बलमेधते ।
असुराणां च रजसि तमस्युद्धव रक्षसाम् ॥१९॥

19. When Sattva increases, the gods,[1] O
Uddhava, gain in strength; when Rajas increases, the
Asuras prevail; and when Tamas increases, the
Râkshasas.

[1] *Gods etc.*—It is the sense-organs which, characterised
by illumination, activity, and inertia, represent the Devas,
the Asuras, and the Râkshasas, respectively.

सत्त्वाज्जागरणं विद्याद्रजसा स्वप्रमादिशेत् ।
प्रस्वापं तमसा जन्तोस्तुरीयं त्रिषु संततम् ॥२०॥

20. From Sattva one should expect wakefulness
in a man; from Rajas dreams; and from Tamas sleep.

306 UDDHAVA GITA

The fourth or superconscious state persists[1] through all the three.

[1] *Persists*—It is unchanged, being identical with the Âtman.

उपर्युपरि गच्छन्ति सत्त्वेनाब्रह्मणो जनाः ॥
तमसाऽधोऽध आमुख्याद्रजसान्तर्चारिणः ॥२१॥

21. Through Sattva men rise higher and higher, up to the sphere of Brahmâ; through Tamas they sink lower and lower, down to the state of vegetable existence; and through Rajas they remain between[1] these two stages.

[1] *Between etc.*—i.e. in the human plane.

सत्त्वे प्रलीनाः स्वर्यान्ति नरलोकं रजोलयाः।
तमोलयास्तु निरयं यान्ति मामेव निर्गुणाः ॥२२॥

22. People dying when Sattva is predominant go to heaven; those dying when Rajas is up remain in the human plane; and those dying when Tamas prevails go to hell. But[1] those who are above the three Gunas attain to Me alone.

[1] *But etc.*—Incidentally the results of a state beyond the three Gunas are extolled in this and several other verses below.

मदर्पणं निष्फलं वा सात्त्विकं निजकर्म तत् ।
राजसं फलसंकल्पं हिंसाप्रायादि तामसम् ॥२३॥

23. One's own duties, if done for My sake or without any desire for fruits, are Sâttvika; work done

THE LAST MESSAGE OF SHRI KRISHNA   307

with a desire for fruits is Râjasa; and that attended
with cruelty etc., is Tâmasa.

कैवल्यं सात्त्विकं ज्ञानं रजो वैकल्पिकं च यत् ।
प्राकृतं तामसं ज्ञानं मन्निष्ठं निर्गुणं स्मृतम् ॥२४॥

24. The knowledge of the existence[1] of the Self
is Sâttvika; that of the body etc., is Râjasa; the
knowledge of a child etc., is Tâmasa; and that which
is concerning Me is beyond the Gunas.

[1] *Existence etc.*—as something distinct from the body
etc.

वनं तु सात्त्विको वासो ग्रामो राजस उच्यते ।
तामसं द्यूतसदनं मन्निकेतं तु निर्गुणम् ॥२५॥

25. The forest is called the Sâttvika dwelling;
the village is Râjasa; a gambling-den is Tâmasa; and
My abode[1] is beyond the Gunas.

[1] *My abode*—i.e. a temple.

सात्त्विकः कारकोऽसङ्गी रागान्धो राजसः स्मृतः ।
तामसः स्मृतिविभ्रष्टो निर्गुणो मदपाश्रयः ॥२६॥

26. The non-attached agent is called Sâttvika;
one blinded by attachment is Râjasa; one who never
considers the pros and cons of an act, is Tâmasa; and
one who has taken refuge in Me, is beyond the Gunas.

सात्त्विक्यध्यात्मिकी श्रद्धा कर्मश्रद्धा तु राजसी ।
तामस्यधर्मे या श्रद्धा मत्सेवायां तु निर्गुणा ॥२७॥

UDDHAVA GITA

27. Faith in the Self is Sâttvika; that in work is Râjasa; faith in irreligion is Tâmasa; and that in service unto Me is beyond the Gunas.

पथ्यं पूतमनायस्तमाहार्यं सात्त्विकं स्मृतम् ।
राजसं चेन्द्रियप्रेष्ठं तामसं चार्तिदाशुचि ॥२८॥

28. Food which is wholesome, pure and easily available is termed Sâttvika; that which is merely palatable is Râjasa; and that which is injurious to health and impure is Tâmasa.

सात्त्विकं सुखमात्मोत्थं विषयोत्थं तु राजसम् ।
तामसं मोहदैन्योत्थं निर्गुणं मदपाश्रयम् ॥२६॥

29. Joy which springs from the Self is Sâttvika; that from the sense-objects is Râjasa; the joy due to ignorance and misery is Tâmasa; and that which is based on Me is beyond the Gunas.

द्रव्यं देशः फलं कालो ज्ञानं कर्म च कारका: ।
श्रद्धाऽवस्थाऽऽकृतिर्निष्ठा त्रैगुण्यः सर्व एव हि ॥३०॥

30. Thing,[1] place, fruit, time, knowledge, work, agents, faith, state, form, and goal—all these verily fall within the range of the Gunas.

[1] *Thing etc.*—"Thing" has been referred to in verse 28, "place" in verse 25, "fruit" in verse 29, "time" in verses 13-19, "knowledge" in verse 24, "work" in verse 23, "agent" in verse 26, "faith" in verse 27, "state" in verse 20, "form" in verse 21, and "goal" in verse 22.

THE LAST MESSAGE OF SHRI KRISHNA   309

सर्वे गुणमया भावाः पुरुषाव्यक्तधिष्ठिताः ।
दृष्टं श्रुतमनुध्यातं बुद्ध्वा वा पुरुषर्षभ ॥३१॥

31. O best of men, all[1] things that are regulated
by Purusha and Prakriti—whatever is seen, heard, or
thought by the intellect—are modifications of the
Gunas.

[1] *All etc.*—Not only the above, but everything in the
universe.

एताः संसृतयः पुंसो गुणकर्मनिबन्धनाः ।
येनेमे निर्जिताः सौम्य गुणा जीवेन चित्तजाः ।
भक्तियोगेन मन्निष्ठो मद्भावाय प्रपद्यते ॥३२॥

32. All these which make for the transmigration
of man are due to the effects of the Gunas. That
man who has conquered these Gunas which are produced in his mind, is attached to Me through the path
of devotion and is fit for absorption[1] in Me.

[1] *Absorption etc.*—hence, liberation.

तस्माद्धिमिमं लब्ध्वा ज्ञानविज्ञानसंभवम् ।
गुणसङ्गं विनिर्धूय मां भजन्तु विचक्षणाः ॥३३॥

33. Therefore let wise men, having obtained
this body which is conducive to knowledge and realisation winnow out their attachment to the Gunas
and worship Me.

UDDHAVA GITA

निःसङ्गो मां भजेद्विद्वानप्रमत्तो जितेन्द्रियः ।
रजस्तमश्चाभिजयेत् सत्त्वसंसेवया मुनिः ॥३४॥

34. The wise, meditative man should worship Me, without attachment to anything else, ever alert, and master of his senses. He should conquer Rajas and Tamas by the culture of Sattva.

सत्त्वं चाभिजयेद्युक्तो नैरपेक्ष्येण शान्तधीः ।
संपद्यते गुणैर्मुक्तो जीवो जीवं विहाय माम् ॥३५॥

35. With his intellect pacified, he should conquer Sattva with the help of desirelessness.[1] By this means a man is freed from the Gunas, gets rid of his subtle body, and attains to Me.

[1] *Desirelessness*—which is a highly purified form of Sattva.

जीवो जीवविनिर्मुक्तो गुणैश्चाशयसंभवैः ।
मयैव ब्रह्मणा पूर्णो न बहिर्नान्तरश्चरेत् ॥३६॥

36. Such a man, freed from his subtle body and the Gunas which spring up in the mind, is wholly filled by Me, the Brahman, and he should have nothing to do with the sense-objects, either outside[1] or inside.

[1] *Outside etc.*—by actual contact or in thought.

CHAPTER XXI

श्रीभगवानुवाच ।
मनुष्यजन्ममिमं कायं लब्ध्वा मद्धर्मे आस्थितः ।
आनन्दं परमात्मानमात्मस्थं समुपैति माम् ॥१॥

The Lord said:

1. Obtaining a human body which gives a glimpse of My nature, a man, by practising the religion of love to Me, realises Me, the All-bliss Paramâtman, who dwells in his mind.[1]

[1] *Dwells etc.*—as the Antaryâmin or Internal Ruler.

गुणमय्या जीवयोन्या विमुक्तो ज्ञाननिष्ठया ।
गुणेषु मायामात्रेषु दृश्यमानेष्ववस्तुतः ।
वर्तमानोऽपि न पुमान् युज्यतेऽवस्तुभिर्गुणैः ॥२॥

2. Freed by a steadfastness in knowledge from the subtle body,[1] which, consisting of the Gunas, brings on the limitation of Jivahood, a man, even though living in a sense-world which is but a phantom, an unsubstantial appearance, is not attached to the unreal sense-objects.

[1] *Subtle body*—comprising the five sensory and the five motor organs, the five Prânas (or according to another version, the five subtle elements), Manas, and Buddhi. This it is that takes on body after body, till one realises the Âtman.

312 UDDHAVA GITA

सङ्गं न कुर्यादसतां शिश्नोदरतृपां क्वचित् ।
तस्यानुगस्तमस्यन्धे पतत्यन्धानुगान्धवत् ॥३॥

3. One should never associate with evil persons, who are solely after the satisfaction of their animal instincts. One who follows a single one of them falls into abysmal darkness,[1] like a blind follower of the blind.

[1] *Darkness*—of ignorance, from which it is extremely difficult to get out.

ऐलः सम्राडिमां गाथामगायत बृहच्छ्रवाः ।
उर्वशीविरहान्मुह्यन्निर्विण्णः शोकसंयमे ॥४॥

4. The far-famed Emperor Pururavas,[1] who had at first been overcome by his separation from Urvashi, sang at the expiry of his grief the following song,[2] out of a feeling of disgust (for his past life).

[1] *Pururavas*—A grandson of Manu and a powerful and accomplished Emperor of the Lunar Dynasty, who fell in love with the nymph Urvashi, who married him on two conditions. These being broken, she left him, to his utter grief. He, however, met her again, first at Kurukshetra and then, through the kindness of the Gandharvas, in the Urvashiloka, where he spent long years of intense enjoyment with her. The reaction which followed this period is described in this chapter.

The episode is as old as the Rig-veda. Vide the 10th Mandala, 95th Sukta.

[2] *Song*—set forth in verses 7-24.

त्यक्त्वाऽऽत्मानं व्रजन्तीं तां नग्न उन्मत्तवन्नृपः ।
विलपन्नन्वगाज्जाये घोरे तिष्ठेति विक्लवः ॥५॥

THE LAST MESSAGE OF SHRI KRISHNA   313

5. When Urvashi was leaving him, the Emperor, beside himself with grief, followed her like a madman, undressed, and crying, "My wife, stay! O you cruel one!"

कामानतृप्तोऽनुजुषन् क्षुल्लकान् वर्षयामिनीः ।
न वेद यान्तीनीयान्तीरुर्वश्याक्ष्टचेतनः ॥६॥

6. With his mind absorbed in Urvashi, he fed his sordid desires, ever unsatisfied, and for years together never knew when the nights came or when they were gone.

ऐल उवाच ।

अहो मे मोहविस्तारः कामकश्मलचेतसः ।
देव्या गृहीतकण्ठस्य नायुःखण्डा इमे स्मृताः ॥७॥

Pururavas said:

7. O the extent of my infatuation! My mind was so much polluted by lust! With my neck in the embrace of the goddess, I never noticed these portions of my life flitting away!

नाहं वेदाभिनिर्मुक्तः सूर्यो वाऽभ्युदितोऽमुया ।
मुषितो वर्षपूगानां बताहानि गतान्युत ॥८॥

8. Befooled by her, I never knew when the sun rose or when it set. Numberless days, amounting to years, alas, passed in this way!

अहो मे आत्मसंमोहो येनात्मा योषितां कृतः ।
क्रीडामृगश्चक्रवर्ती नरंदेवशिखामणिः ॥९॥

9. O the infatuation of my mind, which reduced the person of an Emperor—a crest-gem to a host of kings—into a sort of toy animal for women!

सपरिच्छदमात्मानं हित्वा तृणमिवेश्वरम् ।
यान्तीं स्त्रियं चान्वगमं नग्न उन्मत्तवद्रुदन् ॥१०॥

10. Like a madman, undressed and weeping, I followed that woman as she left me, an Emperor, with all my regal state—as if I were a mere straw!

कुतस्तस्यानुभावः स्यात्तेज ईशत्वमेव वा ।
योऽन्वगच्छं स्त्रियं यान्तीं खरवत्पादताडितः ॥११॥

11. Can valour, splendour, and lordship any more belong to a man like me who followed a deserting woman, like an ass kicked (by a she-ass)?

किं विद्यया किं तपसा किं त्यागेन श्रुतेन वा ।
किं विविक्तेन मौनेन स्त्रीभिर्यस्य मनो हृतम् ॥१२॥

12. Of what avail are learning, devotion to duty, renunciation, scriptural erudition, retirement, and reticence, to a man whose mind has been captivated by women?

स्वार्थस्याकोविदं धिङ् मां मूर्खं पण्डितमानिनम् ।
योऽहमीश्वरतां प्राप्य स्त्रीभिर्गोखरवज्जितः ॥१३॥

13. Fie on me who, though wise in my own conceit, was but a fool, ignorant of my real welfare, and who having attained suzerainty was conquered by women, like an ox or an ass!

THE LAST MESSAGE OF SHRI KRISHNA   315

सेवतो वर्षपूगान्मे उर्वश्या अधरासवम् ।
न तृप्यत्यात्मभूः कामो वह्निराहुतिभिर्यथा ॥१४॥

14. Though I have for years together been
tasting the nectar of the lips of Urvashi, my desire
would not be satisfied, but crop up again and again
in the mind, like a fire kindled by oblations.

पुंश्चल्याऽपहृतं चित्तं कोन्वन्यो मोचितुं प्रभुः ।
आत्मारामेश्वरमृते भगवन्तमधोक्षजम् ॥१५॥

15. Ah, who but the Omnipotent Lord, whose
bliss is in Himself and who is beyond the reach of
sense-knowledge, is able to liberate a mind that has
been enthralled by a courtesan?

बोधितस्यापि देव्या मे सूक्तवाक्येन दुर्मतेः ।
मनोगतो महामोहो नापयात्यजितात्मनः ॥१६॥

16. I was such a fool and slave to the senses,
that even though warned by the goddess[1] with signi-
ficant words, the dire infatuation of my mind would
not pass!

[1] *Goddess*—Urvashi. For the reference see note on
Verse 4.

किमेतया नोऽपकृतं रज्ज्वा वा सर्पचेतसः ।
रज्जुस्वरूपाविदुषो योऽहं यदजितेन्द्रियः ॥१७॥

17. What[1] harm has she done to me, who was
but a slave to my senses! Does a rope hurt a man

UDDHAVA GITA

who, failing to notice its true nature, mistakes it for a snake?

[1] *What etc.*—He is accusing himself. If a man is frightened out of his wits by a piece of rope mistaken for a snake, it is all his fault. The idea is followed up in the next four verses.

कायं मलोमसः कायो दौर्गन्ध्याद्यात्मकोऽशुचिः ।
क गुणाः सौमनस्याद्या ह्यध्यासोऽविद्यया कृतः ॥१८॥

18. O the difference between this dirty body —full of foul smell etc., and unclean—and virtues like those of a flower, and so forth! The superimposition is simply due to ignorance.

पित्रोः किं स्वं नु भार्यायाः स्वामिनोऽग्नेः श्वगृध्रयोः ।
किमात्मनः किं सुहृदामिति यो नावसीयते ॥१९॥
तस्मिन्कलेवरेऽमेध्ये तुच्छनिष्ठे विषज्जते ।
अहो सुभद्रं सुनसं सुस्मितं च मुखं स्त्रियः ॥२०॥

19-20. Does the body belong to the parents, or the wife, or the master, or fire,[1] or dogs and vultures, or one's self,[2] or the relatives? To a thing which cannot be thus adjudged, is impure and has a vile end,[3] people get attached, saying, "Oh, how beautiful is a woman's face, with such a charming nose and lovely smile!"

[1] *Fire etc.*—By which it is consumed after death.
[2] *One's self*—which it affects by the merits or demerits of works done by it.
[3] *Vile end*—being reduced to ashes etc.

THE LAST MESSAGE OF SHRI KRISHNA

त्वङ्मांसरुधिरस्नायुमेदोमज्जास्थिसंहतौ ।
विण्मूत्रपूये रमतां कृमीणां कियदन्तरम् ॥२१॥

21. What is the difference between those who delight in a mass of skin, flesh, blood, tendon, fat, marrow, bones, and various other filthy things—and so many maggots?

अथापि नोपसज्जेत स्त्रीषु स्त्रैणेषु चार्थवित् ।
विषयेन्द्रियसंयोगान्मनः क्षुभ्यति नान्यथा ॥२२॥

22. The man of discrimination should neither associate with women nor with those who are attached to them, for the mind is agitated only by the contact of the senses with their objects, and in no other way.

अदृष्टादश्रुताद्भावान्न भाव उपजायते ।
असंप्रयुक्तः प्राणान् शाम्यति स्तिमितं मनः ॥२३॥

23. A mental wave is never produced by anything that has not been seen or heard. So the mind of a man who controls his senses is gradually stilled and is perfectly at peace.

तस्मात्सङ्गो न कर्तव्यः स्त्रीषु स्त्रैणेषु चेन्द्रियैः ।
विदुषां चाप्यविश्रब्धः षड्वर्गः किमु मादृशाम् ॥२४॥

24. Therefore no association through the senses should be made with women or with those who are attached to them. The passions are not to be trusted even by the wise, not to speak of people like me.

UDDHAVA GITA

श्रीभगवानुवाच ।

एवं प्रगायन्नृपदेवदेवः
स उर्वशीलोकमथो विहाय ।
आत्मानमात्मन्यवगम्य मां वै
उपारमज्ज्ञानविधूतमोहः ॥२५॥

The Lord said:

25. Thus singing, Pururavas, who shone among the gods as well as among kings, gave up the sphere where Urvashi lived, and realising Me, the Ātman, in himself, dispelled his infatuation through that knowledge and attained peace.

ततो दुःसङ्गमुत्सृज्य सत्सु सज्जेत बुद्धिमान् ।
सन्त एतस्य छिन्दन्ति मनोव्यासङ्गमुक्तिभिः ॥२६॥

26. Therefore the wise man should shun evil company and associate with the holy. It is these who by their words take away the attachment of the mind.

सन्तोऽनपेक्षा मच्चित्ताः प्रशान्ताः समदर्शिनः ।
निर्ममा निरहंकारा निर्द्वन्द्वा निष्परिग्रहाः ॥२७॥

27. Saints are independent, attached to Me, calm, even-minded, have no idea of "I" or "mine", are beyond the pairs of opposites, and accept no gifts.

तेषु नित्यं महाभाग महाभागेषु मत्कथाः ।
संभवन्ति हिता नृणां जुषतां प्रपुनन्त्यघम् ॥२८॥

THE LAST MESSAGE OF SHRI KRISHNA 319

28. O fortunate one, among these blessed ones there is constant talk of Me, listening to which people are purged of their sins.

The effect of the association with saints is described in verses 28-34.

ता ये शृण्वन्ति गायन्ति ह्यनुमोदन्ति चाद्दताः ।
मत्पराः श्रद्धानाश्च भक्तिं विन्दन्ति ते मयि ॥२८॥

29. Those who reverently listen to, chant, and appreciate these talks, become attached to Me, acquire faith, and attain devotion to Me.

भक्तिं लब्धवतः साधोः किमन्यदवशिष्यते ।
मय्यनन्तगुणे ब्रह्मण्यानन्दानुभवात्मनि ॥३०॥

30. O pious one, what more remains to be achieved by one who has attained devotion to Me, the Brahman, of infinite qualities, the Bliss and Knowledge Absolute?

यथोपश्रयमाणस्य भगवन्तं विभावसुम् ।
शीतं भयं तमोऽप्येति साधून्संसेवतस्तथा ॥३१॥

31. As a man resorting to the blessed Fire is rid of his cold, fear, and darkness,[1] so also[2] is a man associating with saints.

[1] *Darkness*—which causes the fear.
[2] *So also etc.*—i.e. he is rid of his mechanical engrossment in rituals, his fear of rebirth, and its cause, ignorance.

UDDHAVA GITA

निमज्ज्योन्मज्जतां घोरे भवाब्धौ परमायनम् ।
सन्तो ब्रह्मविदः शान्ता नौर्दृढेवाप्सु मज्जताम् ॥३२॥

32. The saints who have realised Brahman are the supreme refuge of people sinking[1] and rising in the dreadful ocean of transmigration, like a strong boat to people about to be drowned in water.

[1] *Sinking etc.*—attaining lower and higher bodies.

अन्नं हि प्राणिनां प्राण आर्तानां शरणं त्वहम् ।
धर्मो वित्तं नृणां प्रेत्य सन्तोऽर्वाग् बिभ्यतोऽरणम् ॥३३॥

33. As food is the life of beings, as I am the refuge of the afflicted, and as religion is the treasure of people in the next world, so are the saints refuge for those who are afraid of sinking down.[1]

[1] *Sinking down*—to a very low existence.

सन्तो दिशन्ति चक्षूंषि बहिरर्कः समुत्थितः ।
देवता बान्धवाः सन्तः सन्त आत्माऽहमेव च ॥३४॥

34. The sun, when risen, furnishes[1] people with a single, external eye, but the saints furnish them with many eyes.[2] The saints are the true gods and true friends. They are Myself,[3] the Âtman.

[1] *Furnishes etc.*—i.e. only makes external objects visible to them.

[2] *Many eyes*—enabling them to attain relative and absolute knowledge.

[3] *Myself etc.*—So they sum up all the virtues.

THE LAST MESSAGE OF SHRI KRISHNA 321

वैतसेनस्ततोऽप्येवमुर्वंश्या लोकनिःस्पृहः ।
मुक्तसङ्गो महीमेतामात्मारामश्चचार ह ॥३५॥

35. Being thus averse to the sphere where Urvashi lived, and aided also by the association of the saints, Pururavas[1] was free from all attachment, and wandered over this earth, taking pleasure in the Self alone.

[1] *Pururavas*—The word in the text literally means : Son of one (Sudyumna) whose army (on entering a charmed forest) underwent a strange transformation. For the story, see the Bhâgavata, Book IX, Chapter I.

CHAPTER XXII

उद्धव उवाच ।

क्रियायोगं समाचक्ष्व भवदाराधनं प्रभो ।

यस्मात्त्वां ये यथाऽर्चन्ति सात्वताः सात्वतर्षभ ॥१॥

Uddhava said:

1. O Lord, the adored One of the devotees, please describe to me the mode of worshipping Thee through ceremonials—how and through what aids the devotees worship Thee.

एतद्वदन्ति मुनयो मुहुर्निःश्रेयसं नृणाम् ।

नारदो भगवान्व्यास आचार्योऽङ्गिरसः सुतः ॥२॥

2. Sages like Nârada, Bhagavân Vyâsa, and Âchârya Brihaspati, the son of Angiras, repeatedly describe this as the way to liberation for men.

निःसृतं ते मुखाम्भोजाद्यदाह भगवानजः ।

पुत्रेभ्यो भृगुमुख्येभ्यो देव्यै च भगवान्भवः ॥३॥

एतद्वै सर्ववर्णानामाश्रमाणां च संमतम् ।

श्रेयसामुत्तमं मन्ये स्त्रीशूद्राणां च मानद ॥४॥

3-4. O Lord who glorifiest Thy devotees, that instruction which, after it had issued from Thy lotus lips, the Lord Brahmâ told his sons, Bhrigu and

THE LAST MESSAGE OF SHRI KRISHNA 323

others, and the Lord Shiva to the Goddess Pârvati—
that I consider the best and the most suitable means
of well-being for all castes and orders of life including
even the Shudras and women.

एतत्कमलपत्राक्ष कर्मबन्धविमोचनम् ।
भक्ताय चानुरक्ताय ब्रूहि विश्वेश्वरेश्वर ॥५॥

5. O lotus-eyed One, O Lord of the Rulers[1]
of the universe, tell me, Thy ardent devotee, about
this way that unlooses the bonds of Karma.[2]

[1] *Rulers etc.*—Hiranyagarbha etc.
[2] *Karma*—See note I on verse 15, Chapter XIX.

श्रीभगवानुवाच ।
नह्यन्तोऽनन्तपारस्य कर्मकाण्डस्य चोद्धव ।
संक्षिप्तं वर्णयिष्यामि यथावदनुपूर्वशः ॥६॥

The Lord said:

6. There is no end, O Uddhava, to the course
of ceremonial worship, which is really limitless. So
I shall give you a brief but accurate description of
it in order.

वैदिकस्तान्त्रिको मिश्र इति मे त्रिविधो मखः ।
त्रयाणामीप्सितेनैव विधिना मां समर्चयेत् ॥७॥

7. There are three ways of worshipping Me,
viz Vaidika, Tântrika, and mixed. One may worship

UDDHAVA GITA

Me by any one of the three methods that appeals to one.

यदा स्वनिगमेनोक्तं द्विजत्वं प्राप्य पूरुषः ।
यथा यजेत मां भक्तया श्रद्धया तन्निबोध मे ॥८॥

8. Learn it of Me with faith how, having at the due season[1] his investiture with the holy thread according to the injunction of his particular Veda, a man should worship Me with devotion.

[1] *Due season*—i.e. seventh, tenth, or eleventh year.

अर्चायां स्थण्डिलेऽग्नौ वा सूर्ये वाऽप्सु हृदि द्विजः ।
द्रव्येण भक्तियुक्तोऽर्चेत्स्वगुरुं माममायया ॥६॥

9. A twice-born[1] should worship Me, his Teacher, with sincerity and devotion, by means of various presents, in an image, or the sacrificial ground, or fire, or the sun, or water, or in his own heart.

[1] *Twice-born*—Brâhmana, Kshatriya, or Vaishya.

पूर्वं स्नानं प्रकुर्वीत धौतदन्तोऽङ्गशुद्धये ।
उभयैरपि च स्नानं मन्त्रैर्मृद्ग्रहणादिना ॥१०॥

10. Cleansing his teeth, he should first have a bath for the purification of his body. The bath is to be accompanied by both Vaidika and Tântrika Mantras and the use of earth etc.

THE LAST MESSAGE OF SHRI KRISHNA

325

संध्योपास्त्यादिकर्माणि वेदेनाचोदितानि मे ।
पूजां ते: कल्पयेत्सम्यक् संकल्प: कर्मपावनीम् ॥११॥

11. Through the Vedas I have enjoined certain rites such as the morning, noon, and evening prayers. Along with them, he should perform with right determination My worship, which roots out Karma.

शैली दारुमयी लौही लेप्या लेख्या च सैकती ।
मनोमयी मणिमयी प्रतिमाऽष्टविधा स्मृता ॥१२॥

12. Images are of eight kinds—those made of stone, wood, gold, clay, sand, and jewels, as well as painted and mental ones.[1]

[1] *Mental ones*—When the worship is performed in one's heart.

चलाचलेति द्विविधा प्रतिष्ठा जीवमन्दिरम् ।
उद्वासावाहने न स्तः स्थिरायामुद्धवार्चने ॥१३॥

13. Images, which are the temples of God, are divided into two other classes—movable and immovable. In worshipping through the immovable ones, O Uddhava, there is neither[1] the ceremony of invocation nor that of valediction.

[1] *Neither etc.*—Because at the time of installation the deity is invoked to reside permanently in them.

अस्थिरायां विकल्प: स्यात्स्थण्डिले तु भवेद्द्वयम् ।
क्षापनं त्वबिलेप्यायामन्यत्र परिमार्जनम् ॥१४॥

326 UDDHAVA GITA

14. With regard to the movable images there is an option[1] about this, but in the case of the sacrificial ground etc., they are compulsory. Bathing is performed with all except the clay ones etc.[2] In other cases, only wiping is done.

[1] *Option etc.*—according to the particular case; e.g. they should be omitted in the case of a Shâlagrâma, and performed in the case of a sandy image. As regards other kinds of movable images they are optional.

[2] *Clay ones etc.*—implying paintings; these two exceptions require "wiping".

द्रव्यैः प्रसिद्धैर्मेद्यागः प्रतिमादिष्वमायिनः ।
भक्तस्य च यथालब्ध्यैर्हृदि भावेन चैव हि ॥१५॥

15. The worship of a sincere devotee in images should be done with the choicest offerings that are available; in the heart it should be done with only mental offerings.

स्नानालंकरणं प्रेष्ठमर्चायामेव तूद्धव ।
स्थण्डिले तत्त्वविन्यासो बह्वावाज्यप्लुतं हविः ॥१६॥

16. In images, O Uddhava, it is bathing and decoration which are dearest to Me; in the sacrificial ground, the locating[1] of the deities; and in fire, oblations soaked in ghee.

The special points in connection with particular symbols are mentioned here.

[1] *Locating etc.*—Mentally conceiving the principal and subordinate deities as occupying different parts of it.

THE LAST MESSAGE OF SHRI KRISHNA 327

सूर्ये चाभ्यर्हणं प्रेष्ठं सलिले सलिलादिभिः ।
श्रद्धयोपाहृतं प्रेष्ठं भक्तेन मम वार्यपि ॥१७॥
भूर्यप्यभक्तोपहृतं न मे तोषाय कल्पते ।
गन्धो धूपः सुमनसो दीपोऽन्नाद्यं च किं पुनः ॥१८॥

17-18. In the sun, worshipping through prayers etc., is dearest to Me; in water, through water etc. Even water offered by a devotee with faith is dearest to Me—not to speak of perfume, incense, flowers, light, and various kinds of food. But a heap of offerings from one who is not a devotee fails to please Me.

शुचिः संभृतसंभारः प्राङ्मुखैः कल्पितासनः ।
आसीनः प्रागुदग्वाऽर्चेदर्चायामथ संमुखः ॥१९॥

19. After first collecting the requisites of worship and purifying[1] himself, he should have a seat of Kusha grass, and seated thereon facing the east or north, he should worship Me. In the case of an (immovable) image, however, he should face that.

[1] *Purifying etc.*—by a bath etc.

कृतन्यासः कृतन्यासां मदर्चां पाणिना सृजेत् ।
कलशं प्रोक्षणीयं च यथावदुपसाधयेत् ॥२०॥

20. Having located the deities in his own body, he should place the principal Mantra in My image, and purify[1] it with his hand. He should duly[2]

UDDHAVA GITA

purify the pitcher filled with sacred water for sprinkling.

All the steps in the worship have not been mentioned in these verses. They should be supplied from fuller treatises on the subject.

[1] *Purify etc.*—by taking away the flowers already offered, and so on.

[2] *Duly etc.*—by flowers, sandal, etc.

तदद्भिर्देवयजनं द्रव्याण्यात्मानमेव च ।
प्रोक्ष्य पात्राणि त्रीण्यद्भिस्तैस्तैर्द्रव्यैश्च साधयेत् ॥२१॥

21. He should sprinkle that water on the place of worship, on the requisites of worship and on himself, and put in three vessels some of that water and the things prescribed for each.

पाद्यार्घाचमनीयार्थं त्रीणि पात्राणि देशिकः ।
हृदा शीर्ष्णाऽथ शिखया गायत्र्या चाभिमन्त्रयेत् ॥

22. The worshipper should purify the three vessels meant for the water to wash the feet, for the welcome offerings, and for the water to wash the mouth, with the Mantras "*Namas* to the heart", "*svâhâ* to the head", and "*Vashat* to the hair on the crown", respectively, and all with the Gâyatri.

पिण्डे वाय्वग्निसंशुद्धे हृत्पद्मस्थां परां मम ।
अण्वीं जीवकलां ध्यायेन्नादान्ते सिद्धभाविताम् ॥२३॥

23. Having[1] purified his body with air and fire, he should meditate on the subtle and supreme form

THE LAST MESSAGE OF SHRI KRISHNA 329

of Mine as Nârâyana, seated in the lotus of his heart
—which the Siddhas[2] reflect on at the end[3] of the
Nâda.

[1] *Having etc.*—The process of Bhutashuddhi, referred
to here, is briefly as follows: The priest has first to imagine
his body as dried by the air in his stomach and burnt
by the fire at the extremity of his spine, and then revived
by the nectar of the moon in his forehead. In this new
body he has to meditate on the Lord as described in this
verse.

[2] *Siddhas*—See note on verse 12, chapter XIX.

[3] *End etc.*—The symbol Om consists of five parts—A,
U, M, Bindu, and Nâda, ranged according to their degree of
subtlety. Beyond the last stage even is God. An exceedingly
subtle state of perfection is implied.

तयाऽऽत्मभूतया पिण्डे व्याप्ते संपूज्य तन्मयः ।
आवाह्यार्चादिषु स्थाप्य न्यस्ताङ्गं मां प्रपूजयेत् ।।२४।।

24. Identifying himself with that form and
imagining it as pervading his body, he should
mentally worship it; being one with that, he should
invoke it and put[1] it in the image etc., and locating
the deities in its different parts, worship Me.

[1] *Put etc.*—with the appropriate gesture.

पाद्योपस्पर्शार्हणादीनुपचारान्प्रकल्पयेत् ।
धर्मादिभिश्च नवभिः कल्पयित्वाऽऽसनं मम ।।२५।।
पद्ममष्टदलं तत्र कर्णिकाकेसरोज्ज्वलम् ।
उभाभ्यां वेदतन्त्राभ्यां मह्यं तुभयसिद्धये ।।२६।।

330 UDDHAVA GITA

25-26. Having conceived My cot[1] with the attributes such as virtue etc., and the nine Powers, and on that an eight-petalled lotus, with effulgent[2] pericarp and stamens, he should, for the achievement of prosperity and liberation as set forth in the Vedas and Tantras, offer Me, with both kinds of Mantras, water for washing the feet and mouth, welcome offerings, and other things.

[1] *Cot*—of which virtue, knowledge, renunciation, and lordship are the legs; the opposites of these the four side pieces; the nine Powers—Vimala, Utkarshini, etc.—the seat, and so on.

[2] *Effulgent*—Because of the sun, moon, and fire in three of its stamens.

सुदर्शनं पाञ्चजन्यं गदासीषुधनुर्हलान् ।
मुसलं कौस्तुभं मालां श्रीवत्सं चानुपूजयेत् ॥२७॥

27. He should next worship My weapons—the disc Sudarshana, the conch Pânchajanya, the club, the sword, the bow, and arrows, the plough and the mace[1] as also the ornaments—the jewel Kaustubha, the garland and the curl of hair on the chest called Shrivatsa.

[1] *Mace*—or "Musala" in ancient warfare was an iron-tipped wooden pole for hurling, differing materially from the club or "Gada", which was a formidable iron weapon with a handle.

नन्दं सुनन्दं गरुडं प्रचण्डं चण्डमेव च ।
महाबलं बलं चैव कुमुदं कुमुदेक्षणम् ॥२८॥

THE LAST MESSAGE OF SHRI KRISHNA 331

दुर्गां विनायकं व्यासं विष्वक्सेनं गुरून् सुरान् ।
स्वे स्वे स्थाने त्वभिमुखान्पूजयेत्प्रोक्षणादिभिः ॥२६॥

28-29. He should worship with welcome offerings etc., Nanda,[1] Sunanda, Garuda, Prachanda,
Chanda, Mahâbala, Bala, Kumuda, and Kumudek-
shana as well as Durgâ, Ganesha, Vyâsa, and Vishvaksena, the Gurus and the gods[2]—all stationed in
their respective places,[3] facing Me.

[1] *Nanda etc.*—These form His bodyguard, while Garuda
carries Him on his back.
[2] *Gods*—Indra and the other Rulers of the spheres.
[3] *Respective places*—different points of the compass.

चन्दनोशीरकर्पूरकुङ्कु मागुरुवासितैः ।
सलिलैः स्नापयेन्मन्त्रैर्नित्यदा विभवे सति ॥३०॥
स्वर्णघर्मानुवाकेन महापुरुषविद्यया ।
पौरुषेणापि सूक्तेन सामभी राजनादिभिः ॥३१॥

30-31. Having got the means, he should always
bathe Me with water scented by sandal, Ushira,[1]
camphor, saffron, and agallochum, with such Mantras
as the Svarna-gharma[2] hymn, the stanza[3] on the
Mahâpurusha, the Purusha-Sukta[4], the Sâmas called
Râjana,[5] and so on.

[1] *Ushira*—Khus-Khus, the fragrant root of the plant
Andropogon muricatus.
[2] *Svarna-gharma etc.*—A Vedic hymn beginning with
सुवर्णं धर्मं परिवेदवेनम् etc.

UDDHAVA GITA

[3] *Stanza etc.*—The opening verse of the Vishnu-Purâna.
[4] *Purusha-Sukta*—Rig-Veda, 10th Mandala, 90th Sukta.
[5] *Râjana*—beginning with इन्द्रं नरो नेमधिता etc.

वस्त्रोपवीताभरणपत्रस्रग्गन्धलेपनैः ।
अलंकुर्वीत सप्रेम मद्भक्तो मां यथोचितम् ॥३२॥

32. Full of love, My devotee should appro-
priately decorate Me with clothes, the holy thread,
ornaments, leaf-patterns,[1] garlands, scent, and
sandal-paste.

[1] *Leaf-patterns*—on the cheeks or chest or any other
part of the body, with sandal etc.

पाद्यमाचमनीयं च गन्धं सुमनसोऽक्षतान् ।
धूपदीपोपहार्याणि दद्यान्मे श्रद्धयार्चकः ॥३३॥

33. The worshipper should offer Me with faith
various presents such as water for washing the feet
and mouth, scent, flowers, sunned rice, grains, incense,
and light.

गुडपायससर्पींषि शष्कुल्यापूपमोदकान् ।
संयावदधिसूपांश्च नैवेद्यं सति कल्पयेत् ॥३४॥

34. Having got the means, he should offer Me
the following kinds of food—preparations of molasses,
sweetened milk-rice, ghee, different kinds of flour-
cakes and sweets, curd, and vegetable dishes.

THE LAST MESSAGE OF SHRI KRISHNA

अभ्यङ्गोन्मर्दनादर्शदन्तधावाभिषेचनम् ।
अन्नाद्यगीतनृत्यादि पर्वणि स्युरूतान्वहम् ॥३५॥

35. There should take place, daily[1] or on special days, unction, rubbing of scented powders, presenting of a mirror, washing of the teeth, ablution, offering of different kinds of food, music, and dance.

[1] *Daily*—if the worshipper is rich enough.

विधिना विहिते कुण्डे मेखलागर्तवेदिभिः ।
अग्निमाधाय परितः समूहेत्पाणिनोदितम् ॥३६॥

36. Lighting a fire in a pit made according to the rules,[1] with a girdle, cavity, and altar, he should collect it, when kindled, from all sides with his hand.

The mode of worshipping in the fire for additional results is shown here.

[1] *Rules*—as laid down in his particular Veda.

परिस्तीर्याथ पर्युक्षेदन्वाधाय यथाविधि ।
प्रोक्षण्याऽऽसाद्य द्रव्याणि प्रोक्ष्याग्नौ भावयेत माम् ॥३७॥

37. Then spreading Kusha grass round it, he should sprinkle water around. Having put faggots[1] into the fire according to the prescribed rules and placed the different offerings near it, he should sprinkle the sacred water from the pitcher on it and meditate on Me[2] there:

[1] *Faggots etc.*—uttering the Mantra ॐ भूः स्वाहा, etc
[2] *Me*—as the Indwelling Ruler.

334 UDDHAVA GITA

तप्तजाम्बूनदप्रख्यं शङ्खचक्रगदाम्बुजैः ।
लसच्चतुर्भुजं शान्तं पद्मकिञ्जल्कवाससम् ॥३८॥

38. Like heated gold in complexion; with four
arms bearing gracefully a conch, a disc, a club, and a
lotus; serene; wearing a cloth of the colour of lotus
stamens:

स्फुरत्किरीटकटककटिसूत्रवराङ्गदम् ।
श्रीवत्सवक्षसं भ्राजत्कौस्तुभं वनमालिनम् ॥३९॥

39. Wearing a shining diadem, bracelets, waist-
band, and splendid armlets; with the curl Shrivatsa
on the chest radiant with the jewel Kaustubha; and
wearing a garland of wild flowers.

ध्यायन्नभ्यर्च्य दारूणि हविषाऽभिघृतानि च ।
प्रास्याज्यभागावाघारौ दत्त्वा चाज्यप्लुतं हविः ॥४०॥
जुहुयान्मूलमन्त्रेण षोडशर्चावदानतः ।
धर्मादिभ्यो यथान्यायं मन्त्रैः स्विष्टिकृतं बुधः ॥४१॥

40-41. After meditating and worshipping Me,
he should put faggots soaked in ghee into the fire,
perform the two Aghâras[1] and the two Homas,[2] and
uttering the principal Mantra[3] and the Purusha-Sukta,
for each stanza of the latter offer oblations soaked in
ghee, making duly, with the appropriate Mantras,[4]
offering to virtue etc., as well as the offering called
Svishtikrita.

[1] *Aghâras*—pouring of ghee across the fire, uttering
प्रजापतये स्वाहा etc.

THE LAST MESSAGE OF SHRI KRISHNA

335

² *Homas*—pouring of oblations, uttering अग्नये स्वाहा, etc.

³ *Mantras*—i.e. Om namo Nârâyanâya.

⁴ *Mantras*—adding "Swâha" to each name.

⁵ *Svishtikrita*—made to the fire.

अभ्यर्च्याथ नमस्कृत्य पार्षदेभ्यो बलिं हरेत् ।
मूलमन्त्रं जपेद्ब्रह्म स्मरन्नारायणात्मकम् ॥४२॥

42. Then worshipping and saluting Me, the wise man should offer food to My attendants, and thinking of Brahman manifested as Nârâyana, he should repeat the principal Mantra.

दत्त्वाऽऽचमनमुच्छेषं विष्वक्सेनाय कल्पयेत् ।
मुखवासं सुरभिमत्ताम्बूलाद्यमथाऽर्हयेत् ॥४३॥

43. Having offered Me the water for washing the mouth, he should offer the remnants of My food to Vishvaksena. Then he should offer Me things to chew, such as fragrant betel etc., and again worship Me.

उपगायन्गृणन्नृत्यन्कर्माण्यभिनयन्मम ।
मत्कथाः श्रावयन् शृण्वन्मुहूर्तं क्षणिको भवेत् ॥४४॥

44. He should be rapt for some time in singing to and praising Me, dancing, acting My deeds, and listening to and narrating My exploits.

स्तवैरुच्चावचैः स्तोत्रैः पौराणैः प्राकृतैरपि ।
स्तुत्वा प्रसीद भगवन्निति वन्देत दण्डवत् ॥४५॥

UDDHAVA GITA

336

45. Praising Me with various hymns and odes composed by the ancients as well as the moderns, he should prostrate himself before Me, saying, "Lord, be gracious unto me!"

शिरो मत्पादयोः कृत्वा बाहुभ्यां च परस्परम् ।
प्रपन्नं पाहि मामीश भीतं मृत्युमहार्णवात् ॥४६॥

46. Placing his head at My feet and holding them with both his hands correspondingly,[1] he should say, "Lord, save me from the ocean of transmigration, with the shark of Death in it, of which I am (terribly) afraid. I have taken refuge in Thee."

[1] *Correspondingly*—i.e. holding the right foot with the right hand, and so on.

इति शेषां मया दत्तां शिरस्याधाय सादरम् ।
उद्वासयेच्चेदुद्वास्यं ज्योतिर्ज्योतिषि तत्पुनः ॥४७॥

47. Placing[1] the token of My pleasure respectfully on his head, he should perform the valedictory ceremony—if[2] this has to be done—by merging[3] the Light that was put in the image, back in the Light that is in his heart.

It will appear on reflection that the whole process is firmly grounded on Advaita.

[1] *Placing etc.*—in imagination.

[2] *If etc.*—according to the nature of the image or symbol.

[3] *Merging etc.*—Revoking the projection of his spirit in the image (verse 24) into himself.

THE LAST MESSAGE OF SHRI KRISHNA 337

अर्चादिषु यदा यत्र श्रद्धा मां तत्र चार्चयेत् ।
सर्वभूतेष्वात्मनि च सर्वात्माहमवस्थितः ॥४८॥

48. Among the images etc., one may worship Me just in that in which he may have faith at any particular time. For[1] I am the Self of all and dwell in everything as well as in one's own self.

[1] *For etc.*—So no comparison of their merits need be made.

एवं क्रियायोगपथैः पुमान्वैदिकतान्त्रिकैः ।
अर्चन्नुभयतः सिद्धिं मत्तो विन्दत्यभीप्सिताम् ॥४९॥

49. Worshipping Me thus by means of ceremonials, Vaidika as well as Tântrika, a man obtains from Me his desired boon, both here and hereafter.

मदर्चां संप्रतिष्ठाप्य मन्दिरं कारयेद्दृढम् ।
पुष्पोद्यानानि रम्याणि पूजायात्रोत्सवाश्रितान् ॥५०॥
पूजादीनां प्रवाहार्थं महापर्वस्वथान्वहम् ।
क्षेत्रापणपुरग्रामान् दत्त्वा मत्सार्ष्टितामियात् ॥५१॥

50-51. Installing My image, he must have a strong temple built for it, with beautiful flower-gardens attached, and for the continuance of the daily worship as well as gatherings and festivals on special days, he should make a gift of lands, shops, towns, and villages to support the worship etc. By doing so he attains a splendour equalling Mine.

22

UDDHAVA GITA

प्रतिष्ठया सार्वभौमं सद्मना भुवनत्रयम् ।
पूजादिना ब्रह्मलोकं त्रिभिर्मत्साम्यतामियात् ॥५२॥

52. By installing My image a man attains suzerainty on earth; by building a temple for it, the three worlds; by worship etc., the sphere of Brahmâ; and by all the three, sameness with Me.

मामेव नैरपेक्ष्येण भक्तियोगेन विन्दति ।
भक्तियोगं स लभते एवं यः पूजयेत माम् ॥५३॥

53. By worshipping Me with devotion regardless of any other consideration[1] he verily attains Me. This devotion is accessible to him who worships Me in this way.[2]

[1] *Consideration*—such as going to heaven etc.
[2] *In this way*—By *kriyāyoga* i.e. ceremonials etc.

यः स्वदत्तां परैर्दत्तां हरेत सुरविप्रयोः ।
वृत्तिं स जायते विड्भुग्वर्षाणामयुतायुतम् ॥५४॥

54. He who robs the maintenance—whether awarded by himself or others—of a deity or a Brâhmana, is born as a dirty maggot for millions of years.

कर्तुश्च सारथेर्हेतोरनुमोदितुरेव च ।
कर्मणां भागिनः प्रेत्य भूयो भूयसि तत्फलम् ॥५५॥

55. Whatever fate awaits this culprit in the next life, overtakes also those who aid, instigate, or abet him in the deed, or they are sharers in it. The punishment is greater in proportion to the enormity of the sin.

CHAPTER XXIII

श्रीभगवानुवाच ।

परस्वभावकर्माणि न प्रशंसेन्न गर्हयेत् ।

विश्वमेकात्मकं पश्यन्प्रकृत्या पुरुषेण च ॥१॥

The Lord said:

1. Seeing the universe one with Purusha and Prakriti, one should neither praise nor criticise others' natures[1] and actions.

[1] *Natures*—such as balanced, active, and dull.

परस्वभावकर्माणि यः प्रशंसति निन्दति ।

स आशु भ्रश्यते स्वार्थादसत्यभिनिवेशतः ॥२॥

2. He who praises or criticises others' natures and actions quickly slips away from his well-being, for having set his heart on what is unreal.

तैजसे निद्रयाऽऽपन्ने पिण्डस्थो नष्टचेतनः ।

मायां प्राप्नोति मृत्युं वा तद्धज्ञानार्थटक् पुमान् ॥३॥

3. As, when the organs, the effects of Râjasa egoism, are overpowered by sleep, the Jiva losing his outward consciousness experiences either illusive dreams, or deathlike sleep, so does[1] a man who sees multiplicity.

[1] *Does etc.*—finds his mind either outgoing or dull.

340

UDDHAVA GITA

किं भद्रं किमभद्रं वा द्वैतस्यावस्तुनः कियत् ।
वाचोदितं तदनृतं मनसा ध्यातमेव च ॥४॥

4. In duality, which is unreal, what is good or what is bad, and to what extent? Whatever is uttered by the tongue[1] and conceived by the mind is unreal.

[1] *Tongue*—suggests the other organs also. So also "speech" in verses 17 and 35.

छायाप्रत्याह्वयाभासा ह्यसन्तोऽप्यर्थकारिणः ।
एवं देहादयो भावा यच्छन्त्यामृत्युतो भयम् ॥५॥

5. A reflection, an echo, and an illusive appearance,[1] even though unreal, produce some effect. So do things like the body etc., cause alarm till death.[2]

[1] *Appearance*—e.g. silver in the mother-of-pearl.
[2] *Till death*—Another rendering would be—"until they dissolve in realisation".

आत्मैव तदिदं विश्वं सृज्यते सृजति प्रभुः ।
त्रायते त्राति विश्वात्मा ह्रियते हरतीश्वरः ॥६॥

6. The Lord God, the Ātman, the Self of the universe, projects this universe and is projected,[1] maintains it and is maintained, dissolves it and is dissolved.

[1] *Is projected*—Because it is the Ātman that appears as the universe.

THE LAST MESSAGE OF SHRI KRISHNA

तस्मान्ब्रह्मात्मनोऽन्यस्मादन्यो भावो निरूपितः ।
निरूपितेयं त्रिविधा निर्मूला भातिरात्मनि ।
इदं गुणमयं विद्धि त्रिविधं मायया कृतम् ॥७॥

7. Therefore nothing is proved to be other than the Âtman, which is distinct (from the universe). The threefold[1] appearance in the Âtman (that we see) is proved to be without foundation. Know the threefold division consisting of the Gunas to be but the effect[2] of Mâyâ.

[1] *Threefold etc.*—As Âdhyâtmika, Âdhibhautika, and Âdhidaivika.
[2] *Effect etc.*—an illusory appearance, the Âtman alone being real.

एतद्विद्वान्मदुदितं ज्ञानविज्ञाननैपुणम् ।
न निन्दति न च स्तौति लोके चरति सूर्यवत् ॥८॥

8. He who knows this quintessence of knowledge and realisation that I have spoken of, neither praises nor criticises anybody. He moves in the world like the sun.[1]

[1] *Like the sun*—which shines on the saint and the sinner alike.

प्रत्यक्षेणानुमानेन निगमेनात्मसंविदा ।
आद्यन्तवदसज्ज्ञात्वा निःसङ्गो विचरेदिह ॥९॥

9. Knowing by means of sense perception, inference, scriptural evidence, and one's own realisa-

342 UDDHAVA GITA

tion, that whatever has a beginning and an end is
unreal, one should wander in the world free from
attachment.

उद्धव उवाच ।

नैवात्मनो न देहस्य संसृतिर्द्रष्टृदृश्ययोः ।
अनात्मस्वदृशोरीश कस्य स्यादुपलभ्यते ॥१०॥

Uddhava said:

10. O Lord, relative existence is impossible
either to the Ātman or to the body, for they are
the subject and object, the Self-effulgent One and
non-Self, respectively. All the same it is perceived.
So whose should it be?

आत्माऽव्ययोऽगुणः शुद्धः स्वयंज्योतिरनावृतः ।
अग्निवद्दारुवदचिद् देहः कस्येह संसृतिः ॥११॥

11. The Ātman is changeless, transcendent,
pure, self-effulgent, ever-manifest, and like fire[1];
while the body is non-intelligent, like wood. So which
of these has relative existence?

[1] *Like fire*—i.e. illuminer.

श्रीभगवानुवाच ।

यावद्धेन्द्रियप्राणैरात्मनः संनिकर्षणम् ।
संसारः फलवांस्तावदपार्थोऽप्यविवेकिनः ॥१२॥

The Lord said:

12. So long as the Self is related to the body,

THE LAST MESSAGE OF SHRI KRISHNA 343

the organs and the Prânas, relative existence, even though unreal, has a semblance of reality for the undiscriminating man.

अर्थे ह्यविद्यमानेऽपि संसृतिर्न निवर्तते ।
ध्यायतो विषयानस्य स्वप्नेऽनर्थागमो यथा ॥१३॥

13. Even though the universe is unreal, this man never misses having relative existence, as one given to thinking of sense-objects experiences troubles in dreams:

यथा ह्यप्रतिबुद्धस्य प्रस्वापो बह्वनर्थभृत् ।
स एव प्रतिबुद्धस्य न वै मोहाय कल्पते ॥१४॥

14. As a dream is a fruitful source of troubles to a sleeping man, but it no more[1] deludes him when he awakes.

[1] *No more etc.*—So that the man of realisation is free.

शोकहर्षभयक्रोधलोभमोहस्पृहादयः ।
अहंकारस्य दृश्यन्ते जन्ममृत्युश्च नात्मनः ॥१५॥

15. Grief, joy, fear, anger, greed, infatuation, desire, etc., as well as birth and death are observed to belong to egoism, and not[1] to the Âtman.

[1] *Not etc.*—Because they are absent in dreamless sleep.

UDDHAVA GITA

देहेन्द्रियप्राणमनोऽभिमानो
जीवोऽन्तरात्मा गुणकर्ममूर्तिः ।
सूत्रं महानित्युरुधेव गीतः
संसार आधावति कालतन्त्रः ॥१६॥

16. The Jiva identifying itself with the body, the organs, the Prânas, and mind, of which he is the self, and assuming a form made up of tendencies and activities, travels, under the sway of God, hither and thither in relative existence, called by various names such as Sutra[1] and Mahat and so on.

[1] *Sutra etc.*—See note on verse 6, Ch. XIX.

अमूल्मेतद्बहुरूपरूपितं
मनोबचःप्राणशरीरकर्म ।
ज्ञानासिनोपासनया शितेन
छित्वा मुनिर्गां विचरत्यतृष्णः ॥१७॥

17. Cutting asunder with the sword of knowledge sharpened by service unto the Teacher, this aggregate of mind, speech, Pranas, body, and work—which, though without a basis, is manifested in diverse forms—the meditative man wanders over the earth free from attachment.

ज्ञानं विवेको निगमस्तपश्च
प्रत्यक्षमैतिह्यमथानुमानम् ।

THE LAST MESSAGE OF SHRI KRISHNA

आद्यन्तयोरस्य यदेव केवलं
कालश्च हेतुश्च तदेव मध्ये ॥१८॥

18. Knowledge is the discrimination, by means of the scriptures, performance of one's duty, direct perception, tradition, and inference, that whatever is at the beginning and end of this universe, viz its illuminer and cause, is alone in the intermediate stage.

यथा हिरण्यं स्वकृतं पुरस्ता-
त्पश्चाच्च सर्वस्य हिरण्मयस्य ।
तदेव मध्ये व्यवहार्यमाणं
नानापदेशैरहमस्य तद्वत् ॥१९॥

19. As gold, not converted[1] into beautiful ornaments is the same before[2] and after all its modifications, as also in the intermediate stage, even though it may be called by various names, so am I[3] in respect of the universe.

[1] *Not converted etc.*—i.e. freed of names and forms.
[2] *Before etc.*—before their origin and after their destruction, the effect being identical with the cause.
[3] *So am I etc.*—the only unchanging reality in the midst of the phenomena people call the world.

विज्ञानमेतत्त्रियवस्थमङ्ग
गुणत्रयं कारणकार्यकर्तृ ।
समन्वयेन व्यतिरेकतश्च
येनैव तुर्येण तदेव सत्यम् ॥२०॥

UDDHAVA GITA

20. That transcendent entity,[1] My friend, by which the mind with its three states,[2] the three Gunas, and the universe with its threefold division of cause,[3] effect, and agent, are posited both directly[4] and indirectly,[5] is alone real.

Now it is shown that the object is identical with the subject.

[1] *Transcendent entity*—Brahman, the Existence-Knowledge-Bliss Absolute.

[2] *Three states*—wakefulness, dream, and profound sleep.

[3] *Cause etc.*—Adhyâtma, Adhibhuta, and Adhidaiva, respectively.

[4] *Directly*—As is borne out by such Shruti passages as, "Which shining everything else shines", etc. (Katha V. 15), "The Prâna of the Prâna, the eye of the eye", etc. (Brihadâranyaka IV. iv. 18), and so on.

[5] *Indirectly*—Because It alone persists even when everything else has vanished, as in the Sushupti state.

न यत्पुरस्तादुत यन्न पश्चा-
न्मध्ये च तन्न व्यपदेशमात्रम् ।
भूतं प्रसिद्धं च परेण यद्-
त्तदेव तत्स्यादिति मे मनीषा ॥२१॥

21. That which is neither before nor after is also non-existent in the interim. It is a mere name.[1] I am of opinion that whatever is caused or brought to light by some other thing must be that and nothing else.

[1] *Name*—An echo of Chhândogya VI. i. 4—"All modifications are mere names—efforts of speech", etc.

THE LAST MESSAGE OF SHRI KRISHNA 347

अविद्यमानोऽप्यवभासते यो
वैकारिको राजससर्गं एषः ।
ब्रह्म स्वयंज्योतिरतो विभाति
ब्रह्मेन्द्रियार्थात्मविकारचित्रम् ॥२२॥

22. This world[1] of changes which was originally non-existent is a Râjasika projection of the Brahman and appears because of It. But the Brahman is self-existent and self-effulgent. Hence the Brahman alone appears in multiple forms as the organs, the subtle elements, the mind,[2] and the gross elements.

[1] *This world etc.*—i.e. Brahman is both its cause and illuminer.

[2] *Mind*—also suggests the gods.

एवं स्फुटं ब्रह्मविवेकहेतुभिः
परापवादेन विशारदेन ।
छित्त्वाऽऽत्मसन्देहमुपारमेत
स्वानन्दतुष्टोऽखिलकामुकेभ्यः ॥२३॥

23. Clearly removing one's doubts about the Âtman by reasons that lead to a realisation of the Brahman, as well as by a skilful negation[1] of things[2] other than the Brahman, one should turn away from all sense-pleasures, being satisfied with the bliss of the Self.

[1] *Negation*—This is shown in the next few verses.

[2] *Things etc.*—the body etc.

UDDHAVA GITA

नात्मा वपुः पार्थिवमिन्द्रियाणि
देवा ह्यसुर्वायुजलं हुताशः ।
मनोऽन्नमात्रं धिषणा च सत्त्व-
महंकृतिः खं क्षितिरर्थसाम्यम् ॥२४॥

24. The body is not the Atman, for it is material. Neither are the organs, the gods, the Prânas, air, water, fire, ether, earth, the sense-objects,[1] the Manas,[2] the intellect, the Chitta, the ego, and Prakriti —for they are all matter.

[1] *Sense-object*—sight, sound, smell, taste, and touch.
[2] *Manas etc.*—Mind is conceived of in four aspects according to its functions. As Manas it considers the various alternatives to a question, without coming to a definite conclusion about them. This last is the special function of the Buddhi or intellect, the faculty of judgment. As Chitta or mind-stuff it remembers things. And as Ahamkâra or ego it flashes forth the feeling of "I" in connection with all mental states.

समाहितैः कः करणैर्गुणात्मभि-
र्गुणो भवेन्मत्सुविविक्तधाम्नः ।
विक्षिप्यमाणैरुत किं नु दूषणं
घनैरुपेतैर्विगतै रवेः किम् ॥२५॥

25. If the organs, which are made up of the Gunas, are controlled, what credit does it bring to a man who has completely realised My nature, and if they are outgoing, what blemish? What matters it to the sun if the clouds gather together or are scattered?

THE LAST MESSAGE OF SHRI KRISHNA   349

यथा नभो वाय्वनलाम्बुभूगुणै-
गंतागतैर्वर्तुगुणैर्न सज्जते ।
तथाऽक्षरं सत्त्वरजस्तमोमलै-
रहंमतेः संसृतिहेतुभिः परम् ॥२६॥

26. As the sky is not affected by the ever-changing attributes[1] of air, fire, water, and earth, or[2] of
the seasons, so the Absolute, which is beyond egoism,
is not affected by the impurities of Sattva, Rajas, and
Tamas, which cause transmigration.

[1] *Attributes*—viz the properties of drying, burning,
wetting, and soiling, respectively.
[2] *Or etc.*—such as heat and cold.

तथापि सङ्गः परिवर्जनीयो
गुणेषु मायारचितेषु तावत् ।
मद्भक्तियोगेन दृढेन याव-
द्रजो निरस्येत मनःकषायः ॥२७॥

27. Yet contact with sense-objects, which are
the creation of nescience, should be avoided till
attachment, which is a stain on the mind, has been
removed by a strong and systematic devotion to Me.

यथाऽऽमयोऽसाधुचिकित्सितो नृणां
पुनः पुनः संतुदति प्ररोहन् ।
एवं मनोऽपक्वकषायकर्म
कुयोगिनं विध्यति सर्वसङ्गम् ॥२८॥

UDDHAVA GITA

350

28. As a man's disease, carelessly treated, crops up again and again and troubles him, so a mind from which desire and activity have not been destroyed, torments a bad Yogi who is attached to everything.

कुयोगिनो ये विहितान्तरायै-
मनुष्यभूतैस्त्रिदशोपसृष्टैः ।
ते प्राक्तनाभ्यासबलेन भूयो
युञ्जन्ति योगं न तु कर्मतन्त्रम् ॥२६॥

29. Those unsuccessful Yogis who have been led astray by obstacles in the shape of men,[1] despatched by the gods[2] for that purpose, practise, on account of their previous habit, Yoga alone in their future life, and not an extension of work.

[1] *Men*—relatives and friends to whom we get attached.
[2] *Gods*—who do not generally like that men should get beyond their sphere by attaining realisation. Compare Brihadâranyaka I. iv. 10.

करोति कर्म क्रियते च जन्तुः
केनाप्यसौ चोदित आनिपातात् ।
न तत्र विद्वान्प्रकृतौ स्थितोऽपि
निवृत्ततृष्णः स्वसुखानुभूत्या ॥३०॥

30. It is the body which, directed by something,[1] works and is modified[2] till death, but the man of realisation, with his desire quenched by experiencing the bliss of the Âtman, even though he is in the body, is not affected by work.

THE LAST MESSAGE OF SHRI KRISHNA 351

[1] *Something*—e.g. past impressions of work.
[2] *Modified*—e.g. by the food it eats.

तिष्ठन्तमासीनमुत व्रजन्तं
शयानमुञ्जन्तमदन्तमन्नम् ।
स्वभावमन्यत्किमपीहमान-
मात्मानमात्मस्थमतिर्न वेद ॥३१॥

31. The man whose mind rests in the Âtman does not even know the body as it stands, sits, walks, lies down, eats food, or performs any other natural function.

यदि स्म पश्यत्यसदिन्द्रियार्थं
नानानुमानेन विरुद्धमन्यत् ।
न मन्यते वस्तुतया मनीषी
स्वाप्नं यथोत्थाय तिरोदधानम् ॥३२॥

32. Even if the illumined man sees the objects of the outgoing senses, he does not consider them as something real and other than the Self, because they are rejected by inference on account of their multiplicity—as a man, on waking from sleep, dismisses the vanishing dream perceptions.

पूर्वं गृहीतं गुणकर्मचित्र-
मज्ञानमात्मन्यविविक्तमङ्ग ।
निवर्तते तत्पुनरीक्षयैव
न गृह्यते नापि विसृज्य आत्मा ॥३३॥

352   **UDDHAVA GITA**

33. Formerly before illumination the effects[1] of nescience, diversified by the Gunas and works,[2] My friend, were taken as mixed up with the Self; they again dissolve on the dawning of knowledge. But the Self is neither accepted nor discarded.

[1] *Effect etc.*—the body etc.
[2] *Works*—good and bad, engendered by Sattva, Rajas, and Tamas.

यथा हि भानोरुदयो नृचक्षुषां

तमो निहन्यान्न तु सद्विधत्ते ।

एवं समीक्षा निपुणा सती मे

हन्यात्तमिस्रं पुरुषस्य बुद्धेः ॥३४॥

34. Just as sunrise takes away the veil of darkness from men's eyes, but does not create anything, so the knowledge of Me (the Âtman), if skilful, takes away the darkness from a man's intellect.

एष स्वयंज्योतिरजोऽप्रमेयो

महानुभूतिः सकलानुभूतिः ।

एकोऽद्वितीयो वचसां विरामे

येनेषिता वागसवश्चरन्ति ॥३५॥

35. This Âtman is self-effulgent, birthless, unknowable, Knowledge Absolute, omniscient, one, indivisible, and beyond speech,[1] for under[2] Its direction speech and the Prânas function.

[1] *Beyond speech*—Compare Taittiriya II. 9.
[2] *Under etc.*—Compare Kena I. 1-2.

THE LAST MESSAGE OF SHRI KRISHNA 353

एतावानात्मसंमोहो यद्विकल्पस्तु केवले ।
आत्मन्नृते स्वमात्मानमवलम्बो न यस्य हि ॥३६॥

36. The delusion of the mind consists in this that it imagines duality in the Absolute Âtman, for except one's own self the duality has no foundation.

यन्नामाकृतिभिर्ग्राह्यं पञ्चवर्णमबाधितम् ।
व्यर्थेनाप्यर्थवादोऽयं द्वैयं पण्डितमानिनाम् ॥३७॥

37. It is[1] only people wise in their own conceit who consider this duality, consisting of the five elements and perceived through name and form, as irrefragable, and quite gratuitously assume the Vedantic view to be a piece of glorification.

[1] *It is etc.*—A criticism of the Mimâmsaka School, which holds that the Vedantic passages are not to be taken literally since they merely eulogise Vedic acts. In reality, they do not form part of an injunction.

योगिनोऽपक्वयोगस्य युञ्जतः काय उत्थितैः ।
उपसर्गैर्विहन्येत तत्रायं विहितो विधिः ॥३८॥

38. Should the body of a Yogi who is but practising Yoga and is not yet an adept in it, be overtaken by troubles that may have cropped up in the course of it, then the following remedies are prescribed.

Now follow some directions for warding off certain concomitant evils of Yoga practice.

23

UDDHAVA GITA

योगधारणया कांश्चिदासनैर्धारणान्वितैः ।
तपोमन्त्रौषधैः कांश्चिदुपसर्गान्विनिर्दहेत् ॥३९॥

39. Some of these troubles he should burn up through Yogic concentration,[1] some[2] through postures coupled with retention of the breath, and some[3] through austerities, Mantras, and medicines.

[1] *Concentration*—e.g. by concentrating on the sun and the moon he should remove sensations of cold and heat, respectively.
[2] *Some*—e.g. rheumatism etc.
[3] *And some*—e.g. those due to planets, snakes, etc.

कांश्चिन्ममानुध्यानेन नामसंकीर्तनादिभिः ।
योगेश्वरानुवृत्त्या वा हन्यादशुभदान् शनैः ॥४०॥

40. Some evils[1] he should slowly kill through meditation on Me and the chanting of My name, etc., and some[2] through service unto the great Masters of Yoga.

[1] *Evils*—such as lust etc.
[2] *Some*—such as haughtiness etc.

केचिद्द्धिमिमं धीराः सुकल्पं वयसि स्थिरम् ।
विधाय विविधोपायैरथ युञ्जन्ति सिद्धये ॥४१॥

41. There are some strong-willed people who by various means first make the body very strong and of undecaying youth, and then practise Yoga with a view to acquiring extraordinary powers.[1]

[1] *Powers*—For details of these see Chapter X.

THE LAST MESSAGE OF SHRI KRISHNA

355

न हि तत्कुशलाद्वृत्यं तदायासो ह्यपार्थकः ।
अन्तवत्त्वाच्छरीरस्य फलस्येव वनस्पतेः ॥४२॥

42. But that is not praised by the wise, for such effort is useless, since the body is mortal, like[1] the fruits of a tree.

[1] *Like etc.*—But the Âtman is eternal.

योगं निषेवतो नित्यं कायश्चेत्कल्पतामियात् ।
तच्छ्रद्दध्यान्न मतिमान् योगमुत्सृज्य मत्परः ॥४३॥

43. If, in the course of regularly practising Yoga, his body gets strong, the intelligent Yogi who is devoted to Me should not[1] give up practice, pinning his faith on that.

[1] *Should not etc.*—He should not get attached to these powers, which are nothing in comparison with the majesty of the Âtman.

योगचर्यामिमां योगी विचरन्मद्व्यपाश्रयः ।
नान्तरायैर्विहन्येत निःस्पृहः स्वसुखानुभूः ॥४४॥

44. The Yogi who practises this Yoga, relying solely on Me and having no desires, is not thwarted by obstacles and experiences the bliss of the Self.

CHAPTER XXIV

उद्धव उवाच ।

सुदुस्तरामिमां मन्ये योगचर्यामनात्मनः ।
यथाञ्जसा पुमान्सिध्येत्तन्मे ब्रूह्यञ्जसाऽच्युत ॥१॥

Uddhava said:

1. O Achyuta, I consider the pursuit of this Yoga extremely difficult for one who is not a master of his senses. Please tell me in a simple way how a man may attain realisation easily.

प्रायशः पुण्डरीकाक्ष युञ्जन्तो योगिनो मनः ।
विषीदन्त्यसमाधानान्मनोनिग्रहकर्शिताः ॥२॥

2. O lotus-eyed One, often do Yogis who are trying to control the mind feel despondent either owing to their failure to do so, or being exhausted in their struggle to control the mind.

अथात आनन्ददुघं पदाम्बुजं
हंसाः श्रयेरन्नरविन्दलोचन ।
सुखं नु विश्वेश्वर योगकर्मभि-
स्त्वन्माययाऽमी विहता न मानिनः ॥३॥

3. Hence, O lotus-eyed One, O Lord of the universe, sages with discrimination never fail to resort cheerfully to Thy lotus feet, which shower bliss.

THE LAST MESSAGE OF SHRI KRISHNA 357

They are not overtaken by Thy inscrutable Mâyâ
and are never proud of their attainments in Yoga and
work.

किं चित्रमच्युत तवैतदशेषबन्धो
दासेष्वनन्यशरणेषु यदात्मसात्त्वम् ।
योऽरोचयत्सह मृगैः स्वयमीश्वराणां
श्रीमत्किरीटतटपीडितपादपीठः ॥४॥

4. O Achyuta, O Friend of all, is it any wonder
that Thou placest Thyself unreservedly at the disposal of Thy servants who have no other refuge but
Thee? For did'st Thou not gladly mix on terms of
friendship with animals,[1] even though high Potentates[2] lay the ends of their shining crowns at Thy
footstool?

[1] *Animals*—monkeys and bears. The reference is to the
Lord's incarnation as Râma.

[2] *Potentates*—such as Brahmâ.

तं त्वाऽखिलात्मदयितेश्वरमाश्रितानां
सर्वार्थदं स्वकृतविद्धिसृजेत को नु ।
को वा भजेत्किमपि विस्मृतयेऽनु भूत्यै
किं वा भवेन्न तव पादरजोजुषां नः ॥५॥

5. Who that knows what Thou dost to Thy
devotees, would discard Thee, the Self of all, the
well-beloved Lord, the Giver of all boons to Thy
dependants, and who would resort to any other

358 UDDHAVA GITA

master for material prosperity, or for forgetfulness[1]
of the world either? What indeed is inaccessible to
us who adore the dust of Thy feet?

[1] *Forgetfulness etc.*—i.e. liberation.

नैवोपयन्त्यपचितिं कवयस्तवेश
ब्रह्मायुषाऽपि कृतमृद्धमुदः स्मरन्तः ।
योऽन्तर्बहिस्तनुभृतामशुभं विधुन्व-
न्नाचार्यचैत्यवपुषा स्वगतिं व्यनक्ति ॥६॥

6. O Lord, sages, whose joys increase as they
think of Thy favours, can never—not even in the
lifetime of Brahmâ—repay their debt of gratitude to
Thee, who revealest Thy nature, by removing the
evil[1] of all beings, in a double form—outside, as the
Teacher, and inside, as the Indwelling Ruler.

[1] *Evil*—i.e. the hankering for sense-pleasures.

श्रीशुक उवाच ।
इत्युद्धवेनात्यनुरक्तचेतसा
पृष्टो जगत्क्रीडनकः स्वशक्तिभिः ।
गृहीतमूर्तित्रय ईश्वरेश्वरो
जगाद सप्रेमममनोहरस्मितः ॥७॥

Shuka said:

7. Being thus asked by the devoted Uddhava,
the God of gods, whose toy is the world, and who

THE LAST MESSAGE OF SHRI KRISHNA 359

through His Own powers[1] assumes a triple form,[2] said with a loving, beautiful smile.

[1] *Own powers*—Sattva, Rajas, and Tamas.
[2] *Triple form*—as Vishnu, Brahmâ, and Shiva respectively.

श्रीभगवानुवाच ।

हन्त ते कथयिष्यामि मम धर्मान्सुमङ्गलान् ।
यान्श्रद्धयाऽऽचरन्मर्त्यो मृत्युं जयति दुर्जयम् ॥८॥

The Lord said:

8. Well, I shall tell you some excellent forms of religion concerning Me, practising which with faith a man can conquer invincible Death.

कुर्यात्सर्वाणि कर्माणि मदर्थं शनकैः स्मरन् ।
मय्यर्पितमनश्चित्तो मद्धर्मात्ममनोरतिः ॥९॥

9. Placing one's Manas and mind-stuff in Me, with the body and mind delighting in the religion concerning Me, one should calmly do all work for My sake, remembering Me all the while.

देशान्पुण्यानाश्रयेत मद्भक्तैः साधुभिः श्रितान् ।
देवासुरमनुष्येषु मद्भक्ताचरितानि च ॥१०॥

10. One should resort to sacred tracts inhabited by holy men devoted to Me. Among the gods, Asuras, and men, one should imitate the conduct of those alone who are My devotees.

360 UDDHAVA GITA

पृथक् सत्रेण वा महं पर्वयात्रामहोत्सवान् ।
कार्येद्द्रीतनृत्याद्यैर्महाराजविभूतिभिः ॥११॥

11. One should arrange, either single-handed or jointly with others, special days, gatherings, and festivities celebrated in my honour with royal splendours, in the shape of music and dance, and so on.

मामेव सर्वभूतेषु बहिरन्तरपावृतम् ।
ईक्षेतात्मनि चात्मानं यथा खममलाशयः ॥१२॥

12. With a pure mind one should observe in all beings as well as in oneself only Me, the Âtman, who am both inside and out, and unobstructed like the sky.

इति सर्वाणि भूतानि मद्भावेन महाद्युते ।
सभाजयन्मन्यमानो ज्ञानं केवलमाश्रितः ॥१३॥
ब्राह्मणे पुलकसे स्तेने ब्रह्मण्येऽर्के स्फुलिङ्गके ।
अक्रूरे क्रूरके चैव समदृक्पण्डितो मतः ॥१४॥

13-14. O great soul, he who, taking his stand on pure knowledge, thus regards and honours all beings as Myself, who has the same attitude towards a Chandâla[1] as well as a Brâhmana, a thief as well as a patron of the Brâhmanas, a spark of fire as well as the sun, and a ruffian as well as a kind man,—is considered a sage.

---

[1] *Chandâla etc.*—suggesting differences due to birth, work, quality, and nature, respectively.

THE LAST MESSAGE OF SHRI KRISHNA

नरेष्वभीक्ष्णं मद्भावं पुंसो भावयतोऽचिरात् ।
स्पर्धासूयातिरस्काराः साहंकारा वियन्ति हि ॥१५॥

15. Ideas of rivalry,[1] jealousy, pity, and egoism quickly depart from a man who always thinks of Me in all men.

[1] *Rivalry etc.*—concerning his equals, superiors, inferiors, and himself, respectively.

विसृज्य सयमानान्स्वान् दृशां त्रीडां च दैहिकीम् ।
प्रणमेद्दण्डवद्भूमावाश्वचाण्डालगोखरम् ॥१६॥

16. Ignoring the derisive smiles of one's friends, and leaving aside a merely physical view[1] of things as well as shame, one should prostrate oneself on the ground before every creature, down to a Chandâla, a cow, an ass, or a dog.

[1] *Physical view etc.*—based on considerations of birth, position, etc.

यावत्सर्वेषु भूतेषु मद्भावो नोपजायते ।
तावदेवमुपासीत वाङ्मनःकायवृत्तिभिः ॥१७॥

17. One should worship thus in thought, word, and deed till one comes to look upon all beings as Myself.

सर्वं ब्रह्मात्मकं तस्य विद्ययाऽऽत्ममनीषया ।
परिपश्यन्नुपरमेत्सर्वतो मुक्तसंशयः ॥१८॥

362   UDDHAVA GITA

18. To such a man everything is Brahman, owing to the knowledge that comes of seeing the Ātman in all. Seeing the Brahman all round, he is free from doubts and gives up all work.

अयं हि सर्वकल्पानां सध्रीचीनो मतो मम ।
मद्भावः सर्वभूतेषु मनोवाक्कायवृत्तिभिः ॥१६॥

19. This looking upon all beings as Myself in thought, word, and deed is, to My mind, the best of all methods of worship.

न श्रङ्गोपक्रमे ध्वंसो मद्धर्मस्योद्धवाण्वपि ।
मया व्यवसितः सम्यङ् निर्गुणत्वादनाशिषः ॥२०॥

20. My dear Uddhava, once begun, there is not the least destruction for the religion concerning Me, for it is free from desire, and I have Myself adjudged this religion as perfect, on account of its being transcendent.

यो यो मयि परे धर्मः कल्प्यते निष्फलाय चेत् ।
तदायासो निर्थः स्याद्भयादेरिव सत्तम ॥२१॥

21. O best of men, any trifling activity what-soever, such as[1] that due to fear etc., if it is unselfishly meant for Me, becomes religion.

[1] Such as etc.—e.g. flight from fear, or weeping from grief.

THE LAST MESSAGE OF SHRI KRISHNA

एषा बुद्धिमतां बुद्धिर्मनीषा च मनीषिणाम् ।
यत्सत्यमनृतेनेह मर्त्येनाप्नोति माऽमृतम् ॥२२॥

22. Herein lies the wisdom of the wise, and the cleverness of the intelligent, that in this very birth they attain Me, the Real and Immortal, by means of something that is unreal and mortal.

एष तेऽभिहितः कृत्स्नो ब्रह्मवादस्य संग्रहः ।
समासव्यासविधिना देवानामपि दुर्गमः ॥२३॥

23. Here I have given you, in a synthetic as well as an analytic way, a complete epitome of the philosophy of Brahman, which is unintelligible even to the gods.

अभीक्ष्णशस्ते गदितं ज्ञानं विस्पष्टयुक्तिमत् ।
एतद्विज्ञाय मुच्येत पुरुषो नष्टसंशयः ॥२४॥

24. I have repeatedly told you about knowledge, with clear reasonings. Knowing this a man has his doubts dispelled and attains liberation.

सुविविक्तं तव प्रश्नं मयैतदपि धारयेत् ।
सनातनं ब्रह्मगुह्यं परं ब्रह्माधिगच्छति ॥२५॥

25. He who understands your questions which I have adequately answered, as well as this discourse, attains the Eternal, supreme Brahman, which is a secret even in the Vedas.

The importance of the discourse is being brought out in various ways in verses 25-28.

364   UDDHAVA GITA

य एतन्मम भक्तेषु संप्रदद्यात्सुपुष्कलम् ।
तस्याहं ब्रह्मदायस्य ददाम्यात्मानमात्मना ॥२६॥

26. To one who fully communicates it to My devotees, I of My own accord give Myself, for thereby he imparts the highest knowledge.

य एतत्समधीयीत पवित्रं परमं शुचि ।
स पूयेताहरहर्मां ज्ञानदीपेन दर्शयन् ॥२७॥

27. He who daily reads out this exceedingly sacred and purifying episode, is purified by showing Me with the lamp of knowledge to others.

य एतच्छ्रद्धया नित्यमव्यग्रः शृणुयान्नरः ।
मयि भक्तिं परां कुर्वन्कर्मभिर्न स बध्यते ॥२८॥

28. That man who calmly listens to it every day with faith, cherishing a strong devotion to Me, is not fettered by work.

अप्युद्धव त्वया ब्रह्म सखे समवधारितम् ।
अपि ते विगतो मोहः शोकश्चासौ मनोभवः ॥२९॥

29. Friend Uddhava, have you rightly comprehended the Brahman? And has your infatuation, and that grief which was in your mind, left you?

नैतत्त्वया दाम्भिकाय नास्तिकाय शठाय च ।
अशुश्रूषोरभक्ताय दुर्विनीताय दीयताम् ॥३०॥

THE LAST MESSAGE OF SHRI KRISHNA   365

30. You must not communicate this message to one who is haughty, atheistic, deceitful, unwilling to listen, wanting in devotion, and wicked.

एतैर्दोषैर्विहीनाय ब्रह्मण्याय प्रियाय च ।
साधवे शुचये ब्रूयाद्भक्तिः स्याच्छूद्रयोषिताम् ॥३१॥

31. You should impart it to one who is free from these defects, is devoted to the Brâhmanas, dear[1] to Me, good and pure, aye, even to the Shudras and women, should they have devotion.

[1] *Dear etc.*—for the qualities of his head and heart.

नैतद्विज्ञाय जिज्ञासोऽर्हातव्यमवशिष्यते ।
पीत्वा पीयूषममृतं पातव्यं नावशिष्यते ॥३२॥

32. After knowing this, an aspirant has nothing more to know: One who has drunk the delicious nectar has craving for no other drinks.

ज्ञाने कर्मणि योगे च वार्तायां दण्डधारणे ।
यावानर्थो नृणां तात तावांस्तेऽहं चतुर्विधः ॥३३॥

33. My friend, I am to you[1] all that fourfold gain[2]—the whole of it—that people obtain[3] from knowledge, work, Yoga, economics, and politics.

[1] *You*—and all devotees like you.
[2] *Fourfold gain*—viz virtue, wealth, desire, and liberation.
[3] *Obtain etc.*—From knowledge, liberation; from scriptural work, virtue; from natural work, desire; from Yoga,

UDDHAVA GITA

the powers; from economics, wealth; and from politics, prosperity. "Powers" and "prosperity" come under "desire", so the number is maintained at four.

मर्त्यों यदा त्यक्तसमस्तकर्मा
निवेदितात्मा विचिकीर्षितो मे ।
तदाऽमृतत्वं प्रतिपद्यमानो
मयाऽऽत्मभूयाय च कल्पते वै ॥३४॥

34. When a man relinquishing all work surrenders himself to Me, it is then that I like to magnify him most. Attaining immortality he is then fit for oneness with Me.

श्रीशुक उवाच ।
स एवमादर्शितयोगमार्ग-
स्तदोत्तमश्लोकवचो निशम्य ।
बद्धाञ्जलिः प्रीत्युपरुद्धकण्ठो
न किंचिदूचेऽश्रुपरिप्लुताक्षः ॥३५॥

Shuka said:

35. Being thus shown the path of Yoga, and listening to the speech of Shri Krishna, of supreme glory, Uddhava had his eyes filled with tears, and his voice was choked with emotion. He could not utter anything, and remained with folded hands.

विष्टभ्य चित्तं प्रणयावघूर्णं
धैर्येण राजन् बहु मन्यमानः ।

THE LAST MESSAGE OF SHRI KRISHNA 367

कृताञ्जलिः प्राह यदुप्रवीरं
शीष्णौं स्पृशंस्तच्चरणारविन्दम् ॥३६॥

36. O King,[1] controlling through patience, the mind convulsed with emotion and considering himself blessed, he touched the lotus-feet of the Chief of the Yâdavas with his head, and spoke with folded palms.

[1] *King*—Parikshit.

उद्धव उवाच ।
विद्रावितो मोहमहान्धकारो
य आश्रितो मे तव सन्निधानात् ।
विभावसोः किं नु समीपगस्य
शीतं तमो भीः प्रभवन्त्यजाद्य ॥३७॥

Uddhava said:

37. O Parent of Brahmâ, Thy very presence has scattered that thick darkness of infatuation which I had been harbouring in my mind. Can chill,[1] darkness, and fear triumph over one who has resorted to a fire?

[1] *Chill etc.*—Compare verse 31, chapter XXI.

प्रत्यर्पितो मे भवताऽनुकम्पिना
भृत्याय विज्ञानमयः प्रदीपः ।
हित्वा कृतज्ञस्तव पादमूलं
कोऽन्यत्समीयाच्छरणं त्वदीयम् ॥३८॥

UDDHAVA GITA

38. Thou hast out of Thy grace restored to me,
Thy servant, the lamp of knowledge. Who that is
conscious of Thy favour will forsake Thy feet and
seek another refuge?

वृक्णश्च मे सुदृढः स्नेहपाशो
दाशार्हवृष्ण्यन्धकसात्वतेषु ।
प्रसारितः सृष्टिविवृद्धये त्वया
स्वमायया ह्यात्मसुबोधहेतिना ॥३८॥

39. That strong net of affection for the
Dâshârhas,[1] Vrishnis, Andhakas, and Sâttvatas, which
Thou through Thy inscrutable power didst cast
over me to propagate Thy creation, Thou hast cut
asunder with the weapon of knowledge relating to
Thee.

[1] *Dâshârhas etc.*—being all relatives of Uddhava.

नमोऽस्तु ते महायोगिन्प्रपन्नमनुशाधि माम् ।
यथा त्वच्चरणाम्भोजे रतिः स्यादनपायिनी ॥४०॥

40. Salutation to Thee, O great Yogi! Please
instruct me, who have taken refuge in Thee, how
I may acquire an undying devotion to Thy lotus-
feet.

श्रीभगवानुवाच ।
गच्छोद्धव मयाऽऽदिष्टो बदर्याख्यं ममाश्रमम् ।
तत्र मत्पादतीर्थोदे स्नानोपस्पर्शनैः शुचिः ॥४१॥

THE LAST MESSAGE OF SHRI KRISHNA

ईक्ष्यग्र ऽलकनन्दाया विधूताशेषकल्मषः ।
वसानो वल्कलान्यङ्ग वन्यभुक्सुखनिःस्पृहः ॥४२॥

तितिक्षुर्द्वन्द्वमात्राणां सुशीलः संयतेन्द्रियः ।
शान्तः समाहितधिया ज्ञानविज्ञानसंयुतः ॥४३॥

मत्तोऽनुशिक्षितं यत्ते विविक्तमनुभावयन् ।
मय्यावेशितवाक्चित्तो मद्धर्मनिरतो भव ।
अतिव्रज्य गतीस्तिस्रो मामेष्यसि ततः परम् ॥४४॥

The Lord said:

41-44. Go, Uddhava, at My command to My
hermitage called Badari, where, at the very sight
of the Alakanandâ, the sacred river that sprang from
My feet, all your sins, My friend, will be removed,
and you will be purified by touching and bathing
in it. There, clad in bark, living on wild roots and
fruits, averse to pleasures, patient under all hard-
ships, calm and well-behaved, with your senses under
control and mind concentrated, possessed of knowledge and realisation, reflecting on what I have taught
you and what you have already considered, with
your speech and mind attached to Me,—practise
the religion concerning Me. Thereby you will
transcend the range of the three Gunas and attain
Me, the Supreme.

श्रीशुक उवाच ।

स एवमुक्तो हरिमेधसोद्भवः
प्रदक्षिणं तं परिसृत्य पादयोः ।

UDDHAVA GITA

शिरो निधायाश्रुकलाभिरार्द्रधी-
न्यषिष्वदद्वन्द्वपरोऽप्यपक्रमे ॥४५॥

Shuka said:

45. Thus addressed by him whose remembrance takes away relative existence, Uddhava reverently went round him, and as in the act of taking leave he placed his head at his feet, he bathed them with his tears, even though he was habitually free from pleasure and pain; for his heart was stirred.

सुदुस्त्यजस्नेहवियोगकातरो
न शक्नुवंस्तं परिहातुमातुरः ।
कृच्छ्र ययौ मूर्धनि भर्तृपादुके
बिभ्रन्नमस्कृत्य ययौ पुनः पुनः ॥४६॥

46. Stung with the thought of separation from one whom it was extremely difficult to part with, he could not leave him, and overwhelmed with grief, was in a miserable plight. At last, saluting him again and again, and placing the Master's slippers on his head, he departed.

ततस्तमन्तर्हृदि संनिवेश्य
गतो महाभागवतो विशालाम् ।
यथोपदिष्टां जगदेकबन्धुना
ततः समास्थाय हरेरगाद्गतिम् ॥४७॥

THE LAST MESSAGE OF SHRI KRISHNA

47. Then placing him in the recesses of his heart, the great devotee went to Vishâlâ,[1] and following the instructions of the one Friend of the universe, attained oneness with the Lord Hari.

[1] *Vishâlâ*—another name of Badarikâshrama.

य एतदानन्दसमुद्रसंभृतं
    ज्ञानामृतं भागवताय भाषितम् ।
कृष्णेन योगेश्वरसेविताङ्‌‍घ्रिणा
    सच्छृद्धयाऽऽसेव्य जगद्विमुच्यते ॥४८॥

48. He who but tastes with genuine faith of this nectar of knowledge that was imparted to the devoted Uddhava by Shri Krishna—whose feet the Masters of Yoga worship, and that is stored in the path of devotion, which is an ocean of bliss—frees himself, and the world with him.

भवभयमपहन्तुं ज्ञानविज्ञानसारं
    निगमकृदुपजह्‌‍ भृङ्गवद्वेदसारम् ।
अमृतमुदधितश्चापाययद्‌‍भृत्यवर्गा-
    न्पुरुषमृषभमाद्यं कृष्णसंज्ञं नतोऽस्मि ॥४९॥

49. That Revealer of the Vedas who, to take away the fear of transmigration, like a bee extracted the essence of the Vedas, comprising the highest knowledge and realisation, as he had done nectar[1] from the ocean, and gave that to his servants to

372   UDDHAVA GITA

drink—that primeval, perfect Being, Krishna by name, I salute.

 ¹*Nectar etc.*—The reference is to the churning of the ocean by the Devas and Asuras for the sake of nectar. The Lord befriended the enterprise in various ways, and finally in the form of an exquisitely beautiful woman, contrived to distribute the nectar exclusively among the Devas, to the chagrin and discomfiture of the nefarious Asuras.

INDEX

[The Roman Capitals indicate the Chapter number, and the figures the Shloka number.]

ÂTMAN : Its nature V. 8-9; XVIII. 45, 57; XXIII. 6, 24-26, 35.

ATTACHMENT and its effects VIII. 9-11; XVI. 1, 19-22.
—condemned IV. 29; XII. 56-58; XXI. 3; XXIII. 27-28.
—how to overcome VIII. 12-14.

AVADHUTA and his twenty-four teachers II. 32; IV. 31.

BHAKTI-YOGA XV. 27-37.

BONDAGE AND FREEDOM both unreal VI. 1.
—their genesis VI. 3-4.

BRAHMA leads a deputation to Shri Krishna I. 1-6, 21-27, 32.

BRAHMAN the only Reality IV. 16-18; XIV. 7, 16; XIX. 17-19; XXIII. 18-22.

CASTES AND ORDERS OF LIFE : their origin and characteristics XII. 13-20.
—their respective duties XII. 40-49; XIII. 42-43.

CATEGORIES : different versions reconciled XVII. 1-25.

DEFINITIONS : a few of them XIV. 27, 33-34.

DEVOTION extolled VI. 19-20; IX. 2, 12-28; X. 33-34; XIII. 47; XXI. 1; XXIV. 3, 33-34.
—its effect XIII. 45-46; XXIV. 15.
—its means VI. 23-25, 34-41, 46-47; VII. 14-15; XIII. 44; XIV. 20-24; XXII. 50-52; XXIV. 8-12, 16-23.

374 INDEX

DISCOURSE between Shri Krishna and Uddhava: qualifications for its study and its effect XXIV. 24-32, 48.

DISCRIMINATION between Self and non-Self VII. 17, 22-32.

DISPASSION V. 30; IX. 11; XIV. 18; XVI. 18.

DUALITY a fiction XXIII. 3-5, 7, 36-37.

EVEN-MINDEDNESS XXIII. 1-9.

GOD : His incarnation as the Swan VIII. 19-21, 41-42.
—His manifestations XI. 9-41.
—His nature I. 7-19; II. 17-18; IV. 19-21; VI. 28; VII. 20; VIII. 39-40; X. 35-36; XI. 1, 4; XIII. 5; XIV. 9-10; XVI. 28; XXIV. 4-6, 49.

GOPIS VII. 10-13.

GUNAS : their adjuncts VII. 4-5.
—their effects VIII. 2; XIV. 25-26; XX. 1-29.
—should be conquered to attain knowledge VIII. 1, 3, 6-7; XXI. 2.

HATHA-YOGA criticised XXIII. 41-42.

HERMIT LIFE : its duties XIII. 50-55.

HUMAN BODY praised II. 21-23; IV. 28; XV. 11-12, 17.

JIVATMAN AND PARAMATMAN VI. 5-7, XXIII. 15-16.

JNANI'S STATE II. 10-12; VI. 11-18; VIII. 36-37; XXIII. 30-32; XXIV. 13-14.
—contrasted with that of the ignorant VI. 8-10.

KARMA-YOGA VI. 22; XV. 9-11, 13-16.

KNOWLEDGE : its means V. 1-7; VI. 21; VIII. 12-14, 33-35; XI. 42-44; XIII. 38-39.
—and realisation XIV. 1-6, 14-15.

INDEX

375

MERITS AND DEFECTS of things XIV. 45; XV. 1-3, 26; XVI. 2-17.

MIMAMSAKA VIEW OF WORK V. 14-15.
—criticised V. 16-21, 31-34.

MIND : the source of all troubles XVIII. 43-50, 60.
—how to control it XV. 20-25; XVIII. 61.

MONASTICISM : its stages and their duties XIII. 15-37.
—disqualifications for it XIII. 40-41.
—transition to it XIII. 12-14.

PARABLE of the courtesan III. 22-44.
—of the miserly Brâhmana XVIII. 2-60.
—of the pigeon II. 52-74.

POWERS and how they are attainable X. 1-32.

PRABHASA : pilgrimage to it recommended I. 35-38.

PURURAVAS : his attachment to Urvashi and disillusionment XXI. 4-25.

PURUSHA AND PRAKRITI XVII. 26, 29-33.

QUALIFICATIONS for the three Yoga paths XV. 6-8.

RELATIVE WORLD (Samsâra) unreal II. 7-9; V. 10; VI. 2; XIV. 7; XXIII. 12-14.
—compared to a tree VII. 21-34.
—how destroyed XXIII. 17, 23, 33-34.

RELIGION : its varieties XII. 10-12, 21.

SAINTS : their nature VI. 29-33; XXI. 27.
—effects of association with them VI. 48; VII. 1-9; XXI. 26, 28-35.

SANKHYA COSMOLOGY XIX. 1-20.

SELF-EXERTION praised II. 19-20.

376 INDEX

STUDENT LIFE : its stages and their duties XII. 22-36.
—the next stages to it XII. 37-39.

TRANSMIGRATION : its illusory nature XVI. 34-56.

UDDHAVA seeks illumination from Shri Krishna I.
41-49; II. 15-16.
—is advised to renounce II. 3-6, 9-10.
—takes leave of Shri Krishna to go to Badarikâshrama XXIV. 35-47.

WORK of various kinds: its fruits V. 22-29; XXIII.
50-55.

WORLD emanating as sound VII. 17-19.
—not different from God VII. 20-21.
—its dissolution XIX. 21-27.

WORSHIP : its process XXII. 6-49.
—some symbols for it VI. 42-45.
—praised XXII. 2-5.

YADAVAS : their destruction prophesied I. 29-31, 33-34;
II. 3.

YOGA difficult XXIV. 1-2.
—its effect IX. 46.
—never fruitless XXIII. 29.
—should be persisted in XXIII. 43.
—some processes of it IX. 32-45.